TECHNIQUES OF THE WORLD'S GREAT MASTERS OF POTTERY AND CERAMICS

TECHNIQUES OF THE WORLD'S GREAT MASTERS OF
POTTERY
AND
CERAMICS

Consultant Editor:
Hugo Morley-Fletcher

**CHARTWELL
BOOKS, INC.**

A QUARTO BOOK

First published 1984
Copyright © 1984 Quarto Publishing Limited
ISBN 0-89009-546-9

Published by Chartwell Books Inc, a division of Booksales Inc, 110 Enterprise
Avenue, Secaucus, New Jersey 07094

This edition not for sale outside the United States of America, its
dependencies, the Philippines and Canada. Published in the rest of the world
by Phaidon · Christie's Limited, Littlegate House, St Ebbe's Street, Oxford,
England.

This book was designed and produced by
Quarto Publishing Limited
32 Kingly Court
London W1

Editors: Emma Johnson, Lucinda Montefiore
Art editor: Moira Clinch
Editorial director: Christopher Fagg
Art director: Robert Morley
Illustrator: Hussein Hussein
Special thanks to Joanna Swindell, Nick Clark, Philip Chidlow, Hazel Edington,
Joanna Edwards, Judy Martin, Margot Patterson, Ann Berne, Michelle Newton
Additional thanks to John Milson of the Worcester Royal Porcelain Company
Limited

Typeset in Great Britain by QV Typesetting Limited
Printed in Hong Kong by Leefung-Asco Printers Limited
Origination by Hong Kong Graphic Arts Service Centre Limited

Previous page *Decorating pottery —*
from the sixeenth century Italian
manuscript, 'The Three Books of the Art
of the Potter', by Cipriano Piccolpasso.

Contents

The maiolica artist, working in Cafaggiolo in about 1520, revealed his artistry in both the intriguing content and the careful execution of the painting on this maiolica plate. The focal point of the painting on this plate is itself a circular plate – the object of the painted decorator's concentration.

Foreword

This book is not just another history of ceramics: nor indeed is it a purely technical book setting out, in minute detail, the chemical composition and temperatures of each firing required to make a specific pot. It is an exploration of various strands and recurrent themes that play an important part in the world of the maker of pots. I use the last expression advisedly because the first subject that we consider in this book is the division between the craftsman potter, throwing pots on his wheel, and the manufacturer who uses various industrialized processes to produce the ware. Although the potter's wheel is an ancient instrument, the industry of pottery production on a large scale is also many centuries old. These two parallel methods of production have thus long coexisted and each has borrowed, and continues to borrow, from the other.

Potters and potteries throughout the world have tried to surmount similar obstacles, have explored similar avenues of invention and have decorated their wares using similar techiques. The way in which they have responded to their surroundings and the sources of their inspiration — metalwork, the painted image, illustrated manuscripts and the work of other artists — is the theme of the eight chapters which comprise the main part of the book. The last of these chapters concerns itself with a problem inherent in all beautiful pots — the fact that although they are all fundamentally useful in their basic forms, many of them are too richly ornamented to be utilitarian. This is an insoluble problem of a philosophical nature: Is a very beautiful chamber pot still a functional object or is it simply a decorative piece for show?

The purpose of this work is not to offer a general survey of the world of ceramics. The idea is to focus attention on certain salient and vital issues within the vast field of ceramics.

If, having read each or any of the essays on the themes we have discussed, you are encouraged to explore the subject further in specialist works, our purpose in whetting your appetite and drawing your attention to these crucial themes will have been fulfilled.

Hugo Morley Fletcher

The Craft of the Potter

Clay figurines of people and animals are as old as man's first paintings and carvings on rocks. Their early association with magic, ritual or commemoration has remained a feature ever since. Later, however, practicality and function were probably uppermost in the minds of the makers of the first vessels. The so-called neolithic revolution which brought about major developments in agriculture and stock breeding called for the storage of food and water, as well as all manner of household pots and utensils. Clay was the obvious material for this early technology and even the earliest examples are decorated, albeit by the imprint of a fingernail or cleft stick in the unfired clay. Clay has always served two purposes: on the one hand functional, and on the other decorative — using embellishment to make the object a personal expression of the maker. Pottery today has not changed in this respect. Factory-made pottery seeks a recognizable style to distinguish it from other factories, while individual studio potters attempt to create their own unique style. The versatility of clay makes it possible for both these demands to be satisfied.

Clay: origin and types

Clay has two distinguishing properties: it can retain the shapes given it by the various forming techniques, and it can change successfully, that is without faults, into a permanent material when subjected to heat. The choice of clays available all over the world is very great indeed and has allowed potters to create a wide range of ceramic objects.

The discovery of the origin of clay involves a study of the formation of the earth itself. The earth's crust is predominantly made up of granite-type rocks; the very rocks from which potters ultimately derive many raw materials, including most clays. Millions of years ago granite domes, thrust up by the violent activity of hot magma, cooled

MVODO DI LAVORAE AL TORNO

A page from the sixteenth century manuscript, Li Tre Libri dell Arte del Vasaio' ('The Three Books of the Art of the Potter') by Cipriano Piccolpasso.

slowly and were subjected, over a period of time, to hypogenic action. Hot gases, such as carbon dioxide, boron and fluorine, were forced through the domes, decomposing the hard rock and 'weathering' it. The mineral felspar is a product of this decomposition and by hydrolization it becomes clay.

Geologists, while still being uncertain about some areas of clay mineralogy, have long recognized two main groups of clay. The first is primary or residual clay, found where it is formed. China clay is the chief one in this group. It comprises an average 98 percent of the material kaolinite ($Al_2O_32SiO_22H_2O$) which has a regular ordered crystal structure that resists weathering. Its particle size is comparatively large so it is not very plastic; all authorities agree that plasticity has a great deal to do with

the smallness of particle size. Often china clay is almost free of iron and other contaminating minerals like titanium. It is used for its strength and whiteness, and is an essential ingredient of porcelain. It is 'won' from its site by washing from the rock face using high pressure hoses, the micaceous matter being separated out. The only other residual clay of interest to the potter is bentonite, from the montmorillonite group of clays. These have decomposed from basalt rather than granite rock and have the special virtue of plasticity. The extremely fine particle size, 0.03 percent of a china clay particle, makes it too plastic to use alone, but it can impart this desirable quality to other clays, if used in small amounts (three to five percent). Porcelain that is otherwise difficult to handle can be used on the potters wheel with the addition of a suitable bentonite of low-iron content.

The other main group is the secondary or sedimentary clays. These contain disordered kaolinite with an irregular crystal structure that is easily broken down. Over many hundreds of thousands of years these clays have been transported by natural weathering agents — wind, rain and ice. In many cases they have been deposited thousands of miles from their original source. During this process they have picked up mineral 'impurities', especially iron and organic matter, and these, together with constant movement, particularly the grinding action of water, have reduced the particle size of the clays. Secondary clays are generally much more plastic than primary clays and more variable in color. Colors can range from off-white to yellow, pale pink to rusty red and even to deep green, blue or black. Secondary clays also differ in physical structure and chemical composition. The following is a simple list in order of refractoriness.

Fireclays can fire to 1500°C (2730°F). Found in association with coal, they

The Art of Throwing
Throwing is a question of a balance of forces – the pressure of fingers, timed to the split second to react to the varying speeds of the spinning wheel. Clay is coaxed, not dominated; gently at one moment and with firm pressure at another. The potter (above) firmly and skilfully pulls up a cylinder from a 20lb lump of clay.

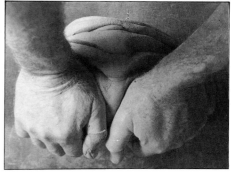

Wedging and kneading *These are two methods of homogenizing plastic clays by hand and eliminating any pockets of air. Wedging (left) involves cutting a large lump of clay in half, diagonally, and slamming one piece down on top of the other. In kneading (above), a process not unlike preparing dough for breadmaking, rhythmic pressure is applied with the palms of the hands.*

were the seat earth on which the primeval forests grew. They are often, but not always, plastic. Potters use them for their high-firing qualities, their rich color, when iron is added, and the speckled effect they can given in a reduction firing.

Stoneware clays fire to around 1300°C (2370°F). This is a general term given to many plastic and reasonably refractory pale-firing clays.

Ball clays fire to 1300°C (2370°F). Some are highly silicious and all are high in plasticity because of their fine particle size. They form the basis of most good throwable, high-firing clay bodies. The English counties of Devon and Dorset have some of the finest deposits of ball clay in the world.

Red clays are fired at around 1100°C (2010°F), but they are very variable; some just reaching stoneware temperatures while others are more fusible and almost collapse at 1000°C (1830°F). Red earthenware clay is commonly used for slipware pots, flowerpots and bricks.

It is not often that potters can dig any clay and use it alone to make their products, so the various properties of the clays mentioned are used as a basis, with other materials added, for producing the 'body'. This is then fired to the correct temperature to give the necessary hardness, color and texture and with oven-

ware, for example, to resist shock. The range of temperatures is one guide — relative porosity might be another — to the main types of pottery.

Types of Ware

Although the dividing lines are not absolute, potters generally do recognize three distinct types of ware: earthenware, stoneware and porcelain.

Earthenware is fired from 700°C (1290°F) at the lowest point of the scale, up to about 1200°C (2190°F). To fire to a higher temperature would either mean deforming the clay or making a weak, brittle article. Traditional earthenware is porous, meaning that the particles are not fused together and it needs glazing all over to make it non-porous. Bright colors are easier to achieve because many of the metals in a glaze will stand the lower temperatures. Most glazes must include lead or borax which have to be heated with other materials until they are red hot, quickly cooled to shatter, and then finely ground to make them safe and nonsoluble respectively.

Stoneware is fired between 1200°C (2190°F) and 1350°C (2460°F) and is a hard nonporous material that only needs glazing for hygienic or aesthetic reasons, since the particles are fused together. Only a small number of metals will stand the high temperature, but the

glazes can be compounded from a wider range of insoluble materials, like the felspars. The generally subdued tones are as much a matter of taste as anything else because brighter, more spectacular colors are possible with stoneware.

Porcelain is extremely hard and nonporous and is fired to temperatures of 1250°C-1400°C (2280°F-2550°F) or beyond. China clay, felspar and quartz are the three main ingredients; bentonite is added to make it more plastic. Its hard white, translucent qualities have been sought ever since the Chinese Tang dynasty. Soft-paste porcelain and bone china are two kinds of imitation true or hard-paste porcelain.

Preparation

However clay is won from the earth, whether by digging from the surface, mining from deeper down or washing from the rock face, certain stages of preparation must be carried out. Although the studio-potter of today may buy ready-made bodies from a supplier, someone else has had to clean them, mix in other ingredients and blend the whole together to bring it to a workable state, either as a dry powder or a plastic body. For potters making up their own bodies certain principles pertain. Depending on what use the clay body is put to, there are materials which can be added to obtain the desired qualities. For example, a throwable clay, free from sand or grog, should be used for fine tableware; the body for large garden pots will have additions of either, or both, of these materials. A hand-building clay is best for coiled forms that will need to be taken from the hot kiln, rolled around in sawdust and plunged into cold water, as is common in the raku process. Most hand-building bodies have liberal quantities of sand or grog. Additions to the clay may alter the physical quality of the body by making it more 'open' and therefore easier to handle, and allowing for a variety of thicknesses. Grogs (fired and ground clays, sand and coarse ground quartz) come into this category.

Other ingredients may alter the chemical composition and behavior of the body. Additions of fine ground quartz, felspar, talc and other minerals have this effect. Lastly, the color of the clay can be changed by adding metal oxides which will stand the firing temperature range. Only the experienced potter can choose the right ingredients in the right proportions and bring

them to a homogenous mixture, suitable for the purpose. There are three commonly used methods of preparing the clay — blunging, dough mixing and wedging by hand. A blunger is used to bring the materials to a liquid 'slip' state. This mixture is then sieved and run onto drying beds. It can be squeezed through a filter press to get rid of excess water and pugged through a machine which chops up the now plastic clay body, mixing and blending it before extruding it out through a tapering barrel exit. Dough-mixing is a method used for mixing those materials which have a high plastic content, like the ball clays, fire clays or other secondary clays. The dry materials are placed in a baker's dough mixer and all the nonplastic materials, like the felspars and quartz, soaked down with water, are added. The plastic mix is then pugged. To mix a clay body by hand without the aid of machinery, you can tread the mass of wetted ingredients together and then wedge or knead the mixture to blend it. Wedging involves cutting a largish lump of clay in half, and slamming one piece down on

top of the other, turning the lump and repeating the actions rhythmically. In kneading, a process not unlike kneading dough for breadmaking, the lump is rhythmically pressed in a spiral or circular movement onto a slightly absorbent surface, like wood. Both these actions eventually homogenize the mass and eliminate air pockets (a modern de-airing pug mill will do the same). If stored in a plastic state, which allows them to age and sour, all clay bodies improve significantly with time. The Chinese are said to have laid down clays for generations.

Forming Processes

There are a number of time-honored methods of making pots and other objects in clay. Most of them were used in prehistoric times and are still used by studio-potters today; it is only in the last 200 years that industry has added different, more mechanized procedures. Generally speaking, they can be divided into handbuilding and throwing techniques. Handbuilding includes pinching, coiling, slab-building and, with the aid of

Pinching and coiling *These are two of the most basic methods of making pots by hand. Pinch pots (far left) are made by squeezing the clay gently with the thumb and fingers to make the desired shape. A coil pot is built up from rolled pieces of clay, wound around a clay base. The Japanese made many hand-made pots (tebineri). The picture below shows (from left to right) a raku tea bowl of the Edo period, a Karatsu water-container, an eighteenth century tea bowl made by the female potter, Rengetsu, and a seventeenth century raku tea bowl.*

molds, press-molding and casting. Throwing requires the use of the potter's wheel to make pots or parts of pots and other objects. Combinations of these methods are possible and have been used by many civilizations — Song potters for example were adept at combining press-molding with throwing. Today more than ever, the artist-potter feels free to use any appropriate technique to achieve the desired effect.

Handbuilding methods

Although smooth, fine-grained earthenware and stoneware clays, and porcelain too, are used for pinching and coiling techniques, many potters would choose clays with an 'open' texture for both of these methods. Clay with a sandy or groggy 'tooth' to it dries out readily from the more uneven thicknesses which these two methods tend to give, and thus it neither warps nor splits. Pinching, as the name implies, is achieved by holding a ball of clay in one hand while the fingers and thumb of the other gently and rhythmically pinch and squeeze the clay round, out and up to form the wall of the shape. The forms tend to be organic and the surface marks can reflect the pressures of the potter's fingers. If the clay is left to stiffen, however, all such evidence can be scraped away to give precise forms and clean surfaces. Some of the finest Japanese tea ceremony bowls, now national treasures, were made by pinching methods, the subtle forms often being enhanced by the marks of the fire. For coiling, the potter uses a similar range of clays. Coils or ropes of soft clay are rolled out and these can be flattened if the potter wishes. Starting from a pinched or pressed-out base, each coil is wound around the form and the ends are joined to form a separate ring on top of the coil below. The coils are 'knitted' into place by upward or downward strokes of the fingers. The positioning of these coils can change the direction of the form: Placing them towards the outside will widen and expand the form; inward moving shapes, even very narrow-necked vessels, are made by applying the coils in decreasing circles. As in all work with clay, timing is essential. If the clay is allowed to stiffen at certain points in the making of the article, there is no limit to the size or shape of coiled pots or objects. Consequently the method is extensively used for more sculptural purposes. For work on a larger scale, the potter usually walks around the pot, rather than sitting and slowly rotating it on a mat or slow wheel. Wooden 'paddles' can be used to thin, beat, swell and alter the shape, and beating marks can be left showing as embellishment, or they can be very smoothly scraped clean. Magnificent coiled pots of truly monumental quality have been made by many cultures. The Nigerian water pots, for example, were produced in this way. The Pre-Columbian civilizations never developed the use of the wheel, but used the coiling technique as one of their main methods of production. Today many studio-potters, especially those interested in form and decoration rather than function, use it as their principal medium of expression.

Two other manual methods of production are slab-building and press-molding. The link between these two methods is in the idea of making vessels or objects from a sheet of clay. The clay can be rhythmically beaten between the palms of the hands, rolled out on a flat surface or squeezed from a machine (a slab roller), which is very like an old-fashioned mangle. Sheets or slabs can also be cut to an even thickness from a block of clay using a taut wire. To make forms entirely from slabs, the clay has to stiffen sufficiently ('cheese' or 'leather-hard' are two expressive terms) to allow them to be cut to shape and joined together. The edges of the pieces are mitered and scored and the 'joints' painted with slip (clay and water mixed to a liquid) before 'luting' them together. This method of building usually produces hard-edged forms.

Press-molding involves the use of molds or formers, made from some absorbent material such as biscuited clay, plaster of Paris or wood. The clay slab is pressed over or into the mold to take its shape. It is then coaxed down or over with the fingers or a damp sponge. Excess clay is cut away and the edges can be treated in a variety of ways. Traditionally this method was used to make oval and rectangular dishes, but much more complex one- and two-piece press molds have long been used to make vessels, figurines and other objects. Press-molding was another method favored by the Pre-Columbians. Soft balls or pieces of clay can also be pressed into the crevices of the mold until the entire inner surface is covered. Any seams remaining when the molds are removed are cleaned or 'fettled' away.

Casting follows as a logical extension of this last method. When potters developed the use of slip (clay in a liquid state), it enabled them to pour it into biscuit or plaster of Paris molds of one or more pieces and make objects of varying complexity. While it is mainly an industrial mass-production method in which the process of minimizing the water content of the slip (deflocculation) has been mastered, casting is used by many craft potters, especially for porcelain sculptural pieces.

Throwing

Throwing on the potter's wheel seems to have first been used in the Middle East sometime during the fourth millenium BC and from that time on it has helped speed up the potter's production and make possible the repetition of a wide variety of symmetrical vessels. Much has been written about the art, mystique even, of throwing pots. Soft clay of a suitable type, held upon a flat surface (the wheel head) and revolved by hand, foot or mechanical device will respond easily to the slightest pressure. All forming methods rely on sensitive handling and well-timed movements. Handbuilding techniques work at an essentially slower tempo than throwing, but throwing also has a rhythm dictated by the clay, the wheel, the form and the potter's skill and temperament.

Throwable clays should be plastic enough to 'pull' upwards or outwards with ease while retaining a given shape as the clay dries. Considerations such as fired hardness or color, however, may claim priority so that a throwing body is always a compromise. The wheel itself usually has a range of speeds, controlled by the potter's foot, either directly in contact with the flywheel that moves the central shaft or, in the case of a cranked shaft, by working a kick bar from the crank. Variations range from the Japanese hand-propelled wheel, at which the potter sits or squats, to the north European stick wheel over which the potter stands. The electric motor is the latest model in this long history of throwing techniques.

The thrower can make one shape from one single lump of clay, can throw several shapes from a larger lump (throwing off the hump) or can throw one pot in several stages. This latter method is used when either the shapes are too large and complicated to throw in one piece, or the clay is not plastic enough to allow such one-piece throwing. To throw in this way, some potters simply add a thick, soft coil of clay to the rim of

Slab-building and press molding *Both of these methods involve making articles from a sheet of clay, but press-molding produces round-edged objects, while a slab-built form is hard-edged. Dishes and figures can be made by pressing the clay into plaster molds of one or two pieces (far left), or several pieces, as in the case of the Bow figures of the girl and fortune-teller (left). For slab-building the sheets of clay are cut to the required thickness and joined together with slip (bottom right). The green-glazed earthenware farm building (below left), of the Han dynasty, was slab-built in this way.*

the form, and continue throwing. Others might add a freshly thrown section, or again allow all the thrown sections to stiffen before assembling the whole pot. However all throwers follow certain procedures. Initially the clay has to be 'centered' on the wheelhead, a process which defies adequate description, as the degree of centeredness can only be recognized by the individual potter. When the clay is centered on the wheel, two or three basic shapes, with numerous subtle variations, can be made. These are the bowl, cylinder and

sphere. At this stage of forming the potter knows whether the whole piece will be finished then and there on the wheel, or whether at a later stage the pot will have to be 'turned' to remove excess clay, to 'finish' the form and complete the foot and base. Methods of throwing vary enormously — some potters use copious amounts of water to lubricate the clay, others hardly any. Some use their hands, and perhaps a sponge, to clear away water while others have a whole range of tools. Ribs of wood or metal are used as aids to throwing and

for skimming away the wet slurry on the form to make it firm for lifting from the wheel. Sticks and callipers are used for measuring, sponges and leathers for compressing edges, and string, gut, or wire to cut under the bases of forms before lifting them away. When the pot has dried to a leather-hard state the potter will use all kinds of tools, mainly metal, to turn away the excess clay from the form as it is held upside down on the spinning wheelhead.

The many appurtenances to thrown shapes — lips, spouts, lids, knobs, lugs

The Potter's Wheel *Throwing pots on the wheel has long been part of the potter's art (right) and this technique has been used to produce a whole range of wares – from the blue and white jars of the Ming dynasty (below) to the splendidly shaped forms of Lucie Rie (far right).*

and handles — are all attended to by the thrower at the appropriate time. Lids and lips are usually made at the same time as the pot, but lugs, spouts and handles are normally made when the clay has stiffened. Much depends on the type of clay used, the tradition of the forms and the character of the potters themselves.

Decoration

Decoration of the ceramic form can start at any time during making. A mark in the wet clay wall of a thrown pot, the impression of fingers on a coiled surface, the intricate enamel painting on an already glazed pot — all are forms of decoration. The main choice for the potter, apart from the vital one of subject matter, whether the form is abstract or representational, is when and how to decorate.

One method is to remove bits of clay from the surface of the form. This could include incising, carving, cutting, fluting, anything in fact that leaves a cut mark in the wet to leather-hard clay. Handbuilding and throwing both employ these methods; the latter involves cutting the clay away from the thickly thrown pot at an early stage and

carrying on throwing from inside the form only, to expand the cut marks into a decorative pattern. All manner of tools are used, from porcupine quills to shaped wire loops. In general the softer the clay, the swifter, more immediate the stroke must be. If the clay is harder, the lines and areas can be cut in a more controlled way. Inlaying of other clays into incisions is an extension of the incising technique. Impressing is also done at the soft stage, but the clay is not actually removed. Any hard object will make an impression and roulettes give continuous patterns around the surface. Piercing goes right through the clay wall and can be left like that or, at a later stage, glaze can be run in to fill the holes and give a window tracery effect. Japanese rice seed decoration, where the seed is pressed through the clay wall and left in place, is a variation of this method.

Adding clay to a form is best done at one of two stages — either when the clay is soft so that clay coils or pads can be joined to it by pressing them on and smoothing them down, or when the form is leather-hard, by keying the surface, applying slip and adding firm clay shapes to the area. The latter method,

called sprigging, was favored by English eighteenth century potters such as Josiah Wedgwood, and the Nottingham and Lambeth salt glaze potters who specialized in hunting scenes. The tiny shapes were first modeled in clay, then cast in plaster to make the molds from which the thin sprigs came away with the aid of a lifting knife.

Decorating with slip is a popular method and slip-trailed, lead-glazed ware was the glory of English seventeenth and eighteenth century pottery. To make slip, clay and water are mixed together to make a creamy liquid. This mixture is then poured over the surface, or the pot is dipped into it. Slip can be stiffened so that it can be piped from a thin-nozzled vessel or bag — not unlike icing a cake. The clays used to make the slips can be mixed together or stained with metal oxides.

Areas and lines of slip can be 'stopped out', (prevented from adhering to the clay), by resist methods of decoration. Damp paper shapes can be stuck on, or hot wax poured or brushed onto the leather-hard clay, prior to dipping, pouring or brushing with slip. The paper is removed later, but the wax is left to burn out in the early stages of the firing.

Sgraffito is the technique of cutting through slip to expose the body underneath, while burnishing is the compression of the slip or body surface to compact the clay and alter its fired appearance and color. Both these methods take place at a time when the clay is leather-hard, but has not yet changed color, which indicates the driest phase. Once the clay has dried to this point, metal oxides can be applied — either by rubbing them dry into the surface or, more commonly, by brush painting them on with a little water and gum. Before biscuit firing was introduced painting, before the glaze was applied to the unfired pot, was the norm. Some potters today still prefer this once-fired or raw-glazed method and paint their decoration either under or over the unfired glaze. The same metals that stain clays or slips are used for painting onto the unfired or biscuited clay or indeed on top of the unfired glaze — a technique called maiolica. Colors for maiolica glazes (an earthenware glaze opacified by tin oxide) are usually ground with water, small additions of gum, and sometimes the glaze itself to help the flow of the brush strokes. The technique is not unlike painting on blotting paper and therefore a swift, controlled skill is called for. At this stage of decoration, the potter can use brush strokes, or pour hot or cold wax (emulsion) on to 'stop out' one color, or one glaze, from another.

Even after the main glaze firings of earthenware, stoneware or porcelain have taken place the possibilities of decorating have not been exhausted because metal oxides, in the form of enamels or lusters, can be painted or sprayed onto the glazed surface. These metals will require another low firing — from 600-900°C (1110-1650°F) is the usual range for enamels and lusters — to fix them to the ware. The Persian minai enamel painters and the magnificent Islamic lusters from Kashan and Spain are the supreme examples of this final stage in the decorator's art.

With all these techniques available, it is simply not feasible to give a definitive list of decorative methods. It must be remembered that combinations of so many of these techniques are used by potters the world over. Today, new methods, based on modern technology (photography and printing processes among them), have added to the already wide spectrum.

Glazes and Glazing

Glazing is a fascinating aspect of ceramics, involving a knowledge of geology and chemistry. The whole area of glazing is seen by some as the high point of the decorator's art. Potters have to consider function as well as exercise aesthetic judgment because glaze, like all decorative materials, should enhance the form to which it is applied.

It is simplest to think of a glaze as a glass that has been melted onto the surface of the clay. There are only a few glass-forming elements, and of these the potter makes use of silica, by far the most abundant and easily accessible one. In fact it is present in many of the minerals potters use. To assist the silica in melting (on its own it would have to be heated to a temperature of around 1720°C/3130°F), potters add fluxes, to bring the temperature down to whatever is required. The third ingredient of a glaze, alumina, is added to help the mixture of silica and flux adhere to the clay. These three, silica, flux and alumina, are akin to the bones, blood and flesh (to use Bernard Leach's imagery). They allow the potter to obtain an infinite variety of glaze qualities, from matt to shiny, soft to hard, smooth to textured. The control

15

of opacity, the large range of colors obtained from the metal oxides, and the way in which the potter fires all these mixtures, completes the outline picture of the skills involved in ceramics.

Certain minerals will make glazes opaque in varying degrees. The amounts of others can be adjusted, or the temperature at which the glazes fire can be altered to give this quality. Either way, a new dimension is added to the glaze by the ability to opacify color and texture.

With all ceramics it is only the metals that can be used to obtain stable colors. Some will withstand the intense heat, while others will volatize and disappear. The blending of metals in glazes, with or without opacifiers, and the effects that various minerals have on them, gives an almost infinite range of colors.

Applying the glaze

Glazes can be applied to clay before it has been fired (raw glazing) or after it has had a biscuit firing — usually at a lower temperature than the glaze firing to follow. One of the earliest methods of application involved dusting the pot with powdered glaze materials. For example, raw lead and copper filings were shaken from a cloth or sieve onto the raw clay surface of a European medieval jug and this gave a characteristic bright copper-green glaze when fired to around 900°C-1000°C (1650-1830°F). Glaze materials mixed with water can be painted on, layer by layer, to build up the required intensity. The most common practice, however is for potters to buy or prepare, finely ground materials, weigh them out after having calculated their proportions, and sieve them with water to make sure they are evenly dispersed and free from lumps and foreign matter. Suspending insoluble materials in water in this way means that the pot or object can be dipped into the glaze, or glaze can be poured or sprayed on at this stage. Being absorbent, the unfired or low biscuit-fired clay sucks in the water, leaving the glaze materials on the surface as a fine

powder. Soluble materials are sucked in with the water so they can not be easily used unless they are first made insoluble by fritting. This is a process where the materials, for example borax and soda, are first heated and fused to a red heat and then shattered by pouring them out onto cold water to facilitate fine grinding. This process of calcining and grinding enables the soluble materials, which are vital for melting silica at the lower temperatures, to be successfully incorporated into earthenware recipes.

Kilns and Firing

Firing work that may have taken weeks or even months to make and decorate is the final trial by fire of the potters art. Everything is staked upon this process, which can easily fail. There is little wonder that the Japanese begin a firing with a religious ceremony, or that present day western potters like to placate the powers that be with small clay effigies.

Procedures for firing clay ware to biscuit temperature or to the higher firings of glazed earthenware, stoneware and porcelain have always followed the same general pattern. This is still true today in spite of some quite startling new developments due to the advent of new lightweight kiln materials. It is important that water in the clay is driven off carefully so that explosions do not occur. Some atmospheric water will remain, even in 'dry' clay, and this will have to be heated gently during the first hour or more of the firing to about 100°C (210°F) — even slower for large or thick pieces of work. Chemically combined water (at the molecular level) only escapes later, so a slow beginning is essential for a biscuit or raw firing. Certain changes in the crystalline structure of the quartz in the clay body have to be reached without undue jumps in the rise of temperature — from 350°C-700°C (600°F-1290°F) and most critically at 573°C (1060°F). At around 800°C-

TYPES OF KILN

Fuel – grass brushwood

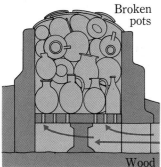

Broken pots

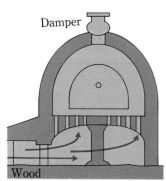

Wood

Damper

Wood

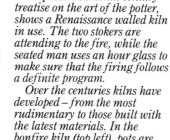

The engraving (right), taken from Piccolpasso's sixteenth century treatise on the art of the potter, shows a Renaissance walled kiln in use. The two stokers are attending to the fire, while the seated man uses an hour glass to make sure that the firing follows a definite program.

Over the centuries kilns have developed – from the most rudimentary to those built with the latest materials. In the bonfire kiln (top left), pots are stacked on top of a bed of fuel and more fuel is heaped over and around the pots. In the open-top updraft kiln (middle left) broken pots and shards have been used to complete the top arch of the kiln. The updraft kiln (bottom left) was used by Greek and Roman potters and variations of it are still used all over Europe and the Near East.

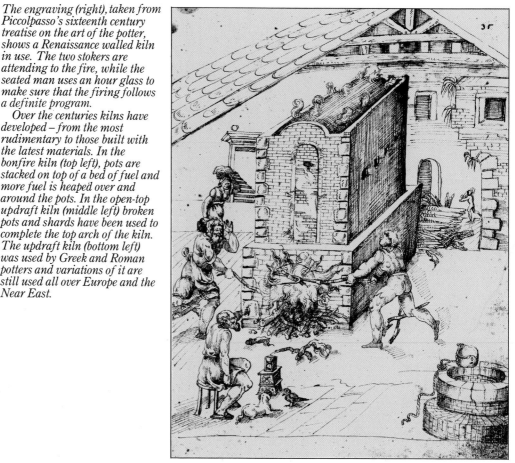

Downdraft kilns were developed in the Far East, where the really high stoneware and porcelain temperatures were achieved. Downdraft kilns work on the same principle (see opposite) whether they are circular, rectangular, or the long kilns built on slopes in southern China and Japan (top right). The ultimate in spectacular kilns must be the Japanese many-chambered climbing kiln (right) in which rows of chambers were built on the sloping hillside and fired from one end. They were boosted at the height of the firing, which took many days, by feeding each chamber with thin slivers of wood until the whole kiln resembled a dragon spitting fire and smoke. An example of a typical European kiln, used particularly by potters in Stoke-on-Trent, England, is the bottle kiln (left). The saggars (fireclay containers) in the kiln were filled with wares.

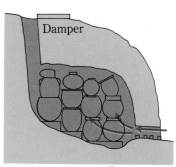

Damper

Fuel – wood

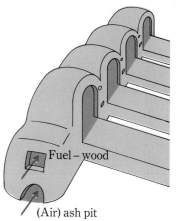

Fuel – wood

(Air) ash pit

900°C (1470°F-1650°F) carbonaceous matter in the clay must be burned out by slowing or holding the rising rate so that there is no 'bloating', or disfiguration. The temperature is then allowed to rise to the full biscuit temperature — for earthenware 1000°C (1830°F) or higher, stoneware 960°C (1760°F) and porcelain about the same, but sometimes lower depending on the clay body.

Biscuit kilns are packed with the pots touching, the small ones inside, the larger ones to form stacks at the bottom. The kiln is well ventilated, especially during the early stages, and some potters like to keep a vent open at the top of the kiln throughout the firing.

At the end of the firing the vent is closed and any other places where cold air could get in are sealed off. Ten to twelve hours is a reasonable and safe period for an average studio kiln measuring about 30-50 cubic feet and stacked with medium-sized to large pots.

The pieces that are packed for a glaze firing must not touch and any glazed portion should not come in contact with any part of the kiln or it will stick as the glaze melts. Kiln furniture and props are coated with a 'wash' of alumina and china clay; some potters spread fine sand over the shelves instead. Stoneware and porcelain pieces that have no glaze on the base can be put directly onto these prepared shelves. Some porcelain is placed on specially made 'setters', or flat porcelain pads. It can also be protected in 'saggars' — fireclay boxes which are stacked in 'bungs'. Earthenware, glazed all over because of its porous nature, is placed on specially made ceramic 'stilts' and 'spurs', small spiked 'feet' which leave sharp marks that have to be ground away after the firing. Salt glazed articles must be 'wadded' when set in the kiln (salt glaze coats everything in the kiln and would adhere the pots to the shelves). Each pot is mounted on three or more small pellets, and wads are made from a mixture of alumina, china clay and a small amount of bentonite with water. Packing a kiln one shelf at a time is an arduous business. A kiln measuring 100 cubic feet could take two people two days to stack. If the glaze on the biscuited clay is dry, the heat can rise fairly rapidly. A temperature of 100°C (210°F) per hour is quite normal, but firing is a very individual task and each potter has a preferred range.

Fuel

Fuels for kilns include anything that will burn or give heat. Electricity, gas, oil or wood (and, until recently, coal) are the main fuels, but such exotic materials as old rubber-tires, dried dung or even solar energy can be used. Potters choose the fuels for various reasons, economic and aesthetic being the two most important. However a major consideration is the choice of atmosphere inside the kiln as this is crucial to the color and texture of ceramics. The atmosphere can be one of oxidation, or of reduction. Oxidation means firing with adequate air to allow good clean combustion. In reduction the kiln is starved of air by the control of fuel consumption and the adjustment of air intakes and flues. If the combustion is then to continue it must take oxygen from somewhere and, if it cannot draw it from outside the kiln, it will take the necessary oxygen from the clays and glazes. This results in speckling in iron-bearing stoneware-bodies — a typical reduction-fired look. It can also produce alternative color response from many of the other minerals used in the glazes.

Similarly, earthenware and porcelain are both affected by the type of atmosphere in which they are fired. Electric kilns (unless fitted with silicon carbide elements) do not take kindly to a reducing atmosphere so are best used for oxidation. With wood on the other hand it is more difficult, though by no means impossible, to achieve a completely carbon-free oxidizing firing.

Electric devices, called pyrometers, can be used for measuring the temperature inside the kiln, but potters also use specially made 'cones' of compressed materials similar to those used in glaze making. They are made to a precise formula, designed to melt at a given temperature. Many potters use both a pyrometer and cones as a double check.

Kilns

It is not always necessary to fire pots in a kiln. The ware can be thoroughly dried out, placed on the ground with brush wood or dried grass piled over it, and when this is ignited, fired to about 700°C (1290°F) or 800°C (1470°F) in as little as twenty minutes, and certainly no more than two hours.

Studio-potters today can choose from many types of kiln, including those built from the latest materials, developed from space-age technology. These kilns can spin fibers of silica and alumina into material that is paper thin, malleable like putty, shaped as a flat board, or to standard brick sizes.

The technology with which the potter works does change but certain age old procedures endure. Moreover the same questions confront the potter now as they did before — what kind of article to make? What type of clays, decoration and kilns to use to make it?

KILN SYSTEMS

The diagrams illustrate the flame paths for different kinds of kilns. In the updraft kiln (left), the heat and smoke are released through an opening, and finally out of a chimney at the top of the kiln. In the downdraft kiln (middle), the heat builds up in the chamber and is pulled first to the top of the kiln, and then down through the pots and out of the end of the kiln. In the crossdraft kiln (right) the heat (fire) enters at the side, is pulled up and over the bag ball and is released at the other side of the kiln.

The Workings of the Manufactory

The coming of the Industrial Revolution hastened the change that had been threatening the manufacture of ceramics for some time. This change was essentially one of shifting the emphasis from the craftsman potter, who produced pots by hand with a few simple tools, to the small factories employing up to a few hundred people, each one working on a specific part of the production process rather than performing the job in its entirety. Perhaps the most illuminating description of a factory in the early days of this change is that of Mrs Philip Lybbe Powys, who visited the Worcester Porcelain Manufactory in 1771 and wrote as follows:

'They employ 160 persons, a vast number of them very little boys. There are eleven different rooms, in which the employment is as follows: First room, a mill for grinding the composition to make the clay; second, the flat cakes of clay drying in ovens; third, the cakes work'd up like a paste, and form'd by *the eye only* into cups, mugs, basins, teapots, their ingenuity and quickness at this appears like magic; fourth, making the things exactly by molds all to one size, but they are seldom different, so nice is their eye in forming; fifth, paring and chipping coffee-cups and saucers in molds, a boy turning the wheel for each workman; sixth, making the little roses, handles, twists, and flowers one sees on the china fruit-baskets, all these stuck on with a kind of paste; seventh, scalloping saucers, &c., with a pen-knife while the composition is pliable, and in this room they make the china ornamental figures; these are done in molds, separate molds for the limbs, and stuck on as above; eighth, the heat of this eighth room was hardly bearable, filled with immense ovens for baking the china, which is put in a sort of high sieve about six feet long; ninth glazing the china, by dipping it into large tubs of liquor, and shaking it as dry as they can; tenth, some sorting the china for pain-

Factory production c1900. *A turner, watched by his 'runner', turns the foot of a piece of Royal Worcester ware.*

ting, others smoothing the bottom by grinding; eleventh, painting the china in the different patterns.'

This description of a factory visit, written by a keenly observant lady who was not a knowledgeable potter, contains a few inaccuracies, such as the reference to the joining of separate parts with 'a kind of paste' when what was really meant was slip (a solution of liquid clay). Nevertheless it is a true account of a medium-sized, contemporary factory which was producing high-quality porcelain by hand, with the aid of simple machinery, and droves of 'little boys' to fetch and carry for the senior potters. A visit to a similar factory today, over 200 years later, would not be very dissimilar. However, the increasing use of electricity has removed the need for much of the physical grind, such as wedging clay or turning handles. A great many changes have taken place within the industry, and it has been necessary to introduce mass-production techniques and special machinery in the most modern factories.

Fortunately, the industry has not yet reached the stage of full automation, as have some automobile factories, but perhaps the day is not far off when this will happen.

Factory-made porcelain
The following is an explanation of all the processes involved in a factory-made piece of porcelain — from the preparation of raw materials, through the making stages to the final decoration. There are many differences to be found in the techniques, according to the type of clay body used — for example pottery and porcelain, or hard and soft porcelain. To help the reader to understand these differences, a simple explanation of the terms is given below.

Pottery is a term which is applied to bodies which are not translucent when fired. It comprises those which are porous unless they are glazed, such as common pottery, earthenware, maiolica (or delft). These types of ware are made from the lower-firing clays, also stonewares, which are dense bodies made of special clays which can stand high-temperature firing and are non-porous without glazing. The latter group can be glazed and, if extremely thin, can have a certain degree of translucency. It is often described as vitreous china or semi-porcelain.

Porcelain can best be divided up into hard and soft. Hard porcelain, or hard-paste porcelain, is sometimes referred to as true porcelain. It is made from the two ingredients known to the Chinese as kaolin and pe-tun-se (in the West, china clay and china stone). The difference between hard and soft is not just in terms of the raw materials used, for the temperature of firing is also relevant. Hard porcelain is fired at a low temperature in the first, or biscuit, firing and then very high in the glaze firing (over 1400°C/2550°F), which vitrifies the glaze and body together.

Soft porcelain, or soft-paste porcelain,

Painted Decoration
The Men's Painting Department of the Royal Worcester factory at the beginning of the century. Large-scale production of pottery was established in England during the second half of the eighteenth century. The 'primitive' industrialization of pottery craft skills through a stage-by-stage process of manufacture has survived almost unchanged into the modern world.

PRODUCTION OF PORCELAIN WARE

PREPARING THE BODY

Pugging

Bone and stone	Water	China clay

Mixing

Sieving and magnetizing

Filter pressing and homogenizing

Plastic body Clay in a solid but malleable form	**Casting slip** Liquid mixture of clay and water

METHODS OF MAKING

Plastic body
The methods of shaping a plastic clay body are jolleying, slab-making, hand pressing or jiggering, dry pressing or sprigging. The major processes of shaping involve the use of molds.

Casting slip
Slip casting is used for making figures and holloware and the liquid slip is set in plaster molds. Molds are constructed for easy removal of the cast, but composite objects are cast in separate pieces.

Drying – final shaping and finishing

Sticking up — leather-hard or dry stages

Slip casting

FIRING AND GLAZING

Sticking up

Biscuit firing
In biscuit firing the composition of the clay body changes; it is made hard and durable by the intense heat. At this stage the ware is inspected so any problems are rectified before the ware passes to the glazing stage.

Underglaze
Basic color is applied to the ware

Spray or dip glazing

Glost firing
Glost firing is the second stage of firing in which the glaze is fused to the surface of the ware.

Glost inspection

ONGLAZE DECORATION

Decorative color and pattern may be hand painted, sprayed, dripped or printed on the surface of ceramic ware. Basic color can be applied as an underglaze immediately after biscuit firing. This is fired at a high temperature and colors (known as onglazes) subsequently added, are fired at lower heat. Some of the metallic oxides used for ceramic color are subject to quite dramatic changes in the firing process. Colored slip is also used as decoration or to build up a relief pattern.

First decorative firing

Second decorative firing

Gilding
Gold decoration is applied last

Burnishing
Burnishing sets and brightens the gold

Final inspection and despatch

Decorating

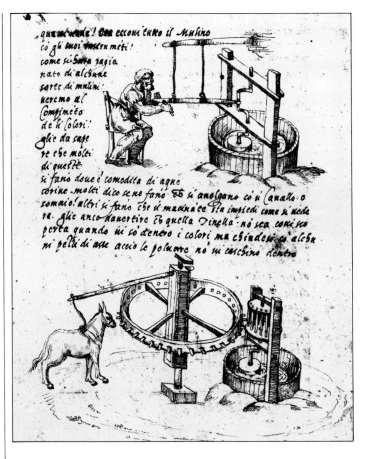

Renaissance and modern technology *A sixteenth century Italian treatise on pottery manufacture by Cipriano Piccolpasso (left), shows a hand-powered and donkey-powered crushing mill, used to grind materials.*

A modern pug mill (below) mechanizes the process of homogenization — squeezing out bubbles of air trapped in the prepared cakes of clay. Homogenization, designed to eliminate blistering in the fired ware, was originally carried out by hand, using a technique called 'wedging': the length of time involved in hand wedging, however, has made this technique prohibitively expensive.

is a translucent body made from materials other than the classic hard paste. The ware is fired to a high temperature in the biscuit firing (usually between 1200°-1300°C/2190°-2390°F) and then glazed and refired at a lower temperature of between about 1000°-1100°C (1830-2010°F) which fuses the glaze on top of the body.

Preparing the body
All clay bodies have to go through an extensive process of preparation in order to bring them to the correct working state. All the different ingredients that go into making up the body are cleaned and processed separately, then blended together in liquid form to produce a solution known as slip. Raw materials tend to vary a great deal and the craftsman potter is able to vary his methods of making — if the body dries too quickly he used more water, if fusing does not take place in the kiln he adjusts the firing time or temperature. However, a machine cannot make adjustments in this way, and it is therefore essential for the raw materials to be consistent. The clays, which reach the factory in a dry state, are mixed with water. Nowadays this process is done in a blunger, a cylindrical or hexagonal vessel container with a mechanized stirrer. The coarser raw materials, such as feldspar, quartz, Cornish stone and flint are nowadays supplied crushed. These require fine grinding in a machine called a ball mill, which consists of a large steel drum lined with quartzite or ceramic blocks, inside which flint pebbles or alumina rods revolve, grinding the hard particles very fine. In the early days of the factory, workers had to use large crushing mills, driven by water or horse power, and later by beam engines.

The raw materials are ground in water and, at the end of each milling, the batch is emptied. After grinding, the slip is passed over sieves, usually of a vibratory type, to ensure that no oversized material enters the clay body. To prevent any possible contamination from small bits of iron, the slip is passed over powerful magnets. It is then ready for mixing.

The blunged and prepared slips are kept separately in storage arks. The slips are pumped into the mixing ark via weighing machines and, after mixing, are pumped into a final storage ark. The body is then ready for use in the liquid slip state. Sometimes it has to be transformed into a more solid body — a process which was first done in a drying kiln, but it is now done in a filter press. Grooved metal trays are pressed tightly together to form chambers, each lined with a filter cloth. The frames and cloth have a central hole so that the slip can be pumped in to fill the chambers. The pumping continues until no more water is being pressed out and this indicates the required consistency. The press is then opened up and the cakes of clay removed.

Although the cakes may look usable straight away, they need to be further prepared by homogenizing. It was at one time felt that the condition of the body at this stage was improved by storage in damp cellars, and some potters still age the body for up to three years. Homogenizing is done by wedging, a method which involves alternately cutting the lump of clay with a wire and slamming one half onto the other with considerable force. The body is then turned 90 degrees each time it is cut, so that it is thoroughly mixed and air bubbles are eliminated. If these bubbles remain in the body they will cause blistering in the fired ware and also impair plasticity and workability. Although wedging is the best method if carried out correctlym it is very time-consuming and has become impractical in industrial usage because of high labor costs. For many years potters used a kneading table, which comprised a set of rollers for wedging the body, but this was not a very efficient method. Nowadays a pug mill is used. This resembles a giant mincing machine, in which the filter cakes are first shredded and mixed. The body then passes through a grid into a vacuum chamber which sucks out the air, and it is then extruded in the form of a large sausage. This is the principal method used, although it has drawbacks. Problems are caused by the shredding process and distortions can occur in firing.

Methods of making
There are two main methods of making — from a plastic body, and by slip casting. Freehand shaping involves throwing, coiling or slab making. These techniques are seldom used by industry nowadays, but throwing was used extensively in the eighteenth century for simple, hollow shapes, such as bowls and teapots, and shapes on which there was no modeled decoration. After such pieces were made they were put aside to dry to a leather-hard state and then the foot was turned on a horizontal lathe by the turner, originally a boy, nowadays an electric device. At this stage it was also possible to incise decoration (sgraffito) or cut the rims into different shapes, such as scallops or nicks or, with the use of concentric lathes, cut diced or ring patterns into the piece.

All objects with modeled decoration on the outside or inside were produced either completely, or partially, with the aids of molds, usually made of plaster of Paris, although often of pitcher (fired) clay. The simplest process to understand is that of sprigging, in which a piece of body is pressed into a mold shape, the surface scraped and the piece, or sprig, carefully picked out. The slip causes the sprig to stick and fuse to the pot during firing. This process is still used today by such firms as Wedgwood for their jasper ware decoration where a colored sprig is contrasted with a different colored body.

All processes using molds work on the principle that the plaster molds absorb some of the moisture content of the body and the piece inside the mold can be removed when dry. The making of the molds by the mold-maker follows an alternating series of positives and negatives: the original model is made by turning a block of solid plaster of Paris or making an original model in clay,

Throwing a pot at Meissen *A craftsman at the Meissen factory in Dresden shapes a pot freehand by throwing it on a wheel.*

plasticine or wax. From this a negative mold is made, which is split into two or more parts to become the block mold. From this positive plaster casts are made, again in two or more parts, and these are known as cases. The negative working molds are made from the cases for actual use. The great advantage of plaster is that it is cheap, but the disadvantage is the fact that the detail wears quickly and the molds do not last for very long.

Flatware is made by hand pressing or jiggering. Hand pressing involves the flattening of a piece of body called a bat, slapping it onto the mold and pressing the body onto the mold with a wet sponge. The edges are trimmed off with a sharp knife and it is left to dry slightly. If the piece requires a foot, a prepared mold shape is placed at the correct position on the still slightly wet pot and squeezed into the mold. When dry, the foot mold, and then the complete dish, is removed. This method is used nowadays for more expensive items, for awkwardly shaped dishes, or those with molded decoration on the inside of the dish. This highly skilled job is done by a presser. Jiggering is done by a jiggerer and is usually undertaken in two operations. A bat is prepared (nowadays by a pressing machine, but at one time by hand) and placed upon a plaster mold which provides the upper profile of the plate. The mold is put onto a revolving

head and the jiggerer presses the bat with his hand while working from the center outwards. He then brings down a template which has the profile of the underside of the plate on it, including the foot, and this is set so that the space between it and the mold corresponds to the required thickness of the plate. When all the excess body has been squeezed away, the mold is put aside to dry, after which the plate can be lifted from the mold. This process can be done mechanically in one operation, but without the pressure of the potter's hands to even out strains in the body, stresses can be set up which can cause a mechanically-made piece to be weaker than a handmade one.

Hollowware — cups, simple bowls, casseroles — is made by a process called jolleying and the craftsman is a jolleyer. Jolleying is a mirror image of jiggering, with the plaster mold forming the outside of the piece and the template the inside of the piece. The simplest way is to form the body into a ball and place it into a revolving mold. The ball of clay is drawn up the sides, and the template is brought down to finish the correct shape. A more refined method, used for the finer wares, such as bone china cups, can be achieved with a lining or liner which is made in the rough outline of the cup and put into the mold instead of a ball of clay. This can be fashioned roughly over a chum, or shaping mold. Unfortunately, with all these jolleying processes, a thin cup can be under great stress in firing, and the finest method of all involves a combination of throwing and jolleying. In this, a liner is thrown by hand on a wheel before it is jolleyed, eliminating most of the strains and stresses which the clay would otherwise 'remember' (as potters put it). Rings are often put on the piece to prevent distortion as the cups are removed from the molds after drying.

The modern mechanical application of jiggering and jolleying is forming by roller machine. In this, a heated die, called a 'bomb', is used instead of the hand-held template and the die revolves as well as the mold. No bats or linings are needed, the piece being made directly from a slice cut from an extruded roll of prepared body. The slice is placed on or in the mold, the bomb performing the spreading and shaping in one operation. This method lends itself to automation by semi-skilled or unskilled hands and allows the use of stiffer clay, thus reducing the risk of distortion. All this speeds up the process considerably, and was

Three ways of shaping clay

'Jolleying' (above) — pressing clay between revolving plaster mold and a template, a jolleyed bowl is hand-pressed onto a prepared mold (above right). This process is used to produce the famous Wedgwood Green Cabbage ware (above right). The Liedler 'bomb' (right) produces molded soufflé dishes semi-automatically. The hydraulic ram presses out the clay body against a circular plaster mold, while a knife trims off the surplus clay.

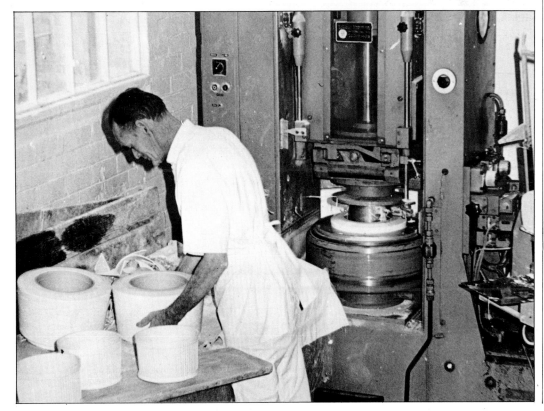

originally designed for mass production; being especially suitable where large quantities of the same shape are required. However, the main drawback is that shapes have to be suitable for such mechanized processes, and refined, beautiful or complicated pieces cannot be produced in this way.

Slip casting is the name given to the making of figures and hollowware from a liquid body. It involves pouring slip into a plaster mold until it is full. The porous plaster removes a quantity of the water from the slip and a solid layer of body — the cast — is built up on the inner walls of the mold. As the water is absorbed, the level in the mold sinks and the larger pieces, at any rate, need topping up with more slip. When the solid body has reached the required thickness, the surplus slip is vigorously poured out and can be used again. The mold is left to dry, the cast shrinks slightly and after a while becomes sufficiently rigid to be taken out of the mold. The molds are in a number of parts so that quite complicated objects can be removed easily, but shapes such as teapots have to be made without handles and spouts, which are cast separately, using thick slip as the adhesive.

Figures often require many separate molds because of undercut parts, such as projections, which make it difficult to remove them from the mold. It often surprises a visitor to a factory to see a figurine in a large number of dismembered pieces awaiting sticking up, looking for all the world like a three-dimensional jigsaw puzzle.

Slip casting is largely mechanized in mass-production processes, with automatic filling and emptying of molds. Some double casting is done in producing solid handles and oblong dishes. This involves applying slip through a casting hole, the cast being formed by two plaster surfaces with the slip filling the whole space. When the pieces are taken from the mold, they have the seam marks of the mold on them, and these marks have to be cut away with a knife. Slip casting can usually produce lighter figures than the alternative method of pressing a solid body into the two halves of a mold and then pressing the halves together until they are joined. The difference in weight would at once be noticeable if one compared the relative lightness of a slip-cast Chelsea figure with the heavy density of a press-molded Bow example.

Dry pressing should perhaps be mentioned, as this was the method by which floor tiles, in the style of the medieval period, were made in the mid-nineteenth century. Dry clay is pressed into a mold to produce thick tiles or other shapes.

The wares require drying and finishing off before the firing commences. Drying involves the removal of water from the clay body, to prevent damage to the piece in the firing. Until recent times, huge drying stoves were used, but nowadays continuous tunnel dryers are used. Finishing can be done before pieces are fully dry; for example turning is done when the ware is almost leather-hard. A shaped foot for the pot can be cut by a turner, and this can be done with the piece fixed upside down on a wheelhead, or horizontally on a lathe. Metal turning tools are used to trim off the surplus clay. There has been very little change in this process over several centuries, and the shape of the foot nowadays remains as characteristic of a particular factory as it was in the eighteenth century.

Sticking up — the joining of parts — can be done at the leather-hard or dry stages. The parts (spouts, handles, pieces of a figure) are joined together with a thick slurry of slip. Technical terms such as towing (taking the seams from plates), sponging (removing imperfections from cups and cleaning them up) and fettling (to deal with castwares in the dry state) are commonly used and most of these techniques have been adapted for automatic or semi-automatic machines nowadays.

Firing

Virtually all ceramics go through two basic kiln firings — biscuit, and glost firing. The first turns the raw materials into a hard body and the second fuses the glaze through the whole body or onto the surface. To use an analogy of the four elements — earth (or clay) is mixed with water dried by air, and finally being hardened by fire.

Factory kilns have probably undergone the greatest change for the better out of all the pottery-making processes over the years. Fortunately the abysmal conditions of work in the bottle ovens are a thing of the past. In areas such as Stoke-on-Trent, where there were hundreds of bottles belching out sulfur-laden smoke, living conditions were badly affected and the town was covered in a black pall, so that from the surrounding hills you could not see the buildings. Gutters could not be made of metal, as they would corrode almost as soon as they were put up. Conditions for the kiln workers were often appalling, because unscrupulous pottery owners would demand a high turnover of firings and send youngsters in to draw the wares out when the heat was still intense. Working in heat of over 150 degrees children inevitably suffered health problems.

Nowadays, the firings are done in tunnel kilns. Trucks, called cars, loaded with the ware, are set onto an automatic belt and passed very slowly through a long tunnel. The temperature slowly rises to its highest point and then drops away until the cars emerge at the other end of the tunnel with the ware cool enough to unload. This method of firing is found to be more economical in the use of fuel, and the kilns are usually gas-fired. Morever, there are no health hazards or pollution. Both biscuit and glost firings are done in tunnels, but between the two firings the ware has to be glazed.

Glazing

The glazing consists of covering the body with a thin layer of glasslike coating to make it more attractive and durable. Glaze can be composed of a number of ingredients, but it is of paramount importance that the glaze fits the body. Otherwise crazing can occur. This is a cracking of the surface into a myriad of cobweb lines. During the firing the glaze melts and special fluxes are introduced into the raw materials to assist this process. The earliest flux was lead, which helped create translucence and a depth of colors. However lead is an extremely dangerous material to handle, causing harmful effects through long exposure, and for many years now leadless glazes, made with borax, have been used.

Glaze is applied in a liquid suspension; at one time all wares were dipped into large tubs, and the surplus glaze was shaken off. The most difficult shapes to glaze were flat plates and dishes, which had to be spun round to spread the glaze. One of the most interesting factory processes was to watch a glazer perform this task with the skill of a juggler, spinning an article which was as slippery as an eel.

Nowadays, most glazing is sprayed on, either by hand or by mechanical aerographing. A low-firing vegetable dye is put in the glaze so that, on examination, it is possible to check that the

Casting a figure *Casting complicated figure subjects has always been a job for the skilled specialist. This photo sequence, taken at the Royal Worcester factory in 1947, shows Bob Bradley, a foreman caster, assembling a pottery figure of the then Princess Elizabeth. Slip is poured into the mold (above), and the molded pieces are then trimmed and cleaned (top right). The individual pieces are ready for sticking up (right), and the complete figure, with supports (below), is then ready for firing.*

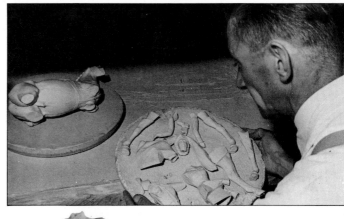

Decoration *From the humblest domestic jug to the exquisite products of the Meissen factory, pottery continues its long tradition as a decorative as well as a functional manufacture. Fine engraving on copper plate (below) contrasts with a simple hollowware (right). Painting, whether of ornamental figures (below right) or vases (opposite) is a primary method of decoration,* *carried to its ultimate perfection in the chinoiserie vase (below right) and elegant peacock figure produced in Meissen studios. Rosebud decoration modeled from individual petals of clay (below left) shows one element of a complex decorative vase in a traditional Meissen design.*

whole area is covered. An assistant, called a retoucher, removes any surplus glaze, particularly from the foot or rim, if the piece is to be fired without the use of supports or pegs.

Decoration

Many pieces are left undecorated in what is called the 'white' state — a simple white glaze — or even in the unglazed biscuit state, although the problem with both of these is that the surface gets dirty. Both bodies and glazes can be colored, and this can be the sole form of decoration. However in the case of industrially made ceramics, colors are used in the form of decorative patterns or colors, either handpainted or, more often nowadays, printed. In a factory, there is a definite distinction between the potters and the decorators, and it is often the decoration which is noted by the general public or knowledgeable collectors, rather than the shape and form.

Ceramic color is almost invariably provided by metallic oxides. These oxides are either used on their own or with a filler, such as alumina, quartz or feldspar for use at high temperature, or a flux for lower temperatures. High temperature colors can be used on the biscuited body, with the glaze fired on top, producing what are known as underglaze colors. The most famous of these is cobalt oxide, which gives a fine blue color. Lower firing colors are put on top of the glaze and are fired into the glaze in subsequent lower temperature firings. These colors which do not have glaze on top are called onglaze colors.

Underglaze colors are usually mixtures of cobalt, chromium and iron, and these can produce a fairly wide range of colors — from the deep blue cobalt to blue-green, if cobalt is mixed with chromium and black. These colors can only be applied onglaze on hard porcelain, and refired into the glaze. Many of these change during the firing into quite different colors due to certain atmospheric effects. Perhaps the most changeable colors are cobalt, and copper. The latter is green at low temperatures, but turns into a beautiful turquoise in alkaline form, or a magnificent *rouge flambé* or *sang-de-bœuf* red if a reducing atmosphere is introduced at the right moment of firing.

One simple form of decoration consists of applying liquid slip of a contrasting color to the body. This can be done by dipping, spraying, brushing, or trailing. The object is to set one color against another or, by cutting through the layers to expose the color underneath. The most complicated style of decoration is *pâte-sur-pâte*, where a low relief is slowly built up on a colored base and, when the slip is fired, a translucent effect is produced. It is possible to get a pot colored different inside and out by a skillful application of slip.

Methods of Decoration

Painting is perhaps the easiest decorative technique to understand, but the process is nowadays so time consuming and expensive that less and less handpainting is being done. Painters obtain their colors in powder form and grind them with a mixture of fat oil and aniseed to produce the right consistency for applying with the brush. The painter's bench or cubicle has an atmosphere of its own — a strange mixture of the smells of aniseed and fat oil and the sight of colors on a tile or in a palette with dozens of brushes of different sizes and shapes. The fat oil is produced from pure turpentine which is allowed to evaporate and the resulting oil is progressively made thicker by pouring it over from one level of dish to a lower one in what is called a fountain. One of the complications of painting is that most pieces have to be fired two or more times, both to accommodate the different firing temperatures of colors, and to help build up the strengths and perspectives of the painting. As all the colors are metallic oxides, they are all translucent. Colors can be sprayed, producing some very attractive flowing effects.

Ground laying is the process that produces wide bands or areas of ground color. In the eighteenth century these were painted on with a brush, but this seldom produced beautifully smooth colors. The ground layer covers the parts to be left free from color with a resist and then paints the rest with a drying oil. The oil is then bossed by striking it with a thick pad to remove the brushmarks. The powdered color is dusted on with a pad of cotton wool and the excess is shaken off. After drying, the resist is removed in warm water. The process is extremely expensive and has mainly been taken over by the use of bands of lithographs.

Printing from copperplate engravings was introduced around 1755 at Worcester. The engraver engraves or etches a pattern onto a copper plate, then the printer takes a pull from the heated copper by filling it with an oil-based color. Wetted tissue paper is then pressed between the rollers of a press (rather like the rollers of a mangle). The tissue is carefully removed from the copper and is passed to the printer's assistants, called transferers, who cut up the tissue, lay the still sticky pattern onto a piece that has been warmed and covered with a size, and rub it hard to fix the design. The tissue paper is then washed off with a sponge, leaving the pattern behind. Finally it is fired.

Printing with a copper plate is a lengthy and labor-intensive process and attempts have been made to semi-mechanize it with the use of a machine called a Murray-Curvex machine which stamps the pattern onto the piece. This greatly reduces the cost, but the results are not as good as the best quality hand printing. One of the drawbacks of copperplate printing is that only one color can be printed at a time. A print can be printed in one color, fired and then colored in by hand or it is possible to register small pieces of different colored prints on the piece, rather like putting a jigsaw together. This method was used by Pratt in the so-called Pratt-printed pot-lids of the Victorian period.

Lithography, known as decalcomania in the United States, is now most widely used method of ceramic decoration. It is mainly onglaze, but it is also suited to underglaze. By this process, full color patterns can be produced very simply in one firing. The lithography printing firm will supply specified or stock patterns in the form of large sheets. In the early days the process was called 'size down' and involved varnishing the ware before the application of the transfer to make it tacky — not unlike transfer printing. This involved a fair amount of skill on the part of the lithographer as it was essential to put the transfer onto the correct place since it could not be moved. Nowadays the need for varnishing has been eliminated by the new method called 'slide off'. The pattern is printed onto special paper by silk screen and then covered with a plastic medium. The decorator soaks the transfer in water, slides the pattern off the paper and sponges and squeezes it onto the ware. During the firing the plastic medium burns away, leaving the fully fired color decoration. This has ousted the size down method, as it requires little skill and is much quicker.

Acid gold etching involves etching part of the glaze with hydrofluoric

Production and Decoration *A complex piece such as this Sèvres vase à bobèches covers many of the aspects of casting and decorating porcelain.*

The flowers were produced separately by hand.

The ground colors were generally done before the panel subjects.

The panel subjects were particularly difficult to do as the color applied with the brush was not that which appeared after the firing.

The gilding was done last; on this vase it is achieved by a technique known as 'honey gilding'. It was tooled and burnished after firing.

The body, in this case a soft-paste or artificial porcelain, was prepared and cast in a mold in its various component parts. These were allowed to dry and were then stuck together with slip. Following this, the whole piece received its first or 'biscuit' firing. It was then glazed and fired again.

and producing a raised pattern onto a receding background. To produce this effect, a deeply cut copper engraving is filled with a resist, such as beeswax, which is transferred onto paper and applied to the glazed piece. The remaining areas are covered with the resist so that only the engraved portions to be etched are left exposed. The piece is immersed in hydrofluoric acid for a few minutes, then rinsed off in water, which removes the resist. Gold is then applied to the engraved portion.

Gilding is usually the last of the decorative processes, as gold fires at the lowest temperature. The method used in the eighteenth century involved gold leaf pounded in a mortar with honey, the so called 'honey gold'. This was fired once, leaving a soft brown-colored gold on the ware after firing. Attempts had been made at an earlier date to put un-fired honey gold onto the ware but this was not very hard wearing. By 1770, at the Royal Manufactory in Sèvres, the process called mercuric gilding was in use — gold in an amalgam of mercury. This 'best gold' process is used by a gilder with a brush, either to produce rims or footlines on a whirler. The whirler is turned slowly with one hand while the brush is held against the piece. Alternatively, more elaborate decorative strokes, curves and flashes can be applied by hand. After firing, the gold appears dull, but after burnishing (by the (by the burnisher) with agate, hematite zircon sand, the gold is bright and shiny. Nowadays a liquid bright gold can be used which does not need burnishing after firing. This gold is used very thinly and is not as hard wearing as burnished gold. Platinum can be used in the same way to produce silver effects.

Even the most simple cup goes through an enormous number of processes. A really complicated ornamental item can have as many as ten firings. Although mechanization and mass production has speeded up these processes, it will probably never be possible to mechanize the production of the finest wares, which will always be made by hand.

1
The Luster Tradition

The story of luster-ware is one of the most fascinating in the history of ceramics. The idea seems to have been born around Baghdad in the ninth century and, with the advance of Islam, it was to be carried the length of the North African seaboard into Moorish Spain. The fifteenth century witnessed a wonderful flowering of luster wares which were the envy of Europe. The Moors, whose skills had brought the wares of Valencia and Malaga to such a peak of brilliance, were finally expelled from Spain in 1492. The tradition, progressively debased, endured there for at least another century. However the idea had fired the imagination of the potters of Gubbio and Deruta and it is a matter of opinion whether the delicate and molded ruby-lustered wares of the former are more beautiful than the massive, but majestically serene blue and gold wares of the latter. Luster did not survive long in Italy. The age of the finest production was but brief. It is unlikely that production began before 1500; by 1550 it was over. Simple wares of a rustic nature continued to appear in Spain, and later in Staffordshire and Sunderland. Luster was also used as a brilliant decorative feature on the Meissen wares of the 1720s and 1770s. However it was not until William de Morgan appeared on the scene, in the nineteenth century, that the technical and artistic skills of the Renaissance were revived and matched.

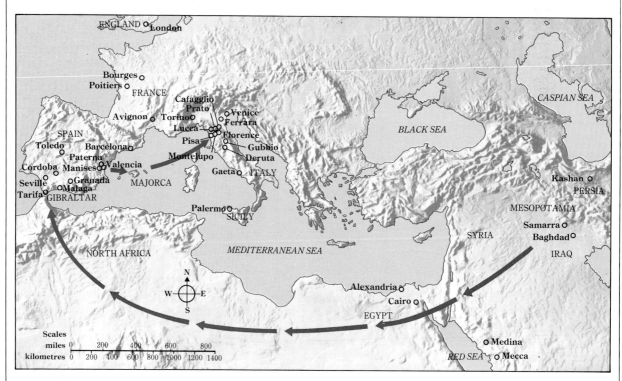

The map (above) shows the spread of luster, from Mesopotamia, across North Africa into Moorish Spain, and then to Italy.

Gubbio Plate *(opposite)*
Date: 16th century
Diameter: 15in (37.5cm)

This sixteenth century Gubbio plate, molded in relief, depicts the infant St John, surrounded by a border of peppers and leaves.

The use of high relief was a style following the fashionable repoussé decoration of metalwork. The ruby-red luster added an exotic sparkle to the table displays which showed the maiolica exhibited together with the metalware.

**Luster Persian
Molded jar**

*Date: 12th century
Height: 13in (32.5cm)*

The elegant shape of this storage jar is well balanced due to the careful use of contrasting surface decoration. The round-faced figures, which are commonly found in work from this area, are complemented by the bulky coats gathered around them, but it is their position above similarly sized panels with overlaid stylized cloud-band or arabesques, that provides the balance and layout of the decorative scheme. The detail (below) shows the tendency of monochrome decoration to give a positive/negative effect. This stylized arabesque motif is usually found in the background, filling the space around more important decoration. In this example the decoration is elevated to greater importance, and a very loose derivative on a white ground is used as a border to give contrast. Further contrast is achieved by the 'fluting' of the body of the jar, which does not exactly follow the order of the decorative scheme.

The Development of Luster in Persian Pottery

The great achievement of the Islamic potter is his discovery of a complex and richly decorative scheme.

In the seventh century AD, when invading Arab armies began their conquests of surrounding countries in the name of Mohammed, there commenced a period of more than one thousand years in which some of the finest ceramics were produced. The unifying force of Islam in this growing empire made it possible for craftsmen to move freely within different states and different cultures, assimilating the decorative techniques and styles of each, and adopting them in their own work. Potters were influenced by the shapes and decorative effects, not just of ceramics, but also of manuscripts, paintings and architecture. With the gradual establishment of centers of wealth and a stable political climate, Islamic potters, together with other artists, came to adapt these new shapes and techniques to create a style of their own. Despite the large geographical area it covered, this pottery displays an inherent unity, and is one of the greatest artistic achievements of our civilization.

The history of Islamic pottery begins in the seventh century and ends in the seventeenth. Within this time span various phases of pottery-making took place, with new techniques and styles evolving after periods of adaptation and experimentation; other styles were sometimes ignored for a time and later revived. Imitations and variations in less well-known centers in the Muslim world eventually influenced pottery in countries as distant as Spain, Italy and India.

Throughout the evolution of Islamic pottery four basic elements were shared by workers using other materials. Decoration in the form of ornamental inscriptions, based on the many varieties of Arabic script had evolved as a direct result of the most important reference the Muslim potter had to hand — the Koran. The rhythms of Islamic calligraphy suited the potter and pervaded all other types of decoration. The depiction of plants passed through various stages of stylization to become purely geometric, while the quintessentially Islamic arabesque became the most useful form with its unique ability to fill a space completely. Figurative iconography, banned from buildings and objects of religious use, was less commonly used by the Islamic potter and was usually subordinated to other elements in an ornamental design; nevertheless figures provide important information about the styles and customs of the period. In early representations, human beings and animals display little movement, being bold and imposing in the design, but by the twelfth century they had become more animated, and are depicted in more delicate and complex drawings.

Islamic pottery is made of either fired clay, earthenware, or 'frit', a harder and more compact

Luster Bowl
Diameter: 8¾in (22.5cm)

Fragments from another bowl have been used to restore the example (right) which shows a seated prince holding a flower and cup. This image, together with particular details such as the almond eyes and nose, is derived from Central Asia — the most likely source being Christian textiles which show a similar iconographic convention.

material developed in the twelfth century. Early Islamic pottery was produced by the local industry and the vessels, invariably made for practical daily use, were wheelthrown. An innate desire to decorate — a desire shared with other Islamic craftsmen — led the potters to incise the surfaces of these vessels, or fashion the pieces of clay in a mold or by hand into particular shapes which were applied to the body. In the larger urban centers, however, techniques like these became simply a basis for the artistic aspirations of the potter; it was not until pigments and colored glazes came to be used in conjunction with painted and carved surface decoration that the truly fine works developed.

Initially, attempts to imitate Chinese porcelain were numerous, as excavations at Samarra, the Abbasid capital, have shown. The greatly valued Tang porcelain reached Mesopotamia by sea routes across the Indian Ocean. For a time, the imitation of

Fatimid Dish
Date: first half 12th century
Diameter: 8½in (21.5cm)

The appearance of this lavishly robed figure carrying a mosque-lamp suggests that he is probably a religious authority — although his position is undetermined. The shapes on this dish have been basically defined by broad brushstrokes, while the

detail has been carefully worked out with the use of a stylus to remove the still wet slip, achieving a feeling of lightness, and resulting in a sophisticated and successful use of monochrome.

whiteness of such porcelain was attempted by covering the earthenware with a mixture of tin oxide and clear lead glaze — a combination used centuries before by the Egyptians. The early Islamic tin-glazed work, with its blues and greens, closely resembles the loosely controlled Tang glazed ware. However the glazing techniques of the Islamic potters progressed dramatically, and their methods began to anticipate the Chinese; these methods were later to be exploited in the Renaissance Italian maiolica and in European painted pottery.

Perhaps the greatest technique of all developed by the Persian potter was that of luster-ware. This new technique of the ninth century made Samarra, and in particular its Abassid capital of Baghdad, an important pottery center. The technique of painting in luster had been discovered by the glass-makers of Syria and Egypt who began applying it to their vessels at the end of the ninth century. The Mesopotamian potters probably used it to imitate the appearance of bronze, brass or gold, which was particularly effective when applied to dishes with relief molding, and the technique was later to enjoy popularity in the Near East and in Moorish Spain. The pigment, composed of silver, copper and sulphur oxides, was painted onto a glaze that had already been fired; a second firing in a special reducing kiln resulted in a thin metallic film. The luster was applied to both a transparent lead glaze, occasionally stained with patches of green, and to an opaque white tin glaze, as the Syrians and Egyptians had done; by using various tones, this produced a polychrome effect. A monochrome palette was in widespread use by the middle of the ninth century.

The luster technique of the Mesopotamian potters was passed on to the Fatimid potters in Egypt and subsequently to Persia but, in the twelfth century, a highly important technical discovery was made. In an attempt to imitate the appearance of Song porcelain, the potters discovered a way of producing a stronger, harder and whiter body clay than earthenware. By using the earlier Egyptian technique of mixing potash, quartz and white clay, they had a material which lent itself admirably to fine carved and pierced decoration, and in particular to painted designs requiring great linear control and tonal variety. Vessel shapes from the twelfth century onwards were of great elegance and refinement.

The earliest Persian luster-ware dates from the end of the twelfth century, and was made in the city of Rayy. Large-scale figures, used to fill the complete face of the dish, were a direct influence from Fatimid potters, but by the beginning of the thirteenth century the potters of the city of Kashan had developed the technique by painting in luster with touches of blue and turquoise. It was about this time that another major technical breakthough was made. Underglaze painting became possible after the discovery that colored pigments, such as cobalt and manganese remained perfectly stable under an alkaline glaze, while they had been apt to run under a lead glaze. This economical technique eventually supplanted all others.

In an attempt to increase the number of colors in their palettes twelfth-century potters developed a technique of painting both under and over the glaze. The overglaze colors were applied to the fired vessel in the form of a paste which was subsequently fixed by a second firing. Many examples of this 'minai' ware depict narrative scenes derived from contemporary manuscript illumination. Fluent drawings were made in this way by the potters of Rayy in Syria, who like those in the city of Kashan, began production at the end of the twelfth century, and also made luster and underglaze painted ware. The introduction of Arabic script and use of arabesques allowed the potters to demonstrate their fine decorative abilities. Many of the important potteries were, however, to be destroyed or severely disrupted by the Mongol invasions which had begun in the 1220s. Only the potteries of Kashan were able to resume production in the second half of the thirteenth century, and luster pottery continued to be made, although it was principally used to decorate architectural tiles.

Egyptian Bowl
Date: 13th-14th century
Diameter: 11½in (29.5cm)

The use of proverbs and quotations from the Koran is frequently found in Islamic decorative art. This bowl and fourteenth century tile (above) show specific use of inscriptions but in two contrasting ways — incised lines have been used on the bowl while on the tile the script is molded and stands in relief.

Hispano-Moresque bowl

Date: 15th century
Size: 9 x 20in (23 x 50.5cm)

An early fifteenth century bowl, painted in coppery red and gold luster, depicting a sailing vessel. The mainsail bears the arms of ancient Portugal. Although formerly attributed to Manises, excavations at Malaga have revealed similar pieces, and it is now thought to have originated at that ceramic center. The detail (left) shows the Almohad influence, evident in the representation of the leaves and the stylized 'tree of life'.

A painting from a Book of Hours (c 1500) by a Flemish artist. The pottery examples of Manises luster-ware indicate the spread of luster to Europe.

The Wares of Moorish Spain

*The technical and artistic skills of Moorish potters led to the
production of superlative luster ware in Muslim Spain, especially in
Valencia and Malaga.*

The luster tradition spread with the expansion of the Islamic Empire in which it had originated. In AD 710, less than a century after the death of the Prophet Mohammed, the Berber chief, Tarif, crossed the straits from North Africa to Tarifa in Southern Spain. A year later another chief landed with 7,000 men at what is now Gibraltar; Islam had already engulfed Persia, Syria and Mesopotamia. Cordoba and Toledo were soon captured and the Muslim invaders advanced rapidly through the Iberian peninsula into Southern France. They were halted there in 732 by Charles Martel at the Battle of Poitiers.

To the European rulers invasion by an alien race, who conformed to a different religion, must have seemed an unmitigated disaster, but there were unexpected compensations. In 756 the Umayyad prince, Abd ar-Rahman, became independent Amir of Cordoba. To mark the status of what was now his capital he embarked on an ambitious building program. He originated the Great Mosque, and the court at Cordoba became a center for artists and scholars in letters, music, law, religion and medicine from both East and West. The most celebrated of the Umayyad rulers, Abd ar-Rahman III (912-961) built the fabulous palace city of Madinat az-Zahara nearby, for which craftsmen, and various treasures of silk, marble and pottery, were imported from Syria, Mesopotamia and Byzantium. This palace was sacked and largely destroyed in 1013 in wars between rival Muslim kingdoms.

Excavations on the site of Madinat az-Zahara have yielded sherds of pottery of a high technical standard. One particular fragment from a bowl bore a painted equinelike head and part of a longish neck in gold luster which could have been that of a camel. The discovery of this fragment of luxury ware at such a well-documented site, gave rise to the speculation that Spain was producing high-quality luster wares as early as the tenth century. However, this fragment has been identified as an importation from the East. Sherds found at Medina Azzara have proved that Spain was, at this time, producing some good quality tin-glazed earthenware, but none of the contemporary lustered fragments discovered were made from local clays.

During the eleventh and twelfth centuries the Umayyad government slowly crumbled as the Muslim territories were split into small principalities and kingdoms, fighting each other for ascendancy. During this troubled period luxury industries, including the making of fine pottery, were severely restricted to the few places where some order could be maintained. Nevertheless, some fine pottery was made in Spain during the thirteenth century and, typically, it was decorated with cobalt blue, a new pigment obtained from imported ore. A list of pottery objects, stored in a warehouse, was compiled by a Toledan Muslim at a date not later than 1066. It refers to golden pottery, but it could be that these objects were imports from Egypt, where most of the skilled luster decorators were then working.

The demand for gold luster pottery continued for several hundreds of years, and the knowledge of how it was made spread widely. In spite of this the main producers of this elegant, refined pottery were confined, during the twelfth, thirteenth and fourteenth centuries, mainly to Mesopotamia, Persia and Syria. Some of these objects have been excavated at the Alcazaba at Malaga and, although they were once thought to be local products, the luster is too close to the Fatimid type for this to be likely, although it is always possible that they were made by immigrant artists from Egypt after the decline of the Fatimid.

Written references to luster pottery made in Malaga begin to appear after the middle of the thirteenth century. Lustered pottery was also being made at this time in Almeria and Murcia but, according to the documents, the Malaga production was without equal. It is largely on this written evidence that the best of Moorish pottery, including the fabulous 'Alhambra' and the famous winged vases, is attributed to Malaga. A more concrete piece of evidence that Malaga, under the Nasrid Dynasty (1238-1492), produced very superior pottery is the lustered bowl on the base of which appears the word 'Malaga' in Arabic. Fragments excavated at Fostat in Egypt have been found similarly marked.

Examination of surviving pieces of what is now universally known as Malaga ware amply justify the reputation of that center. Although some writers attribute the Alhambra vase to an Islamic factory in Granada, it cannot be disputed that the potters at Malaga had assimilated all the technical skills required for the production of luster-ware. Their pottery of the Nasrid period introduced a decorative style that was not slavishly dependent on Egyptian models, but used an amalgamation of Syrian and Hispano-Moresque decoration. It is evident from archival records and from archaeological excavations that a considerable quantity of luster pottery was ex-

**Hispano-Moresque
Wing-handled Vase**
*Date: 1465, Valencia
Height: 22in (55.5cm)*

*The Italians had a great love
for lustered Hispano-
Moresque pottery. Tuscan
families had commercial
banking connections in
Spain and large quantities
of Hispano-Moresque luster-
ware were imported into
Italy. This is a late example
of the 'Alhambra' vase. The
vine leaf decoration is typical
of the finest productions of
Valencia. The arms are those
of the Medici family. The
fact that a piece was made
with the arms of the greatest
art patrons of the day on
shows quite clearly the
standing of the wares of
Valencia. This vase was
once the property of Horace
Walpole, one of Britain's
most influential collectors.*

ported from Malaga; specimens have been found in England, Sicily, Flanders, Alexandria and Fustat.

Political strife and the continuous advances of the Christian kings, culminating in the surrender of the city of Malaga in 1487, must have brought the production of Malagan luxury wares to an end. Luster production may have ceased even before this. An Egyptian writer who visited the Alcazaba in 1465 gave a good description of three great water jars of Malagan 'porcelain', which he admired for their workmanship, but he did not mention seeing any luster decoration. After the fall of Malaga, the Nasrid King held on in Granada until the combined army of Castile and Aragon captured the city. Soon after this a royal edict proclaimed the expulsion of all non-catholics from the peninsula.

The political unrest and economic insecurity of Muslim Spain caused many of its craftsmen to migrate from place to place in search of greater religious tolerance, better markets or new employment. In the early part of the fourteenth century some potters from Murcia arrived at the Valencian pottery centre at Manises, bringing with them a knowledge of the techniques of luster production. In 1362, two master potters from Manises, Juan Albalat and Pascasio Martin, were commanded by Cardinal Aubert Audoin to make tiles for his palace at

Avignon, as it was more economical to have the pottery made on the spot than to ship it from Manises. The two tilemakers were skilled in 'obra de Malicha' (Malaga work) and agreed to produce whatever pottery the Cardinal required. They possessed all the secrets of their art, including the knowledge of how to construct the special kilns required for luster production. A few years later two other Valencian potters were to be found even further afield. These were Jehan de Valence (the Saracen) and his companion working at Bourges and Poitiers for the Duke of Berry.

One notable Murcian name associated with Manises from 1325 to 1533 is that of Murci, Morci or Almurci, as it was variously spelled. The potting tradition of this family was probably begun by the Moorish brothers Abdelaciz and Abraham Almurci. Generations of the family seem to have specialized in tiles and to have received continuous royal patronage. They made tiles for Spanish royal palaces and also for the Italian Castle of Gaeta and the Castel Nuovo in Naples.

Large commissions, such as a tiled pavement, can be traced through documents to a particular master potter, but not so with household objects. They carry no workshop or factory marks, not even amid the profuse decoration that is often on the backs of luster plates, bowls and dishes. The production of luster-

Hispano-Moresque Armorial Jar
Date: Late 15th century
Height: 12¼ in (31cm)

This 'albarelo', or pharmacy jar, was made in Valencia in the late fifteenth century. It is decorated in blue and luster, with the arms of Aragon, trailing bryony (wild clematis) and stylized acacia leaves. Many jars of this type were commissioned by pharmacies and hospitals and also by princely houses which, for political reasons, had their own private dispensaries. The Italian pharmacy jars or 'albarelli' differ from their Spanish counterparts. They are very seldom enriched with luster and the decoration usually incorporates a riband on which the name of the medicament is fired.

ware in the Valencia region was not limited to Manises, for documents of the fifteenth century mention luster-ware being made at Mislata, Paterna and Alacuas.

In the early part of the fifteenth century, Valencian pottery had not yet broken away from the influence of Malaga and Granada. The repertoire consisted largely of stylized leaves and flowers, Kufic and cursive lettering, the tree of life, palmettes and pine cones. Later in the century a wide variety of new decorative patterns were introduced. These included scrolling tendrils with leaves and flowers resembling the wild clematis, fish scale designs, reticulated patterns and acacia-like leaves, as well as imbrications, embossing and gadrooning. The Kufic letters and words of dedication gave way to Latin words in Lombardic capitals and fragments of prayers to God or the Ave Maria. Sometimes the sacred monogram I.H.S. is placed in the center of plates or on the front belly of jugs, just like a coat of arms, surrounded by one or other of the decorative patterns already mentioned. In the last quarter of the fifteenth century, as the range of decorations changed so also did the shapes, probably under the influence of contemporary metalware shapes, which were then following the Renaissance fashion. Much use was made at this time of molds to produce a *repoussé* effect. Bowls were made taller by placing them on splayed, footed stems. The gadrooning effect, which in earlier times had been achieved by skillful imitation painting, was now produced with the aid of molds, and appears as real as on a piece of metalware.

By the beginning of the sixteenth century Spanish lustered pottery was becoming less highly regarded, both at home and abroad. The decline in demand was partly the fault of the potters themselves, who failed to move with the times. In 1516 Charles I became King of Spain and from 1519 to 1556 he was also, as Charles V, the Holy Roman Emperor. His love for Renaissance art was well known. Consequently the Spanish potters lost the Royal patronage, commissions from the nobility diminished and they were obliged to compete with ever-increasing imports of pottery from Italy, the Netherlands and Flanders, as well as porcelain from China. Another factor in the decline of the Valencian luster-ware was the rise of the pottery at Talavera de la Reina. The artisans of this Castillian center provided their clients with a fashionable Italian style. Their tiles and other pottery won the patronage of Philip II (1556-1598) and his court.

By the end of the century Talavera pottery had become an indispensable commodity for both nobility and commoners. In addition, vast quantities of pottery were being shipped from Talavera to the New World, but this outlet was completely closed to the Valencian potters. The excessive tax imposed on goods made in one place and transported to other localities in Spain effectively prevented the Valencians from sending their products to the Western ports serving the New World. A further severe blow came in 1609 when the government ordered the expulsion of all Moorish people from Valencia. As the potteries were mostly manned by 'Moriscos', this Act caused considerable disruption in the industry. The production of luster never stopped completely however, not even when the Manises potters began to concentrate on producing other items in the fashionable Italian pictorial style of Talvera and Seville. Thus the opening years of the sixteenth century marked the turning point from Spanish luster to the beginnings of the Italian style of pottery.

Castel Durante Dish
Date: 1525
Diameter: 17.5 in (44 cm)

The skill of the Maestro Giorgio, and the inventiveness of the maiolica painters of Castel Durante, are shown at their best on this large dish. The

center, or 'well', is decorated with maidens bathing in a pool. Winged and garlanded heads of putti are painted on the nearside of the pool; the surrounding border is decorated with grotesques and military trophies. The bathers are taken from two different engravings by Raimandi: the central group is from 'The Three Graces', after Raphael (left), and the group on the right is from an engraving after Raphael's design for 'The judgement of Paris'. The luster is applied at strategic points on the rim and well, giving depth to the design. The underside of the plate is signed and dated by Giorgio (far left).

Luster of Renaissance Italy

*In the early sixteenth century Italian craftsmen adapted the Islamic
tradition of decorating ceramic ware with luster, to enrich their
pictorial, polychromed designs. This craft centered on the small town
of Gubbio in Umbria, flourished only briefly.*

The beauty of Eastern ceramics had been well known to the Italians for a long time. Islamic pottery, including luster-ware, had been in widespread use for the embellishment of religious and civic buildings. A common form of decoration consisted of shallow pottery bowls or 'bacini' inset into outside walls. In the Pisan region alone it is thought that some 1,400 bacini were used to decorate the facades of buildings, and some 600 of them are still *in situ.* Except for a few Egyptian Fatimid examples, not many of them are decorated in luster. A fair number, however, are in polychrome and are of Magreb origin, some possibly Hispano-Moresque.

It is not certain who brought the bacini and why they were relegated to the outside of buildings. According to one theory they were brought back in the eleventh century by the crusaders as trophies of their victories over the pagans and were displayed on the facades of churches to demonstrate how great and powerful were the Christian forces. But there had been more direct contact between the Italians and Islam before the first crusade of 1095. From about 740 to 1061 Sicily was a part of Islam and ruled by a succession of Islamic princes. After the conquest of the island by the Normans the Islamic art and traditions were not lost. One of the Norman rulers, Roger II (1130-1154), became known as the 'Pagan' because he favored the Arabs so much. He used Arab troops for his military campaign in Southern Italy and Arab architects for his buildings, creating a Norman-Saracenic style. His magnificent coronation mantle, woven in the royal workshop at Palermo, bears an Arabic inscription in Kufic style and the Hijra date 528 (1133-4).

The Italians' admiration of the luster pottery of Islam increased further during the fourteenth and fifteenth centuries. More than any other region of Italy at this time Tuscany had good commercial relations with Moorish Spain. Merchants from Pisa, Lucca, Florence and Prato kept banks and warehouses in Barcelona and Valencia and imported large quantities of luster-ware from Spain. Many pieces, decorated with heraldic shields, were individually commissioned, which testifies to the high reputation of the Hispano-Moresque ware. In fact, the decoration of Italian maiolica of the fourteenth and early fifteenth centuries is strongly influenced by, and sometimes a direct copy of Hispano-Moresque models. The only difference between the

San Sisto Bacini
Date: Late 11th century
Diameter: 9in (22.5cm)

This eleventh century bowl of the Egyptian Fatimid period, is decorated in luster on an opaque white glaze. It is one of the 'bacini' found on the facade of the Church of San Sisto in Pisa. Similar bacini, with or without luster, were widely used to decorate the walls of churches and public buildings. They usually depict characters in the repertory of the court — in this case a drinker.

Italian and Spanish products of this period is the absence of luster on the Italian wares.

The word 'Maiolica' derives from Majorca or Majolica, the largest port of the Balearic Islands, which was a port of call between the Italian and Spanish ports. Although the imported luster came from as far as Manises or Barcelona it had all gone via Majorca and so became known as maiolica. The name was first applied only to the luster-ware, but in time it evolved to cover the whole range of tin-glazed pottery. That the Hispano-Moresque ware was considered particularly desirable is shown by the pains the Italian artisans took to imitate their style. They had no trouble in reproducing the patterns, including the Arabic script, but they remained in ignorance of how to produce the luster tones. They imitated the effect as best they could using fine manganese or an orange-yellow color. Besides manganese and yellow the Italo-Moresque palette included green and a dark blue. The latter was sometimes used as a

monochrome decoration.

During the fifteenth century, Italy, and Tuscany in particular, was awakening to a new era — the Renaissance. The humanist spirit of the Renaissance brought about gradual changes in the decoration of maiolica. From the mid-fifteenth century the maiolica painters, using a wider range of colors, slowly abandoned the Moorish and Gothic modes and moved towards a definite pictorial style. Maiolica, made for the humanists of the Renaissance, was painted to illustrate themes reflecting the new interests of the patrons. The development of this 'istoriato' style meant that Italian maiolica was evolving from utilitarian products to articles of luxury and high art.

The storytelling mode was used by all the maiolica making centers, but their styles were influenced by the corresponding regional schools of painters. The development of pictorial designs was further encouraged by the increasingly widespread distribution of engravings and prints. It was through the circulation of this printed material that some of the works of the great contemporary masters found their way onto maiolica wares. By the beginning of the sixteenth century maiolica seemed to have little scope for further development; everything had been achieved. Only one thing was absent — true luster decoration. How this technique eventually reached Italy remains a mystery. Some say it was brought by potters emigrating from Spain after the Christians had reconquered the land. Others believe that Italian potters migrated to Spain in search of the secret. How ever it came about, luster first appeared on examples from Deruta which date from the outset of the sixteenth century. Once begun, luster production at Deruta continued for many years and became world renowned. The color combination of Deruta is a dark blue design on a white background with a luster of a dark gold tinge.

Because of the technical difficulties of production, and the restriction of luster to one color, the decorative effect appears to best advantage on an uneven surface. It is probably for this reason that the pictorial work on Deruta luster-ware appears rather stiff and severe, but is more lively on surfaces which are molded in low relief. Good examples are the plates with gadrooned borders, or the vases shaped like pine cones.

Although luster originated in the East the Deruta painters seldom used patterns of Egyptian or Hispano-Muslim origin. Most of their work consists of large plates painted with portraits of beautiful ladies surrounded by borders, filled with exotic flowers on a white background, giving an overall effect of cut velvet. The method of luster production gradually became known elsewhere and other Italian centers of luster sprang up. Probably second only to Deruta in importance is Cafaggiolio, in the vicinity of Florence, which was patronized almost exclusively by the Medici. It appears that the workshop there was manned by artisans mostly from Montelupo. According to the statutes of the Potters' Guild at Montelupo, in the revised edition written in 1510, the potters in the town were so numerous that 'almost all the population is fed by their industry'. The brassy yellow, golden yellow or red-gold luster of Cafaggiolo, as also the luster pattern of the stylized flowers and leaves, is very reminiscent of the wares of Muslim Spain. But perhaps the most important center for sixteenth century luster in Italy was Gubbio.

Gubbio, a little fortress town in Umbria, not far from Assisi, was already famous in the sixteenth century for having once been delivered from a killer wolf by St. Francis of Assisi. Many people today may not remember this thirteenth century miracle, but the luster wares of that name are familiar to all collectors. They are renowned for the magical luster effects produced by the Master of Gubbio, Giorgio Andreoli. He is remembered for the rich, ruby-red luster produced in the third firing. (It is doubtful that he ever painted maiolica for the second firing). The approximate date for the commencement of lustre production at Gubbio is given on a dish at the museum at Arezzo, dated 1518. It is decorated with grotesques and bears - the arms of the Aldobrandini. It has some affinity with the maiolica from Castel Durante, but is enriched with a luster of gold and ruby tones, characteristic of the work of the master of Gubbio.

The importance of Giorgio's magic touch was well recognized in his own day. Although he was born in the North of Italy, in 1498 he was granted citizenship of Gubbio by the Duke of Urbino. He was made 'Lord

Deruta Dish
Date: 16th century
Height: 15.4in (39cm)

Deruta was probably the first Italian center to produce lustered maiolica and apparently only used the ruby-red color on a few early sixteenth century pieces. This dish, painted in luster, depicts a lady in profile and bears the inscription 'My hearth has only hope'. The detail (right) shows the border of flowers on a white background.

Caffaggiolo Blue and White Armorial Tondino
Date: c 1570
Diameter: 9in (22.5cm)

The coat-of-arms at the center of this dish is that of the Medici. The Caffaggiolo pottery was actually set up in the confines of their castle towards 1490. This is an interesting combination of stencilled luster decoration and blue and white 'd'all porcellana' painting of a clearly oriental cast.

of the Citadel' and exempted from paying taxes for twenty years. His art was later recognized by Leo X, the great Medici Pope who was the patron of Raphael and Michelangelo. In 1519 the Pope gave this 'excellent Master of the art of maiolica' permanent exemption from taxes. Maestro Giorgio, whose works had brought so much prestige and revenue to the town of Gubbio, died in about 1553, but the traditional craft was carried on by his two sons, Cencio, who was the master potter, and Unaldo, who was the painter in charge of that department.

Because the luster colors were applied in a third and final firing, objects made at other centers were often sent to Gubbio to receive this final embellishment. The process has been described by the Cavaliere Cipriano Piccolpasso who wrote a treatise on the potters' art in the year 1556 or 1557. The work was divided into three books entitled *Li Tre Libri Dell Arte Del Vasaio*. In the second book the author makes it quite clear that in his day the art of luster was still a closely guarded secret and that the process was applied to finished ware. He wrote: 'This I have seen at Gubbio in the house of Maestro Cencio of that place and they follow this method in painting it. They leave the place where it is to be put on, so that no sort of color is put there; that is to say, in making for example on a little plate an arabesque or rather a grotesque these leaves that should properly be in green are left blank, the outlines only being drawn. The wares are finally fired like the others, then when they have been fired these blanks are filled with maiolica (pigment) which is made thus ...'. The description is accompanied by a drawing of a design and Piccolpasso proceeds to give detailed recipes for making both the ruby-red and the gold maiolica. He also gives instructions for the building of the special reducing kilns and the method of stacking and firing the wares. 'Having been brought thus far, you should know that the kiln having thus been set, always in the blessed name of God, the fire is lit and increases little by little, as is done with other wares.' Piccolpasso's precise instructions then specify the kind of wood to be used for

the different stages of the baking and the times required. At the end the kiln is left to cool quickly and when cold 'the wares are taken out and put to soak in a tub of washing-lye or lessive. Then they are rubbed one at a time with a piece of cloth; this done, they should be given another rub with another dry piece and with ashes, that thus they may reveal all their beauty.' But even at the time that Piccolpasso was writing his famous treatise the technique of luster making was still somewhat unpredictable: 'Frequently, out of a hundred pieces, barely six are good, but it is true that the art is essentially beautiful and ingenious and when the works are good they are paid for in gold'.

The luster decoration at Gubbio was applied to ware that was already richly polychromed, which made it appear particularly lively and robust. Like Deruta, the Gubbio luster is at its best on objects with raised decoration. On such pieces the reflection and refraction of light produces a sparkling, prismatic optical effect, with all the colors of the rainbow dancing before one's eyes.

By the second half of the sixteenth century the art of luster, and of maiolica generally, had reached its peak. More and more patrons were beginning to interest themselves in and to collect the porcelain objects which were then reaching Europe in larger quantities than ever before. In fact, Piccolpasso refers to and illustrates some maiolica designs in blue and white in the manner of oriental porcelain.

The quest for the secret of porcelain had been started in Italy as early as 1470 by the alchemist Maestro Antonio of Venice. A little later other trials were carried out, rather unsuccessfully, in Ferrara, Pesaro and Torino. In the 1568 edition of Giorgio Vasari's famous *The Lives of the Most Eminent Painters, Sculptors and Architects*, it is written that Buontalenti 'in a short time will be making vessels of porcelain'. Buontalenti was the artistic director of most of the Medici artistic ventures at this time. In 1575, Andrea Gusoni, the Venetian Am-

Armorial Dish
Date: c 1525
Height: 10½ (27cm)

The original polychrome decoration left blank spaces for the luster, which was added later at Gubbio. The dish bears the arms of a cardinal, and this is surrounded by a border of trophies and grotesques.

bassador at the court of Florence, sent a report to Venice stating that the secret for making Indian (that is oriental) porcelain had been rediscovered at Florence. Of course the 'discovery' was only of a substitute, not the real hard-paste porcelain. Even so, it was closer to porcelain than was maiolica.

On the death of the patron, the first Grand Duke of Tuscany, the Medici venture into porcelain-making came to an end. However, with the rise to power of the mercantile companies in the seventeenth century, and the foundation of the Dutch East India Company, more and more oriental porcelain reached European ports. It was at first collected and used with discriminiation by the nobility, but eventually this strong and practical ceramic material found its way to the tables of ordinary people.

The increasing familiarity with porcelain, and the great market demand for it, brought about a revival of ceramic research in Europe. St Cloud in France was the first centre to produce soft-paste porcelain on a large scale. Later, the composition of true porcelain was discovered at Meissen in the first decade of the eighteenth century. European tin-glazed pottery production competed unsuccessfully with the new material. Most of the skilled potters and decorators began working in the new porcelain industry and the output of tin-glaze rapidly declined, although some naive folk art productions still continued. However, the gleaming luster of Italian maiolica at its best disappeared. The fashionable designs on oriental and European porcelain did not include luster, which was anyway unpredictable and costly, so its use on maiolica was abandoned. It was not until the nineteenth century that luster production started again.

**William de Morgan
Dish**
Date: c 1880
Diameter: 14in (35cm)

*This dish, depicting a
fantastic animal, was
painted in red luster. De
Morgan animals are very
reminscent of medieval
bestiary, but his
backgrounds, with stylized
leaves and flowers (see detail
right), reflect an Eastern
influence.*

*This detail of a fourteenth
century Islamic tile, has a
similar leaf design to the
dish above, indicating the
influence of the Islamic
decorator's art on later
craftsmen.*

William de Morgan and the Revival of Luster

The revival of luster in England in the nineteenth century owes much to the Arts and Crafts Movement, and to the decorative techniques of the artist-potter, William de Morgan.

The nineteenth century was a period during which the artistic styles of the past were revived one after the other without discrimination. It was also a period of industrialization and technical research and of great international exhibitions, of which probably the greatest was the 1851 exhibition held in London in Paxton's 'Crystal Palace'. This marked the triumph of mass-produced, machine-made goods. At the time voices were raised against industrialization and the lack of educated design. It was not until some time later that the anti-industrialization lobbyists were to have their own high priest in William Morris.

Morris was an admirer of Ruskin and of the Middle Ages and a friend of Burne-Jones and other Pre-Raphaelites; the revival of luster in England owes much to this circle. The prime mover was William de Morgan who had an unusual background for a potter. Born in London in 1839, the son of a professor of mathematics at University College, he studied art and was admitted to the Academy School in 1859. He first met Morris in 1863, and later met Burne-Jones and other members of the Morris circle, including Dante Gabriel Rossetti and Ford Maddox-Brown. It was at the instigation of Morris that De Morgan gave up painting and became interested in designing stained glass windows, and eventually in ceramics.

De Morgan began his career in ceramics in 1869 by decorating ready-glazed tiles with his own designs at a studio in Fitzroy Square. His interest in luster decoration was stimulated by his involvement with stained glass. He noticed that the silver used for the decoration of glass panels was producing a yellow stain, but that when it was overfired it became irides-

Luster Bottle
by Bernard Moore
Date: Early 20th century
Height: 9¾in (25cm)

Bernard Moore, the Staffordshire potter, tried throughout the 1880s and 1890s to produce a flambé glaze similar to the Chinese copper-reds and the work of De Morgan. Moore's rouge flambé glazes were excellent and show how he mastered the technique of high-temperature reduction-fired copper glazes. Whereas De Morgan used wood fired kilns to achieve his luster decoration, Moore used gas fired kilns.

cent. He found he could produce similar and better effects on tiles by painting with silver or copper and firing in a reduction kiln. De Morgan became more and more interested in pottery and began experimenting with slips, glazes and clays, but after he set fire to the roof of 40 Fitzroy Square he moved, in 1872, to Chelsea. In 1882 he moved to Merton Abbey, close to the workshops of Morris & Company.

The majority of the De Morgan output consisted of the tiles for which he became so well known. Large quantities were bought ready for decoration from other manufacturers, but he also produced some of his own, particularly when he was at Chelsea and Merton Abbey. His tiles were used to decorate walls, the surrounds of fireplaces and the interior of boats, and his designs ranged from flowers to dolphins and fantastic beasts. He also made large dishes decorated with fabulous animals in rich red luster on a white background. De Morgan retired in 1907, but his work was carried on by his partners Charles and Frank

Passenger and Frank Iles. In 1917 De Morgan died, but the popularity of his luster had rekindled interest in the technique and various imitators sprang up.

By 1900 the demand for decorative tiles was enormous and attracted the attention of the Pilkington Tile and Pottery Company at Clifton Hearsley near Manchester, one of the largest in the country. This firm produced tiles and architectural faience and employed artists of international repute, such as Alphone Mucha, Walter Crane, Lewis F. Day and C. F. A. Voysey as consultant designers. Also employed there from 1896 was a celebrated ceramic artist called Abraham Lomax, who assisted William Burton, a talented young chemist, in experiments in the production of crystalline glazes. Having achieved this, an art pottery production was launched, which was expanded in 1903 following the successful formulation by Lomax of a new glaze. E.T. Radford, a master thrower, was taken on and the new ware was

**Pilkington Peacock
Plate** *(left)*
Date: Early 20th century
Diameter: 19in (48cm)

Wedgwood Ship Plate
(above)
Date: 1930
Diameter: 12½in (32cm)

named 'Lancastrian'. This proved very successful and exhibitions were arranged. The shapes were based on Greek, Persian and Chinese forms, but the glaze effects were original and very good. In particular, the new 'ultramarine blue' which a critic described as 'a queer poisonous blue', seemed to stand out from all the others. New developments in glazes, variations such as uranium orange, orange vermilion and kingfisher blue were to give Pilkington's 'Lancastrian' an international reputation.

Late in 1905 a new method of making iridescent luster was discovered. The technique was very reliable, with a kiln success rate of well over 90 per cent. The Lancastrian production began to attract other famous ceramic artists and designers, · in-

cluding the young Gordon Mitchell Forsyth, whose influence on the factory became very great. Walter Crane and Lewis Day also contributed designs, as did Richard Joyce, Charles Cundall, William Salter Mycock and Gladwys Rogers. Exhibited abroad at international exhibitions the 'Lancastrian' luster acquired wide appreciation, both in Europe and America. It was discovered and illustrated by many studio yearbooks. In 1913 King George V gave the ware the title 'Royal Lancastrian', but the outbreak of the First World War constituted a blow from which the enterprise never recovered. Forsyth and Cundall joined the RAF in 1914 and William Burton retired the following year. Forsyth returned after the war, but finally left in 1920. Like Burton, he had been one of the driving forces in the art pottery department. The post-war economic depression, and the further depression in the thirties caused a worsening decline and few new articles were produced. By 1937 the firm's art pottery division had closed down.

2
Sèvres:
Luxury for
the Court

The Sèvres porcelain tradition started just outside Paris at Vincennes, when the manufactory there began to experiment with the production of soft-paste wares. These experiments occurred in the late 1730s, a little later than the experiments of other porcelain manufactories in Europe. Both the form and the decoration of the wares produced at Vincennes and Sèvres were influenced by the contemporary French schools of design. The Meissen factory in Saxony, by contrast, took its inspiration for its earliest creations from the forms and decorations of Chinese and Japanese porcelains. Similarly, in France the Chantilly manufactory, which started production some 15 years before Vincennes, also produced wares inspired by the Japanese porcelains that belonged to its owner, the Prince de Condé.

In 1738 Louis XV became indirectly involved with experiments to produce porcelain when he granted permission for rooms in the old royal chateau of Vincennes to be used for this purpose. Two brothers, Gilles and Robert Dubois, fugitives from the Chantilly manufactory who knew how to work in soft-paste porcelain, were installed there with a capital of ten thousand *livres*. The money came from two wealthy and powerful brothers, Jean-Louis-Henri Orry de Fulvy, a counselor of state and Intendant des Finances, and Philibert Orry de Vignori, Contrôleur Général des Finances. The Dubois brothers were joined in 1741 by other workers from Chantilly, including the potter Francois Gravant. He was more successful than they were at developing the soft-paste body, and the two brothers were dismissed by Orry de Fulvy. The establishment was administered from this date by an assistant to Orry de Fulvy,

Charles Adam, who confidently put a great deal more capital into the venture.

By 1745 Francois Gravant had produced competent results from his work and applied for a royal patent. The Council of State granted the patent to Charles Adam on 24 July 1745, and Gravant was handsomely paid for passing on his porcelain techniques. From this date, porcelains were sometimes marked with the royal symbol of crossed 'L's — the mark that was later used on almost all wares produced by the company.

Workers at the factory were forbidden to leave and work elsewhere without permission, and other factories were not allowed to make porcelain in France without the consent of the Council. The ownership of the Vincennes manufactory was transferred to a new company with seven shareholders, and the organization was enlarged in 1747 under Orry de Vignori's successor, Jean-Baptiste Machault d'Arnouville as Contrôleur Général des Finances. Machault engaged a managing director and artistic directors to organize the production of porcelains on a commercial scale.

Vincennes initially produced wares based on porcelains from factories such as Meissen and Chantilly that had by this time developed their own European styles; however at Vincennes the quantity of these wares was small compared to the production of shapes that stemmed from silver designs of the period. In 1745 Jean-Claude Duplessis, a gold-and silversmith and a *bronzier* by training, was given charge of the modeling studio at Vincennes This led to the great influence that metalwork forms had on the shapes produced at Vincennes and Sèvres,

---

Vincennes Vase *(Vase Duplessis à Enfants)*
Date: 1753
Height: 9½in (24cm)

The basic form of this bleu céleste, two-handled vase, which is one of a pair, was designed by the silversmith Jean Claude Duplessis; it was decorated by Antoine

Caton. This ground color, bleu céleste, — sometimes called bleu Hellot after its inventor, Jean Hellot, the factory's chemist - was first used in 1753.

These vases are typical of the early wares of Vincennes in which the influence of Meissen is still clearly visible. The floral decoration is directly derived from Meissen flower painting, itself inspired by contemporary botanical woodcuts.

just as the appointment of J.J. Irminger, goldsmith to Augustus the Strong of Saxony, had influenced the forms produced at Meissen in the 1720s. The team of specialists who were to establish the various workshops and studios of the manufactory grew from this period. Robert Millot became kiln master in 1746, in charge of operating and developing the kilns and firing procedures. The technique for preparing gold and applying it to the porcelain was obtained from a Benedictine monk, Father Hypolite, and the gilding studio was placed under the guidance of Louis Massüe from 1745. The studio for painted decoration was run by Jean-Jacques Bachelier, a man much younger than his colleagues, who was a flower and genre painter. The responsibility for developing the materials used in the paste and the decoration fell to the respected chemist, Jean Hellot. He invented several of the distinctive ground colors that were to be used so extensively at Vincennes and Sèvres. From 1745 all of these artists and craftsmen worked under the aesthetic direction of Hendrik Van Hulst, a Dutch portrait painter living in Paris who was also a member of the French Académie de Peinture et de Sculpture. He chose what designs were to be used for models and how they were to be decorated. Van Hulst died in 1745, but by this time he had imposed his taste upon the products that were to become the basis for the later productions of the Vincennes and Sèvres manufactories.

In 1753 a new company was formed to control the porcelain manufactory. The King took a major shareholding and the privileges of the Royal Patent were taken from Charles Adam and put in the name of Eloi Brichard — the future Fermier Général. The title 'Manufacture Royale' was formally given to the company. From that year all the products were marked with the royal cypher of crossed 'L's enclosing a letter that indicated the date of manufacture. The letter 'A' represented 1753 and the successive letters of the alphabet represented the following years — 'B' for 1754 and so on. By 1778 the alphabet was exhausted so double letters were used, beginning in that year with 'AA'. This dating system lasted throughout the revolution until 1793.

It was also decided in 1753 to move the Manufacture Royale to a specially commissioned factory built on a new site. The new location was at Sèvres, which lies on the banks of the river Seine between Paris and Versailles; it was also close to the Château of Bellevue, then a home of the Marquise de Pompadour who encouraged the King's interest in the new porcelain manufactory. The building was designed by the architect Lindet, and was completed in 1756. From then on, all production of the Manufacture Royale ceased at Vincennes. However, the cost of the new building and the move to Sèvres created new financial difficulties. In 1759 Louis XV bought out his fellow shareholders; as a result the manufactory became Crown property and any losses were paid from State funds. The Sèvres enterprise was assigned to the control of a commissaire-administrateur who appointed a directeur-régisseur to carry out the day-to-day running of the business. The former post was filled by a minister of State, Dominique-Jacques de Courteille, until 1767, and later by Henri-Léonard-Jean-Baptiste Bertin.

Boileau de Picardie was directeur-régisseur from 1759 until his death in 1772, when Melchior-Francois Parent took over the position. Parent was not successful; in his term of office the manufactory sales dropped and in 1778 the Comte d'Angivillier was appointed to help re-establish the commercial viability of the enterprise. This was no easy task, for although the objects produced at Sèvres were of good quality and popular appeal, they were too expensive to reach a large market. In May 1759, the weekly newspaper *La Feuille Nécessaire* noted that Sèvres porcelains were 'so expensive that people can only hope to look...without paying such a high price'. However, the Comte d'Angivillier succeeded in keeping the income of the manufactory high enough so that it needed only limited state support until the end of the eighteenth century. He even arranged an agreement with the Parisian dealer, Dominique Daguerre, to export products for sale in London from 1788. Despite the theoretical popularity of Sèvres porcelain in England, this venture was not successful again because of the high cost of the porcelain.

In the 1760s great efforts were made to improve the soft-paste material, which was difficult to control in the kiln. At the same time research was being undertaken on the production of hard-paste porcelain. The chemists knew that to make the latter material they had to find a source of kaolin in France, and this was discovered in 1768. In June 1769 the chief chemist at Sèvres, Pierre-Joseph Macquer, announced to the Académie Royale des Sciences that a new process had been developed using kaolin from Saint-Yrieux near Limoges. It was not for about three years that hard-paste porcelain wares were produced on a commercial scale, each piece marked with a crown painted above the crossed 'L's mark of the manufactory. The hard-paste wares were produced in separate studios to the soft-paste wares, and workers tended to specialize in working with one material or the other. The production of soft-paste porcelain was reduced as the hard-paste wares became more popular, but was not eliminated until the end of the eighteenth century because certain types of decoration could not be achieved on hard-paste.

Some of the earliest productions of the Vincennes and Sèvres manufactory were sculptural groups, flowers and wares without ground colors. During the 1750s, many of these sculptures, particularly of children in different roles, were based on drawings supplied to the manufactory by François Boucher. From 1757 to 1766 the sculptor Etienne-Maurice Falconet took charge of the sculpture studio and he produced numerous models in marble based on his own works, as well as on the works of other sculptors and designers. The figures were of both contemporary and mythological subjects. Louis-

Vincennes Wine Cooler
Date : 1753
Height: 7¼ in (18.5cm)

The bleu lapis ground was the earliest ground color evolved at Vincennes. It was first used, as in the present instance, with tooled gilt decoration.

Simon Boizot became *chef* of the sculpture studio in 1773; under him many new figures and groups were produced in the neo-classical style. By this time, the manufactory had acquired many designs in the form of drawings or published engravings, for the painters and sculptors to use as inspiration.

The figures were modeled by specialists in the sculpture studio. They were reproduced from plaster molds (many of which still survive) by specialist molders called *mouleurs*. After this the *répareur* would chase the leather-hard clay with details that could not be formed in the mold. The *répareurs* were responsible for this important finishing work on most of the porcelains that went into the kilns, while the *tourneurs* and *anseurs* (turners and handle makers) produced the final forms of the porcelain wares. These workers often signed their pieces with a letter or a symbol incised into the clay under the base of the object.

The decoration of Vincennes and Sèvres products established distinctive features from the mid-1750s. The soft paste porcelain body had an attractive creamy-white tone which was often decorated, with loosely painted floral sprays (page 54) or with monochrome scenes of figures in landscapes. After the introduction of a range of ground colors, a painted scene such as flowers, birds or figures would be set in a white reserve within the panels of ground color, and then framed by patterns of gilding. The most popular ground colors were dark blue (*bleu lapis* from before 1753 to 1763 and *bleu nouveau* from 1763), turquoise blue (*bleu céleste*) and yellow (*jaune*) both introduced in 1753, green (*vert*) introduced in 1756 and pink (*rose*) introduced in 1757. These colors were particularly appealing on soft paste wares, while on hard paste they had a harsh appearance.

The gilded decoration on Vincennes and Sèvres wares is distinctive and was used on nearly all its products from the early 1750s. The gold was fired onto the porcelain at a low temperature, then chased and burnished. Typically, a piece was gilded around the rim and base and on areas such as handles and piercings, highlighting features of the modeling. On occasion, gilding was used in patterns over the ground color, and was also used to frame the painted reserves. In the rococo period this frame might have taken the form of trails of flowers on a trellis, and later, in the neo-classical period, more stylized patterns of abstract tooled decoration on a plain band. From about 1773 gilding was also used at Sèvres as a backing for 'jeweled' decoration. The enamelor Joseph Coteau developed this technique and used drops of opaque and translucent enamel, imitating pearls and colored 'jewels', set onto gold foils which had been formed in steel dies. These were applied in patterns to the body of the object. This jeweled decoration was particularly popular in the early 1780s, but it was expensive to carry out. Early in the nineteenth century highly burnished gilding was applied to wares over large areas, so forming an alternative to a ground color.

The distinction of Sèvres porcelain lies in the fluent forms and the rich, painted and gilded decoration. By the 1780s there were several privately owned porcelain manufactories operating in Paris, but although many of their shapes were based on the simpler tableware forms popularized by Sèvres, their decoration was far plainer. The only factory outside France to be greatly influenced by the lavishness of Sèvres porcelains was the Chelsea factory in London, especially in the gold anchor period. Generally the lavishness of the Sèvres wares had surprisingly little influence on the porcelains of other manufactories in Europe, (although their style of surface decoration was widely copied), and Sèvres faced little competition in the production of their extravagant wares; mainly due to the fact that there was not enough demand for such expensive porcelains.

Sèvres Green Ground Basket
Date: 1756
Height: 8¾in (22cm)

In December 1757 the artist François Boucher, whose work had such a strong influence on both painted and modeled decoration at Sèvres, acquired a basket of this form (left). It cost 240 livres. Like so many Sèvres forms it is of an entirely original shape. Unlike much that the factory made it is deceptively simple and relies solely on plain green, tooled gilding and subtly shaped basketwork for its effect.

Sèvres Jewelled Cup and Saucer
Date: 1781
Height of cup: 2¾in (7cm)
Diameter of saucer: 5¼in (13.5cm)

Jeweled decoration of this type was one of Sèvres' most original contributions to the art of ceramics. Numerous pieces were presented by Louis XVI to the Comte and Comtesse du Nord, later Tzar Paul I and his Czarina, Maria Feodorovna du Nord, during their visit to Paris in 1782. The painting on this cup and saucer was done by Capelle and the gilding by Etienne-Henri Le Guay.

Sèvres Biscuit Group of Leda and the Swan
Date: c 1765
Height: 12½in (32cm)

This group is after a 1764 model by Étienne Maurice Falconet. Like many of Falconet's subjects it is derived from a painting by François Boucher. Biscuit figures such as this were generally intended to form table decorations to accompany grand dinner services. This group is a typical example of the table-top sculptures that the Sèvres manufactory produced in large quantities during the eighteenth century.

Louis XV gave a fine dinner service (part of which is illustrated below) to the Duchess of Bedford in June 1763. Her husband, the fourth Duke of Bedford, of whom an etching is shown after a painting by Sir Joshua Reynolds (left), was a diplomat serving in Paris. This was a more lavish service than most bestowed by Louis XV, due to its large size and cost.

Sèvres Tureen and Two Plates, from the Bedford Service
Date: 1763

This splendid service decorated with a bleu lapis ground color with gilt vermiculé pattern, consisted originally of 183 objects. It was supplied with a series of vases and groups of animals and human figures, all in white biscuit, to decorate the center of the table.

Detail of the Soup Tureen
The ornate gilding and relief decoration on the foot of the soup tureen shows how richly ornamented the Bedford service was, even by the lavish standards of the Sèvres factory. The design for the tureen was by Duplessis, the court silversmith, whose shapes were one of the essentially original features of the whole of Sèvres' production.

Sèvres Dinner Services

*Some of the most splendid State dinner services ever made were
produced for Louis XV, and as diplomatic gifts to foreign monarchs and ambassadors. Here the
richly-colored wares were offset by figures and groups in biscuit,
another of the factory's major achievements.*

A major part of the Vincennes and Sèvres manufactories' productions was devoted to supplying tablewares. The dining room had long been the showplace of fine plate and metalwork, and in the eighteenth century it became a setting for some of the most lavish porcelains. Porcelain is ideal for serving food, being adaptable to all forms of dishes required. Of all the wares produced at Vincennes and Sèvres, it was the models for dinner and tea services that only needed tiny adaptations to remain fashionable over a series of decades; years that witnessed some of the most pronounced changes in fashion. Rococo tableware forms remained popular throughout the neoclassical period until the end of the eighteenth century; only the manner of decoration changed to suit the taste of the decade.

The sales registers preserved in the Sèvres archives are full of the names of the buyers of dinner services, services that vary enormously in extent and price. Nearly all of the French royal family purchased these tablewares; there are also the names of noblemen and merchants from all over Europe. The largest quantities were sold to the Parisian *marchands-merciers* who from their fashionable shops influenced taste while selling objects and furnishings of the highest quality to the rich. The chief *marchands-merciers* dealing in Sèvres porcelain were Lazare Duvaux and Simon Poirier. Some of these dinner services were presented by the Kings, Louis XV

and Louis XVI, to royalty and to diplomats from other European Courts.

To make a dinner service of any substantial size, several decorators were given particular tasks so that the work could be carried out in a uniform manner. At Sèvres the experienced painters and, to a certain extent, the gilders specialized in various types of decoration. André-Vincent Vieillard, for example, painted figures of children in the manner of Francois Boucher, while Jean-Louis Morin often painted scenes of docks or of military encampments on vases. At the Meissen manufactory, and at factories such as Chantilly, Mennecy and St Cloud, artists were not allowed to sign their work. They painted in the styles of the factory, such as the Kakiemon palette of Chantilly or the *chinoiserie* style associated with J.G. Höroldt and his pupils at Meissen. However at Sèvres the artists were called upon to paint in a common style only when working on a large service, or when working on pieces of a standard pattern; they were given a certain artistic freedom when engaged on individual pieces.

Each of the grand dinner services produced at Sèvres consisted of plates, soup plates, four shapes of serving dishes — square, round, oval and shell-shaped — lidded tureens with trays, wine coolers in various sizes, liquor bottle coolers, ice pails, montieths and other serving dishes and trays, custard and ice cups and salt cellars. In the largest services, the

Plate from the Prince de Rohan Service
Rohan Service.
Date: 1771
Diameter: 9¾in (24.5cm)

This plate is decorated in the rich rococo style with the expensive turquoise blue (bleu céleste) ground color. A.J. Chappuis, a leading painter of ornithological subjects at Sèvres, was the decorator. The plate belongs to a service which Louis XV's ambassador to Vienna, Louis René Edouard, Prince de Rohan (right) commissioned, and it is of a scale commensurate with his lavish entertaining. It consisted of 368 pieces. The plates, such as this, were 36 *livres each, and the whole service cost over 20,000 livres. This was the largest service supplied by the factory for a nonroyal client.*

Sèvres Plate from Catherine the Great Service
Date: 1778
Diameter: 10in (26.5cm)

This plate is part of the largest service the Sèvres factory was to produce. It was ordered by the Empress of Russia (left) whose initial E for Ekaterina appears in the center. The cameo motifs round the borders (detail right) are inlaid into the surface of the porcelain. The original colored designs for this service, a plate of which cost 242 livres, still survive in France.

Pieces from Louis XVI's Service
Date: 1783-1792

This service, ordered by Louis XVI (left), is the last great project the Sèvres factory undertook before the Revolution. The beautiful white 'body' is almost entirely submerged beneath the richness of the decoration. This was a dinner service whose sheer quality almost certainly precluded its actual use. The detail (right) shows the decoration of an elaborately painted mythological scene.

number of pieces altered according to the amount of people they were to serve. The Bedford dinner service survives as one of the earlier of the grand dinner services produced at Sèvres. It also remains remarkably complete, with such rarely produced items as knife handles and biscuit figures — which had mostly become separated from similar services by the twentieth century — still surviving.

The models of tableware produced from the 1750s proved to be so popular that they were rarely changed until the nineteenth century. Thus more effort was devoted to the variety and quality of the painted decoration on each element of a service.

The neoclassical style of decoration became fashionable in France from the middle of the 1760s and in 1776 the Empress, Catherine the Great of Russia, commissioned a large dinner service to be made for her at Sèvres in the 'newest classical style'.

Entirely new forms were designed for all of the elements of the service — from the egg cups to the wine coolers. The 797 piece service cost over 300,000 livres. All of the pieces were decorated with painted imitations of ancient cameos and with the monogram of the Empress. This service was by far the most expensive produced at Sèvres.

In 1783 Louis XVI ordered a lavish dinner service for his use at Versailles, to be made at Sèvres. It was to consist of 445 pieces, and the production was planned for execution over 20 years. Only a portion of this service was completed by 1793, when production ceased after the execution of the King. The decoration of the elements of this service was entrusted to only the most experienced painters and gilders. Each fully decorated plate cost the King the phenomenal sum of 480 *livres*, so each object was more costly than the pieces of the Empress of Russia's service.

Sèvres Porcelain Circular Plaque,
(designed to fit on a fall-front sécrétaire)
Date: 1775

The production of plaques such as this and the seven smaller ones around and below it on the sécrétaire (far right), was a speciality of Sèvres during the reign of Louis XVI. It is not clear whether the initiative came from the factory, from the cabinetmakers, from the marchands-merciers, who were the interior decorators of the day, or from their patrons. It is known, however, that plaques were produced with specific pieces of furniture in mind, and often for a specific place on the pieces. It is also evident that plaques were ordered with the greatest care and were not interchangeable. As a result, although the factory did produce self-framed pictures to hang on the wall, most of its plaques had no independent existence, and they were destined from the outset to be part of a larger object.

Sèvres Plaques

*Flat and curved pieces of porcelain, destined to adorn
specific pieces of furniture, were a speciality of the Sèvres factory. The decoration of the
porcelain often echoed the marquetry of the cabinetwork.*

One field in which the Sèvres manufactory excelled in the eighteenth century was in the production of porcelain plaques with painted and gilded decoration. These plaques were produced in small quantities from the mid-1750s, and by the mid-1760s the popular practice of decorating furniture with porcelain plaques specifically designed for this purpose had developed. Plaques painted with royal portraits and with scenes of figures or landscapes were also placed in gilt wood frames on walls — a fashion which began in the early 1760s. The firing of a plaque had to be carefully controlled as flat objects tend to warp in the kiln.

Charles-Nicholas Dodin was one of the most skilled painters at Sèvres in the eighteenth century; he worked there for almost 50 years, which was longer than most of his colleagues. His name or mark is to be found on most of the few fine porcelain wall plaques that were produced from the 1750s to the 1790s.

One such plaque, dated 1783, now mounted onto a piece of furniture, was copied by Dodin from Francois Boucher's painting *Rinaldo et Armide*, which had been presented by Boucher as his *morceau de réception* (diploma work) at the Salon of the Académie Royale de Peinture et Sculpture in 1734. The painting, which is now in the Louvre in Paris, was apparently sent to Sèvres in 1783 to be copied onto porcelain. This was unusual since the artists at Sèvres generally copied paintings by using engravings or drawings of them. The work of the porcelain painter must have been frustrated by the fact that enamel pigments have a totally different color before and after firing, and the object in progress must have looked an extraordinary mixture of tones. Dodin signed the front as well as the reverse with his name, which is unusual for Sèvres porcelain, perhaps because the time taken to paint a plaque of this size was so considerable.

Sèvres porcelain plaques are thought to have first been placed on furniture in 1755 when a group of plaques copying Cantonese enamels was made and then mounted on a pair of cabinets for Jean-Baptiste Machault d'Arnouville by the Parisian *ébéniste* Bernard van Risenburgh. It is thought that the idea came from cabinets produced in Holland in the late seventeenth and early eighteenth centuries, which were set with enamels imported from China. However the idea of placing a highly colored surface decoration on furniture was not new in France; in the previous decades colored wood marquetry, *pietra dure* pla-

ques and lacquer or *vernis* (varnish) panels had been used. Porcelain was used for the tops of small tables because it was much more durable than delicate marquetry.

In the neo-classical *sécrétaire* (above), the shaped plaque in the drawer front, the triangular plaques above and the circular plaque were made to be set into gilt bronze mounts that were specifically designed for a *sécrétaire* of this model. This *sécrétaire* was made by the *ébéniste* Martin Carlin, who was commissioned to make many of the most important neo-classical pieces of furniture decorated in this manner. The plaques are decorated with *bleu céleste* ground color and bear the date letter 'X' for 1775. Undoubtedly, the *marchand-mercier* Simon Poirier and his successor Dominique Daguerre commissioned much of the furniture decorated with Sèvres porcelain plaques, since the two men enjoyed a near monopoly of the plaques on sale from the manufactory.

One of a Pair of Sèvres Vases *(Pot-Pourri Fontaine)*
Date: c 1760
Height: 11¾in (30cm)

This remarkable conception, in which three of the Sèvres ground colors are used together, is part of a pair which was once the property of Madame de Pompadour. The use of three ground colors on one piece of porcelain is very unusual — decoration with two ground colors is more common on Sèvres porcelain. The design stands strikingly apart from contemporary German porcelain.

One of a Pair of Wall Lights
Date: c 1761
Height: 17¼in (43cm)

This wall light, one of a pair, is listed in the same room as the vase Pot-Pourri Fontaine (right) in the 1764 inventory of Madame de Pompadour's belongings. It is decorated with the same three ground colors found on the pot-pourri vase.

Sèvres Vases

*No factory produced so elaborate a range of vases: the complexity
of the shapes was matched by a richness of decoration in enamel colors
and finely chiselled gilding. These very splendid pieces were
confined to the Royal circle.*

Neither the form nor the decoration of most of the wares produced at Sèvres pretended to be oriental. However there does exist a pair of vases decorated with oriental figures made at Sèvres in about 1760 (opposite). The figures are painted simply and are placed in bare Chinese-style settings incorporating exotic vegetation and Chinese porcelain vases. They were probably copied from late seventeenth century or early eighteenth century European engravings, based on scenes found on Chinese lacquer screens and Cantonese enamel plaques which had by then been imported into France.

These vases do not carry the signature of any molder, painter or gilder. One vase, however, does bear the crossed 'L's mark of the manufactory under the base. The painting is attributed to the celebrated porcelain painter Charles-Nicolas Dodin, who was active at Vincennes and Sèvres between 1754 and 1803. This attribution is possible because there are about 12 other pieces of Sèvres porcelain, all dating from between 1760 and 1763, which have similar painted reserves in a Chinese style. On this small group of wares the only painter's mark to be found is

that of Dodin, who is therefore assumed to have painted the entire group. The shape of these vases is described in the Sèvres archives as a 'Vase Pot Pourri Fontaine, ou à Dauphin', because of the design of the flowing water around the base section and because some of these vases have a small porcelain dolphin fitted into a hole in the base section. The shape is first mentioned in the Sèvres sales registers in 1756, and it seems likely that at least eight of the model were produced by the mid-1760s, of which five survive today.

These vases were each designed to contain pot-pourri in the tall central section, hence the pierced lids which allow the scent of the dried flowers to filter into the room. The lower section of each vase has four circular holes at the sides intended to hold small bulb plants such as croci or miniature hyacinths. The plants could be watered through the two lozenge-shaped holes at the front and rear. Originally, these apertures were probably fitted with dolphin-shaped porcelain stoppers, but these are now lost. When the plants died or were out of season, the four round holes might have contained Sèvres porcelain flowers on gilt bronze stems.

**Sèvres Pink and Green
Ground Vases**
Date: 1759
Height: 9¾in (25cm)

*Decorated by Charles
Nicholas Dodin, these vases
have the same form as the
pair of vases belonging to the
garniture of five vases once
owned by Madame de
Pompadour. The original
pair of vases (Pot-Pourri à
Bobechès) would probably
have stood one on either side
of the chinoiserie vases (Pot-
Pourri Fontaine) which in
turn flanked the pot-pourri
vase (Vaisseau à Mat).*

Sèvres Vase à Consoles
Date: 1769
Height: 18in (44.5cm)

The decoration of this vase represents the apogee of Sèvres skills under Louis XV. Here ground color of an unusual mattish blue is enriched with gilding and encloses grisaille panels which are in turn set off by brilliant and luxuriant floral swags in colored enamels. Once again a wholly new conception, this vase displays a perfect marriage between form and decoration. The factory records reveal that the decoration was carried out by Jean-Baptiste-Etienne Genest — the charge was 56 livres. The detail (below) shows the almost excessive opulence of Genest's decoration

Sèvres Vase Bachelier Rectifié
Date: 1779
Height: 2ft 4in (71cm)

Sèvres produced a satisfactory hard-paste porcelain in the early 1770s but much work continued in the more attractive soft-paste. This vase, and its companion, were in the 'cabinet de conseil' at Versailles until the Revolution. Two painters were at work on this vase. The reverse has a martial trophy by Charles Buteux. The side illustrated is decorated by Antoine Caton.

Detail of Vase *The detail shows the fine quality of Antoine Caton's painting, which depicts a scene from the life of Belisarious.*

A Sèvres pot-pourri vase of the celebrated *Vase Vaisseau à Mât* form exists in a private French collection; it has the same three ground colors, a painted reserve of Chinese figures and is decorated with the same gilding patterns as on the two vases *Pot Pourri Fontaine*. They were obviously made to stand together as a *garniture de cheminée* (a set of porcelain vases to decorate the mantleshelf of the chimney-piece); this is confirmed by a brief entry in the Sèvres sales registers. On 30 May 1760 a garniture of five vases was sold for cash to an unnamed purchaser. The entry reads as follows:

'1 Vaisseau en trois couleurs		720 livres
2 Pots pourris fontaines Idem	480	960 livres
2 Idem à bobèches Idem	360	720 livres
		2400 livres'

The Sèvres manufactory produced many garnitures of vases of varying shapes and sizes in groups of three or five, but the one listed here was more elaborate than most and it seems to have been the only one where three ground colors were used together. Although the purchaser of this garniture cannot be identified in the Sèvres archives, the set is mentioned in the 1764 inventory of Madame de Pompadour's belongings. It stood on the mantlepiece of the bedroom in her Parisian home. It is likely that these elaborate vases were made either for her or for Louis XV to present to his mistress as a gift.

The Sèvres manufactory produced an immense variety of vases through the eighteenth century, keeping pace with changes in fashion. Not only were these vases produced in widely differing shapes, but also with very inventive decoration. One example of a vase in the early neo-classical style (opposite) is bodly modeled with consoles and foliate motifs. This vase dates from 1769 and is decorated with a battlescene painted in varying shades of gray (*en grisaille*) set in a gilded frame, with ribbons and flowers on a dark blue ground. Another example of Sèvres' wide production is a pair of neoclassical vases made in 1779, based on the shapes of antique vases and painted with scenes depicting episodes from the life of Belisarius, set in reserves on a dark blue (*bleu nouveau*) ground. The sharp contrast of the deep blue ground color and the thickly applied gilding gives the vases a strong feeling of opulence. This pair (one of which is shown above) formed part of the decoration of the *Cabinet du Conseil* at Versailles until the French Revolution (1789).

3
The Blue and White Tradition

The use of cobalt blue in the decoration of ceramics has played an unequalled role in every great pottery tradition from Europe, the Islamic world and the Far East. Cobalt oxide is unique in producing a good blue color on ceramics across a wide range of firing temperatures, from low-fired earthenwares and medium-fired stonewares to the most highly fired porcelains in reducing or oxidizing atmospheres.

The first identified use of cobalt blue on ceramics is probably that of the sought-after Tang dynasty blue glazed earthenware; it was introduced as early as the first half of the eighth century AD, disappeared with the fall of that dynasty and was not reintroduced until the fourteenth century in China.

Excavations early this century in the ruins of Samarra unearthed a group of wares, mostly small dishes with simple decoration of palmettes or Kufic inscriptions in cobalt blue on a soft tin glaze. These were technically little different from the later European Maiolica and Delft. Samarra was built and occupied by the Caliphs between 836 AD and 892 AD, and then virtually abandoned, so these wares can be confidently dated to the ninth century. The early history of Islamic ceramics is still very uncertain and it is quite possible that archeologists will discover the use of cobalt before this date.

The great Chinese tradition of blue and white

Blue and White Meiping Vase
Date: 1403-1424 (Yongle period)
Height: 14½in (36.5cm)

The baluster vase with rounded short neck is a classic shape in Chinese ceramics. This example shows that the sense of balance and spacious freedom of design, temporarily suborned by the influence of Islamic metalwork designs, have re-asserted themselves. The very broad and generous proportions of this Meiping vase is characteristic of an early Ming example; the proportions were less satisfactory when eighteenth century potters tried to imitate the shape.

Japanese Arita Blue and White Ewer *(with Dutch silver mounts)*
Date: c 1664
Height: 9 in (23 cm)

In the third quarter of the seventeenth century when imports from China were restricted due to the chaos caused by the change of dynasty, the Dutch traders turned increasingly to Japan. The shape of this ewer is derived from a Dutch or German origin. The decoration is taken from the Chinese style of the mid-seventeenth century known as 'Transitional' which was widely copied in Europe in tin-glazed earthenware. Japanese porcelains of this type differ from the slightly earlier Chinese examples in having a softer and grayer blue color and a thicker glaze. Dutch records show that thousands of comparable wares were exported from Japan during this period.

Chelsea Plate
Date: c 1753 (red anchor period)
Diameter: 9in (23cm)

Blue and white Chelsea porcelain is extremely rare; only a handful of pieces survive today. Though blue and white porcelain was produced in large quantities by factories catering to the growing middle class of the period, Chelsea, with its rich and aristocratic clientele, was not much concerned with producing domestic wares. The design of the plate is of Japanese derivation while the shape is purely European.

porcelain that restarted in the fourteenth century has continued with no major interruptions to the present day; it dominates the whole field of ceramics and has been an overriding stimulus to potters everywhere. The magnificent dishes of the fourteenth century and the great classic wares of the fifteenth century were collected and treasured by the rulers of the Moslem world; many of these wares are now to be found in the museum in Tehran and in the vast collection at the Topkapu Saray in Istanbul. A few pieces found their way to Europe before the sixteenth century through trade with the Arabs, and these were mounted in silver — a testimony to the regard in which they were held. It is easy to understand how wonderful these early imports must have seemed with their mysterious and beautifully painted designs of 'Far Cathay'; Europe and the Middle East had nothing to compare with the brilliant and translucent material of these wares.

When the Portuguese and Dutch traders began to import blue and white porcelain in the sixteenth and seventeenth centuries it became an obvious yardstick with which to compare the wares of the local potters. It stimulated the production of the blue and white Delft ware and, to a lesser extent, the Maiolica and faience of the rest of Europe. No European potteries could match the quality of the porcelains of the Kangxi period (1662-1722) which still grace so many country houses in the form of garnitures of vases and other wares. Attempts were made to emulate Chinese porcelain in the form of soft-paste porcelain in Italy in the sixteenth century and in France in the seventeenth century, but it was not until the eighteenth century that the production of hard-paste porcelain was achieved. During that century, in Europe, porcelain colored with overglaze enamels became pre-eminent, and blue and white wares were relegated to the domestic level. However many fine pieces continued to be produced. In Persia and Turkey extremely beautiful copies of Chinese porcelains were made from the sixteenth century; indeed sometimes the painting on these wares was better than that on the Chinese originals, although the quality of the porcelain itself was never matched.

The popularity of blue and white ceramics continued throughout the eighteenth and nineteenth centuries and remains unabated today. It is still frequently used on modern commercial wares despite the fact that modern potters have a vast range of colors and techniques to choose from.

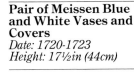

Pair of Meissen Blue and White Vases and Covers
Date: 1720-1723
Height: 17½in (44cm)

By 1720, David Köhler and Johann Melhorn had perfected the technique of underglaze blue decoration, but the secret was lost on the death of Köhler in 1723. After this short period of production, blue and white wares ceased to be a part of the Meissen repertory until later in the century. The soft blue color and the delicacy of the painting, combined with the high quality of the porcelain developed at Meissen, make these rare wares much sought after.

Blue and White Double-Gourd Vase
Date: c 1350-1375
Height: 20in (50.5cm)

Massively potted in five parts and luted together, this remarkable base exemplifies the robust quality and astonishingly vigorous character of the mid-fourteenth century underglaze blue porcelains. The design is cluttered — the painter still unused to treating the surfaces of the vase as a space to be explored rather than occupied. The design is also linear; the dense peony scrolls issue on two sides from specific outcrops of rock, rather than follow the contours of the vase. Given that it was apparently the Near and Middle East which provided the earliest markets for massive wares of this type, it is appropriate that the other recorded extant example of this type with unfacetted lobes is in the Topkapu Saray collection, Istanbul.

Detail of Vase *An area between the two large lobes of the body shows the effect after firing of imprecisely applied ground cobalt pigment. Specks of mineral have been dropped onto the biscuit surface, and the centres of the peony petals are almost black where the coarsely-ground mineral has all but penetrated the glaze flux. The effect is known as 'heaping and piling'.*

Detail of 18th Century Blue and White Vase
(left) The painter has deliberately imitated the earlier accidental 'heaping and piling' by dotting the lotus petals in the paler areas.

Chinese Blue and White

By painting and firing ground cobalt onto a newly-discovered combination of china clay and china stone, Chinese potters laid the foundations and provided the inspiration for most of the subsequent developments in ceramic production around the world.

More clearly than any other field of Chinese art, Chinese porcelain reflects the cross-cultural fertilization brought about by the effects of international overland and sea trade. Nowhere are these cultural exchanges more obvious than in the decoration and design of Chinese blue and white porcelain. For centuries 'Mohammedan blue' (Chinese blue and white ware), produced from a mineral arsenide of cobalt, captivated the Middle and Near East. When the countries of the Mediterranean Basin discovered this porcelain in the later Middle Ages, whether as a gift from a Middle Eastern potentate or by conquest, it acquired lavish European mounts to emphasize its rarity. It joined princely treasuries as fitting company for gems and precious metals and it appeared later in Dutch and Flemish still life paintings to complement rich silver gilt vessels. Its rare appearance for sale in Europe in any quantity created a sensation before the latter part of the seventeenth century. The wartime capture by the Dutch of two Portuguese carracks laden with Far Eastern freight in 1602 and 1604 drew massive interest from throughout Europe to the quayside auctions in Amsterdam, where the contents of the prizes were dispersed.

Chinese blue and white porcelain is remarkable for the speed with which it appears to have matured, both technically and artistically. Like Chinese archaic bronzes of the early second millenium BC, it has curiously obscure origins. No pieces documented either by an inscription or by a dated archaeological context apparently predate the extraordinary pair of large temple vases, painted with dragons and dated in accordance with 1351 AD (based on a Chinese calendar date). These vases were acquired by Sir Percival David, a renowned British collector, in the 1930s and they are now one of the glories of the Percival David Foundation in London.

However it is clear that earlier blue and white ware does exist and pieces of an earlier era, acquired from an excavation of one of the numerous grave sites in South Asia, will almost certainly be documented at a later date. Extensive groups of small, poor-quality blue-painted porcelain jarlets, boxes and miniature ewers have already been randomly discovered; indeed, a number of examples have been found

Underglaze-decorated storage jar *(guan)*
Date: Mid-fourteenth century
Height: 13in (32.5cm)

One of only two recorded examples, this jar is a tour-de-force of the early potter's art in its combination of techniques. The body is painted <u>under the glaze</u> in a dark blue and a particularly rich copper-red which is an exceptionally rare combination for the period. The jar is also applied with bands of small beads around large panels of foliage standing away from the body on short spurs. Under any circumstance, this reticulated effect is difficult to control without precise firing of the kiln, and it is an extraordinary achievement for an early porcelain maker.

Blue and White Dish
Date: c 1400
Diameter: 15in (37.5cm)

This dish is painted in a more fluid manner than the next dish (opposite), which it antedates slightly. The wide, flat flanged rim is painted with 'breaking waves', one of the most dramatic painted border compositions introduced during the Yuan period, and perfectly suited for a flat rim to 'frame' the central floral meanders. Although the composition owes much to Islamic design in its two-dimensional quality and repeated motifs, there is a fluidity and irregularity in details which make the dish more visually interesting.

Detail of Blue and White Dish
Running borders provide dramatic frames for many Chinese designs, in architecture, textiles and metalwork as well as in ceramics. Wave patterns are particularly effective, though the early designs are not entirely symmetrical. Later in the Ming period, large rocks are placed at regular and symmetrical points in the design, breaking up the rhythm and allowing the waves to break violently against them. Flower scrolls, another popular design, are often very accurate in their depiction of specific varieties of flowering shrubs and fruit blossoms.

associated with Southern Song coins, but the evidence provided by these coins is not considered to be precise and certainly does not place these pieces accurately in a particular decade. If the production and decoration of blue and white porcelain did mature exceedingly fast, then this type of imprecise evidence is even less useful. It is noteworthy that the largest, most accurately dated archaeological recovery of early fourteenth century ceramics — a shipwreck off Korea dated around 1330 — included no blue and white.

There is evidence of a large freight of newly-potted celadons, ying qing and some jun yao stonewares, and even 'antique' lacquer, to Japan, but this straightforward commercial voyage included no porcelains painted under the glaze either in cobalt blue or in the contemporaneous ground copper oxide used to decorate the underglaze-red wares. However this shipwreck certainly does not constitute conclusive evidence as to the nonexistence of Chinese blue and white before 1351.

All the evidence suggests that the demand for the earlier products of underglaze blue (and copper red) wares came from abroad. The small pieces went in immense quantities to the Philippines and to the islands off the southern coast; the largest wares went to silk route entrepots for distribution in India and Iran. The elegant blue and white wares of the fifteenth century have always been treasures of the Chinese Imperial collections, but evidence for the solid, massively-potted, strongly and boldly painted wares of the period 1330-1400 comes mainly from archaeological and literary sources outside China. These sources suggest that while some of the wares were transported by camel back along the tortuous and treacherous overland tracks north and south of the Taklamakan desert to Samarkand and Baghdad, many more served (as they have always done), as impermeable and heavy ballast along the shipping routes to protect the lighter, perishable, more valuable exports.

A successful piece of early underglaze-decorated porcelain, such as the massive Yuan double-gourd vase (page 72), has conquered major technical problems, problems that western potters only came to face, much less overcome, four hundred years later. The ground mineral cobalt was painted in suspension straight onto the dried, but unfired, biscuit surface, and the vessel itself was often assembled from several wheel-thrown or slab-constructed clay elements luted together with a clay

Blue and White Saucer Dish
Date: 1403-1424 (Yongle period)
Diameter: 13½in (34cm)

A studied composition depicts a tied cluster of lotus blossoms and leafy fronds; while the sloping well (the area between the rim and the flat center) has a very symmetrical meander of peony, below waves breaking less violently than in the other dish (opposite). The considerable consistency of design suggests the use of stencils to give at least a balanced basis for these seemingly freehand compositions. Sometimes it is possible to spot guidelines used by the painters, but they were extremely skillful at incorporating these marks into the main composition.

Blue and White Dish
(above)
Date: 1465-1487
Diameter: 11¾in (30cm)

**Blue and White
'Palace' Bowl** *(below)*
Date: 1465-1487
Diameter: 6in (15cm)

Both these porcelains date from the Chenghua reign which generated wares that excel not merely as superlative designs but also in the quality of the porcelain body. The proportions are superb; delicate touches like diminutive curves on the edges of rims add to the visual impact. The dish (above) is obviously intended to be seen from the top, and the interior is a well-balanced arrangement with the border panels carefully spaced. But even the underside (middle) has been considered, with the floral design spaced around the imperial reign mark below the lip.

The Chenghua six-character mark is visible below the rim at the top.

The foot-rim has been carefully thinned and cleaned off.

The inside is left unglazed, as on nearly all other early Ming dishes.

Chenghua six-character mark.

The rounded underside of a bowl is a particularly difficult surface on which to organize an elaborate design. In this case three long, leafy sprays of fruiting lychee are symmetrically strewn arond the clean-cut fine-grained foot.

slip. The porcellaneous body required controlled high-temperature firing to cause the vitrification of body and glaze; the cobalt, too, required an extremely high temperature to 'turn' it from a matt black pigment into the extraordinarily rich tone that appears even on the earliest examples. Sometimes this was not possible as the mineral, ground too coarsely, penetrated the surface of the glaze, or fired as much darker specks in the blue washes on the surface of the body. This 'heaping and piling' effect was so characteristic an element of fourteenth and some fifteenth century wares that the Jingdezhen potters in the eighteenth century laboriously recreated it, attempting to emulate their ancestors' great ceramic achievements. But these later essays meant deliberately, and symmetrically, dotting the larger area of blue wash with darker specks, and this application lacks the random, accidental quality of the misfired early designs.

The 'blue' porcelains belonging to the early fifteenth century Ming emperors are far more refined than the products of sixty years earlier. The design is far more restrained, the robust quality is harnessed, the sizes are often much smaller and the potting is crisper and thinner. Some pieces are even identified with the 'nien hao' (the reign mark) of the appropriate emperor, which suggests how extremely acceptable blue and white had become in a Chinese context; the use of an imperial 'seal of approval', even on pieces from Palace kilns, was unprecedented. Although smaller in scale, the vessels were nevertheless painted with far more spacious and delicate designs. The immensely elaborate and dense combinations of floral patterns, under the Yuan and earliest Ming emperors, were replaced with single bouquets of tied flowers, and simple meanders of carefully-detailed flower blossoms.

The combination of superb quality porcelain bodies, new forms of decoration and a clear orientation towards the taste of the imperial court, created a range of porcelain which has influenced the world's ceramics ever since. The potters of late fifteenth century Rome referred to these Chinese wares when they produced the glassy-bodied, limpid-blue 'Medici' porcelains in which both body and design were a pastiche of the original. It was the blue and white tradition which stimulated western demand, and even when transfer-printing revolutionized ceramic production in the West, creamwares and soft-paste porcelains were normally printed in blue, rather than other ink transfers. The quantity of seventeenth and eighteenth century blue and white available in the West is still enormous. This is due to the fact that a large quantity of pieces were used to fill out the holds of merchant ships belonging to the East India Company. It proved to be a handy and commercially profitable way of carrying fragile and light spices, tea and textiles home from Batavia and Canton.

Only two pigments known to the early Chinese porcelain painters — cobalt blue and copper oxide — could cope with the immense heat required to fuse biscuit body, glaze and colors into the superb wares of the Yuan and early Ming period. It was therefore a technical consideration which forced the Chinese to rely on these two, and particularly on cobalt blue at an early date; for this reason the cobalt color established itself in Western eyes as the *sine qua non* of decorated Chinese porcelain.

Blue and White Dish
Date: c 1600 (late Ming)
Diameter: 19¾in (50cm)

This dish belongs to a type known as 'kraak porselein' by Dutch collectors; it was this thin, vividly blue, mass-produced porcelain which first gave most Europeans the chance to own famed Chinese porcelain. It was exported in vast quantities by the Portuguese East India Company in the latter sixteenth century and, more important, by the Dutch equivalent, the V.O.C., in the early seventeenth century; the styles and designs had a crucial influence on the development of the European ceramic industry. By tradition, the term 'kraak' is held to refer to the Portuguese merchantships, 'carracks'; but equally possibly, it may derive from the 'kraak' shelf on which domestic crockery was displayed.

Arita Blue and White Apothecary's Bottle

Date: c 1665-1685
Height: 16in (40cm)

The shape of this apothecary's bottle, or gallipot as it would originally have been called, was probably copied from Dutch glass. A wood dummy may have been made and sent from Europe to Japan. The decoration includes paradise flycatchers and branches of tree-peony. Notice the double lip or string-rim for securing a cover over the mouth. The detail (below) shows bronzing which is peculiar to Japanese blue and white.

The initials I.C. on the base of the bottle are probably those of Johannes Camphuys (1634-1695), who was born in Haarlem and joined the Dutch East India Company twenty years later. In 1671 he was stationed at Deshima and took charge of the Company's operations in Japan, and in 1684 moved to Batavia on his election to Governor-General of the Dutch East Indies.

Japanese Blue and White

Derived from China and Korea, Japanese blue and white came into its own when the Chinese Ming Dynasty collapsed.

Pure white porcelain decorated, beneath a transparent glaze, with designs painted in cobalt-oxide blue is a concept and production so singularly Chinese that any other adjective rings odd. Blue and white is the fortune-making 'Ming vase' of popular saleroom legend, hunted for in many a loft and attic. In later and daintier forms it was the darling of the Aesthetic Movement, collected for the cabinet towards the end of the nineteenth century. It has imprinted itself on the Western mind and has been responsible for the development of European porcelain; it appears even in that sturdy product known as English bone china, especially the ever-popular willow-pattern design.

The main component of porcelain clay is kaolin, named after Kao-ling, the hill in China where it was originally found. The other two components are feldspar, a crystalline mineral consisting mainly of aluminum silicates, and quartz, or silicon dioxide. The Chinese name for the feldspar and quartz-containing material is petuntse, and while in China the porcelain clay was artificially compounded, in Hizen province in Japan (modern Saga prefecture) a natural material was discovered already mixed in the right proportion.

Japanese blue and white also derives largely from Chinese originals, but its first inspiration appears to have been Korean, for during Keicho (1596-1614) and Genwa (1615-23) periods a rather coarse blue and white porcelain was produced at kilns run by Koreans scattered over most of Hizen province. This manufacture of porcelain was undoubtedly the most significant development in Japanese ceramics during the Edo period (1603-1868), and there is some difference of opinion as to when the Japanese (and their Korean mentors) were first successful in producing it. It is traditionally believed that in 1616 a naturalized Korean named Ri Sambei discovered a large deposit of porcelain clay at Izumiyama near the town of Arita in Hizen. Sambei was one of the many potters brought back to Japan when Hideyoshi's armies

returned from the second Korean campaign in 1594. After settling in Kyushu he at first made Karatsu pottery, but soon after his discovery of the clay-beds, Sambei established a porcelain kiln at Tengudani. Such was his success that within a few years many of the neighboring kilns had changed production from Karatsu ware to the new blue and white porcelain. Many of these kilns were also run by Koreans, and the industry expanded so quickly that in 1637 the Nabeshima clan issued an order controlling the number of Japanese kiln workers in order to protect the livelihood of the Koreans. Only 800 Koreans were to be permitted to make porcelain, and ten years later a further order limited the number of Arita kilns to 150, and pottery wheels to 155. The use of kaolin was also regulated, for the local Nabeshima rulers recognized the economic importance of the new

Arita Apothecary's Bottle
Date: c 1665-1685
Height: 16¼ in (41cm)

In this slightly simpler apothecary's bottle there is only a single lip, and the same monogram which

appeared on the base of the bottle (opposite) has here become the sole form of decoration. The reference is probably to the same individual.

porcelain industry and were determined to maintain their control of it.

The decoration of early Japanese blue and white porcelain, (produced in the first half of the seventeenth century), naturally follows the Korean style of sparse decoration employing fast and attractively spontaneous brushwork. Ceramics of this type were appreciated by the Japanese tea masters, both for their strong, straightforward shapes and the freedom and simplicity of their designs. All were intended for native use and, unlike the export ware of the second half of the century, are quite free of any Dutch East India Company influence. Blue and white cobalt underglaze wares are called, in Japan, *sometsuke*, meaning 'dyed', and there is a perceptible difference between them and the Chinese porcelains. The Chinese wares have a hard, smooth glaze and the edges of bowls and plates are thin, even sharp. Japanese wares tend to be thicker and heavier, the glaze seems almost soft and the edges are thicker and rounded. Old Chinese porcelain sometimes shows signs of wear on the edges where the glaze chips off in a characteristic manner, giving a moth-eaten appearance called, in Japanese, *mushi-kui*. The glaze on Japanese wares, perhaps because of the more rounded edges, breaks rather than chips off, and seems to be incorporated into the body and a part of it. On Chinese porcelain the foot-rim is sometimes beveled rather than square-cut, having been ground into shape after firing, or it may show specks of the sand or gravel on which it was placed in the kiln. Japanese porcelains usually have a clean, square-cut foot-rim, often covered with glaze, for they were placed in the kiln on several small cones or pyramids for firing and the marks of these supports can often be seen inside the foot-rim.

In 1641 the Tokugawa shogunate had forbidden all European trade except that with the Dutch East India Company, whose officials were strictly regulated and, except for annual visits to Edo to present gifts, confined to tiny Deshima island in Nagasaki harbor. When the Ming dynasty of China suddenly collapsed towards the middle of the seventeenth century, the Dutch turned to Japan for the manufacture of their export porcelain, and Japanese production, from being almost exclusively manufactured for local consumption in the first half of the seventeenth century, was largely made for export in the second half. This sudden turn of events had a profound effect on both the ceramic industry of Japan and the history of European porcelain. The small groups of potters making porcelain in the Arita area were abruptly put in the position of matching the output of the vast and highly organized Chinese kilns at

Shoki-Imari Pear-Shaped Vase
Date: First half 17th century
Height: 9½in (24cm)

In the early years of the seventeenth century some stoneware and pottery kilns turned to making the new porcelain. The earliest types (Shoki Imari) were made with a poor quality porcelain clay with a high iron content, and the decoration comprised simple yet powerful designs drawn in cobalt oxide under a glaze of a bluish tinge. The subject of the decoration on this vase is the 'Three Friends' or Shochikubai — Pine, Bamboo and Plum. The earliest style of painting reflected Korean styles as transmitted through Korean stoneware, but a more sophisticated approach was soon developed, sometimes representational as here, and sometimes using striking abstract or geometric patterns.

Kakiemon Blue and White Dish

Date: Early 18th century
Diameter: 15¾in (39.5cm)

The dish (above) has a lightly ribbed well, and the foliate rim is dressed with a chocolate-brown glaze. The subject of the design is Chinese, and like most fine quality Kakiemon blue and white of the late seventeenth and eighteenth century, the body is a milky white with a close-textured, almost greasy glaze over a rich, translucent cobalt blue. From a technical viewpoint these pieces represent a peak in the Japanese production of blue and white.

Arita Blue and White Dish

Date: 17th century
Diameter: 15in (37.5cm)

Although Chinese armorial porcelain is well-known and comparatively plentiful, Japanese examples are rare. Japanese porcelain became very acceptable to the Dutch East India Company from 1653 onwards, because of the shortage of Chinese wares, and this unusual dish (left) bearing a fanciful Iberian coat-of-arms dates from the second half of the seventeenth century.

Three Pieces of Japanese Blue and White
Date: All 17th century
Height: 8in (20.5cm), top;
10in (25.5cm), left;
15⅛in (38cm), right

The Arita apothecary's bottle (top) is decorated with birds, peonies and pomegranates surrounding a monogram. The jar (left) is decorated with birds of paradise in display among chrysanthemums, and is probably from the Kakiemon kiln. The pear-shaped bottle (right) is decorated with a flowering shrub and a band of stylized leaves at the neck.

Cheng-te Chen, obliging them to increase production to a previously unheard-of extent, and to cope with both designs and shapes which were quite foreign to them. Inevitably, an element of mass-production crept in, yet the quality of these export wares is, on the whole, remarkably fine. Potting and decoration maintain a high level, despite some repetition of designs. The records of the Dutch Company at Deshima mention the importation of 'porcelain paint' (cobalt blue) into Japan in 1650, and then increasingly extensive shipments until 1656; the Japanese porcelain industry was clearly undergoing major changes. The first documented export of Japanese porcelain is recorded as taking place in 1653, when a ship carrying over two thousand gallipots left Japan for the Dutch East India Company's great warehouse at Batavia, now known as Jakarta, on the Island of Java. These gallipots were almost certainly what are today usually called apothecary's or medicine bottles, and their shapes, with a typical double lip or string-rim for securing a covering over the mouth, probably derived from German stoneware or German and Dutch glass.

The Dutch were in the habit of sending wood samples of the shapes they required to China, and the same method was employed with the Japanese. The vast quantities of porcelain which the Japanese produced for the Dutch East India Company went not only to Holland but to India, Persia, Ceylon, Siam and other parts of South East Asia; the trade in blue and white porcelain was indeed worldwide. But although the Japanese succeeded in producing literally millions of pieces of porcelain for export in a period of less than forty years, the family kilns of Arita could never be as efficient, or in modern terms, cost-effective, as the vast centralized Chinese kilns at Cheng-te Chen. The relative inexperience of the Japanese in large-scale production made their porcelains expensive, and wars with England and France had a disastrous effect on the Dutch economy. By the time that the Dutch had recovered, the Ching emperor, Kangxi, had reorganized the kilns at Cheng-te Chen, and they were again in full production. The Dutch East India Company returned to its old source, and by about 1690 the great days of Japanese export blue and white porcelain were over.

Arita Nine-sided Baluster Jar (left)
Date: Late 17th century
Height: 20½in (51.5cm)

This blue and white jar is a typical example of the large decorative pieces produced in Arita in the second half of the seventeenth century. The three shaped panels contain a design of peonies and two mythical birds known as ho-ho.

Arita Octagonal Baluster Jar
Date: Late 17th century
Height: 16¾in (42cm)

Although the design elements in this jar are similar to the one above, the general effect is different and serves to show how the porcelain painters of Arita contrived to ring the changes with a fairly limited subject matter.

European Blue and White

The centuries old desire of European potters and porcelain manufacturers to imitate the blue and white porcelains of the Orient culminated in the development of the Delft potteries, and later, in the production of blue and white wares at Meissen.

European use of blue decoration on pottery can be seen at its best in the large tulip vases made in Holland predominantly for the royal courts of Britain in the seventeenth century. The idea of 'bulb' vases is undoubtedly based on Persian vases of a slightly earlier period, and the Dutch combined this idea with the shape of Chinese pagodas and the stacking effect of graduated water-trays until they arrived at an obelisk form.

There can be little doubt that several of the Delft potteries derived much of their inspiration from the expert engraving of Daniel Marot, the French Huguenot artist. At the age of twenty Marot was already ranked with the great masters, such as Jean Bérain and Lepautre. The Revocation of the Edict of Nantes in 1683 cut short his promising career at the French court at the age of twenty-four, and he subsequently moved to Holland and entered the service of Prince William, as his architect. It is from this time that the productions of the Delft potteries became more architectural in construction and the painted designs grander and more opulent. Almost certainly these designs were based on Marot's engravings.

The marriage of William III of Orange and Mary (later Mary II of England) had a profound effect on Delft productions destined for the export market. Their courtship provided many royal commissions, and the marriage offered an opportunity to decorate Hampton Court Palace (set outside London, on the Thames) with lavish productions from the various Dutch factories. The De Grieksche 'A' (the Greek 'A') factory in Delft received several commissions for

Tulip Vases
Date: c 1690
Height: 5ft 3in (160cm)

Close ties with architectural details of the period are apparent in the modeling of these tulip vases. The obelisk seems to have held a fascination for architects, sculptors and modelers throughout the seventeenth and eighteenth centuries. The female mask nozzles on the bases resemble Flemish and other European cornice sculptures and gargoyles. Commemorative wares were produced in great quantities during this period; the busts surmounting the bases probably depict Queen Mary. It is not unlikely that an order from the court specified representation of the monarch as decoration for the top of the bases. The caryatid supports (see detail right) look like bowsprits and possibly recall Dutch seafaring skills. The recumbent lion-and-ball feet are derived directly from the Buddhist lions so often depicted in Chinese works of art. The bases demonstrate the skill of the Dutch potters in overcoming the problem of firing cracks appearing in large pieces. They made the

vases in sections, each part being made to fit neatly into another. This must have been done with exactitude as no tier from one vase fits into the corresponding space on the other. The result is a stable form which gives the impression of one piece rather than a vase made in sections.

THE INFLUENCE OF DANIEL MAROT

The architecture of Daniel Marot, court architect of William III, undoubtedly had influence on the forms produced at the Delft potteries. However it was his engravings which contributed most to blue and white decoration on Delft wares. The decoration on the oval plaque (right) comes directly, but with mirrored image, from Marot's engraving 'Troisième Sieuxe de Perspectives' (left).

There does not appear to be a surviving engraved source for the decoration on the tile (left), so it is not possible to be definite about the role of Marot. However, similar tiles, known to have been in the dairy at Hampton Court in England, exist. As Marot designed the dairy, and the tiles are documented as coming from De Grieksche A factory in Delft, where Marot's engravings had great influence, the attribution to Marot should be fairly safe.

Hampton Court, and a bill dated 1695 records an order for tiles for the dairy and ornamental objects for the palace. Included among the latter order were tall tulip vases with the royal coat-of-arms and motto. These were decorated according to sketches made by Marot and the actual vases can still be seen at Hampton Court Palace. The pair illustrated were conceivably made for a contemporary courtier.

The construction of the vases is particularly interesting, as the potting of large pieces had tended to be unsatisfactory for a number of reasons. Firstly, potters found it exceptionally difficult to handle and regulate the thickness of a large body. Secondly, the overall weight produced stresses too great for the lower parts in the unfired state, and this resulted in distortions, particularly during firing. Thirdly, larger pieces required plenty of kiln space; however, if there was an inability to regulate satisfactorily the heat of the kiln, the temperature varied inside the kiln; this in turn caused the clay to fire unevenly and some parts therefore baked faster than others. When this occurred during the firing of large pieces, sags and tears in the body were not uncommon. These problems are particularly evident in the early attempts by Meissen to make large animals for the Dresden Palace. Large firing cracks appeared at the point where water escaped at different speeds, according to the thickness of the clay. The tulip vases, on the other hand, demonstrate the ingenuity and skill of the Dutch potters in overcoming these problems.

Blue and white decoration is directly derived from Chinese porcelain of the Ming dynasty. The Dutch imported vast quantities of Chinese blue and white porcelain through their East India Company, and this had a direct influence on their own ceramic productions. The fascination of the East dominated European art throughout the seventeenth century and well into the eighteenth century. The imported Ming wares often depicted Chinese seated in a landscape and under pagodas, and the Delft painters followed or improvised on these traditions. However, the European painters never fully understood these subjects and Chinese figures tended to have European proportions, with oriental features. Similarly the importance the Japanese placed on the tea ceremony was never fully comprehended or portrayed by the European factories. The Dutch artists tended to overpaint the areas of white, filling the whole space with details, while the Chinese managed to convey the scene with just a few brush strokes. In the earliest Delft productions designs were faithfully reproduced from the Wanli examples (Chinese porcelain named after an emperor in the Ming Dynasty), and it was only in the third quarter of the seventeenth century that the Dutch artists began to paint adaptations of Chinese subjects and purely European themes. Prior to this you only occasionally find a European figure in a landscape, usually with a border of Buddhist symbols or oriental foliage.

The skills of the Dutch artists, enhanced by experimentation, enabled them to handle the cobalt-color very successfully. Accuracy in drawing, and the ability to spread the color evenly gave their pieces a finish that has never been surpassed in European pottery painting. Elsewhere in Europe, blue and white decoration had dominated ceramic production for several centuries. Before the discovery of the eastern sea route small amounts of Chinese porcelain had found their way to Europe via the silk route, and the Turkish and Near Eastern potters had been quick to incorporate elements of Chinese decoration into their own output. However it was the Italians in the fifteenth and sixteenth centuries who were to develop this style of decoration. Elements of Chinese decoration can be seen on maiolica dishes, noticeably the so-called *alla porcellana* foliage decoration, frequently used on the reverses of *istoriato* wares. The Florentine wares produced during the second quarter of the fifteenth century show a distinctive use of cobalt blue in impasto (thickly applied blue pigment), a purely European taste. Designs of oak-leaves, fleur-de-lys, birds and animals feature strongly. In the middle of the sixteenth century the Venetians produced blue and white wares in a novel manner by enriching blue *istoriato* and landscape subjects with *bianco-sopra-bianco* (opaque white on a bluish background). In the latter part of the sixteenth century an artificial porcelain was produced at the Medici court for a short period. This was decorated in blue with symmetrical flower and foliage designs, often incorporating *grotteschi* and Islamic features. The productions, however, were small in quantity and, while distinctly Italian, had little influence on contemporary wares.

The seventeenth century was dominated by the wares of Holland, although other areas of Europe also used blue and white. Most important of these was Rouen in France towards the end of the seventeenth century. Their wares were strongly influenced by the engravings of Jean Bérain and Marot and were decorated with lambrequins and arabesques to a great extent. Carefully drawn baroque strapwork cartouches enclosing coats-of-arms were constantly used as decoration. This was also used on the soft porcelain productions of St. Cloud and Tournai. In

Dutch Delft Blue and White Plate
Date: 1700-1720
Diameter: 16¼in (41cm)

The baroque influence on this liturgical dish is very obvious. The pedimented niche flanked by pillars and strapwork are baroque architectural styles, particularly associated with Daniel Marot. The vases of flowers are European in form, but the floral arrangements are still Chinese in style. The crowded design is typical of European blue and white decoration in that it fills most of the surface. The family who commissioned the dish have had their initials added at the bottom, in a way similar to those which appear on Flemish religious 'donor' paintings.

Meissen Augustus Rex Blue and White Vase and Cover
Date: c 1723
Height: 17¾in (45cm)

The production of a satisfactory blue and white ware at Meissen posed immense problems. David Köhler, the factory's colorist, succeeded in producing a satisfactory cobalt color in 1719. In April 1723 he died and his skill went with him to the grave and the factory ceased entirely to produce quality blue and white wares. Though overtly Chinese in style, neither the shape of the vase nor the detail of the chinoiserie painting really resemble the wares it tried to imitate or rival.

Frankfurt Blue and White Dish
Date: c 1700
Diameter: 18¾in (47cm)

This dish is most probably a direct copy of a Chinese 'kraak porselein' dish of the late Ming dynasty, copious quantities of which were imported into Europe by the East India Companies.

porcelain discovery

Germany blue and white was used in the Delft manner, but places like Nuremberg incorporated religious subjects to great effect.

It was Johann Böttger's discovery of the secret of porcelain manufacture in Germany (during the year 1708-9) that was to cause the decline of patronage in pottery. The Dutch strove to attain colors that could be produced on porcelain but even with their *doré* decorated wares, they could only manage to copy the Meissen production. Owing to the high esteem in which Chinese blue and white porcelain was held by the Saxon court, Johann Böttger strove to produce an acceptable color, but all the surviving specimens of blue and white seem to date from shortly after his death in 1719. At Meissen the factory records show that by March 1720 David Köhler and Johann Gottfried Mehlhorn had solved the difficult problem of obtaining a satisfactory underglaze blue for porcelain, and blue and white wares were exhibited at Leipzig and Naumberg during 1720. Unfortunately, the secret of making this highly successful blue died with Köhler in April 1723 and the production at Meissen in later years was very much of a secondary nature. However, the wares produced in this short period showed high technical skill, and although most were copied from Chinese prototypes, they still achieved a fair measure of success, though the figures resemble European magicians more closely than Chinese dignitaries.

The ensuing popularity of porcelain throughout Europe meant that most factories experimented at some stage with blue, but with varying degrees of success. Vincennes used solid blue ground colors with reserved panels for colored decoration, but most factories used blue for more simple decoration — usually on ware of a utilitarian nature. In Doccia towards the end of the eighteenth century new methods of handling blue were used with stencilled or *a stampino* designs. The process of transfer printing invented in England was hardly used on the Continent until the nineteenth century when it was used mostly in imitation of the Wedgwood and other Staffordshire productions.

Caffagiolo Blue and White Dish
Date: c 1505

In the wares of this pottery, set up in the 1490s by the Fattorini family at the castle of the Medicis, we find the first clear indications of the influence of Chinese porcelain on European pottery. The message almost certainly arrived via Venice, which had strong mercantile links with the Near East.

Florentine Oak Leaf Jar
Date: c 1432
Height: 8in (20cm)

This piece was made at the workshop of Guinta di Tugio. The thickly applied cobalt was a speciality of these early Tuscan potteries. Their wares were very solidly potted and the glaze was built up in layers or 'coperte' in order to achieve the rich, almost enameled effect.

Worcester Porcelain Basket
Date: c 1756
Length: 15in (37.5cm)

This rare and delightful basket is an example of the fine Worcester wares of the 1750s that dominated the blue and white porcelain production in England. The shape of the basket is derived from a silver original, but the painting is a whimsical

version of a Chinese scene commonly found on Chinese porcelain exported to England in the mid-eighteenth century (detail right). The painting is done with great care and delicacy in a pale and slightly grey blue under a thin even glaze.

The great advantage Worcester had over its closest rival Bow was its ability to produce blue and white wares which could withstand boiling water without cracking. Blue and white wares were indeed intended largely for domestic use, and pieces of this size and elegance are untypical. The detail (right) shows some of the different decorative techniques employèd.

Pierced decoration — derived from pierced silver baskets, this would have been cut out at the 'leather hard' stage before firing.

Underglaze blue decoration of a European flower scroll

Relief molding — a technique used with particular skill at Worcester, often forming cartouches on the sides of vessels.

English Blue and White

*These humble counterparts to the enamelled wares
were usually destined for domestic use but a whole range of restrained
masterpieces resulted from their production.*

The English porcelain factories, unlike most of their continental counterparts, were run as commercial enterprises and thrived or floundered in accordance with their success in the marketplace. Blue and white porcelain was cheaper and easier to produce than the enamelled wares which required further firings. Therefore blue and white porcelain became the backbone of the production of those factories which were catering for the daily requirements of the expanding middle classes. It is interesting to note that Chelsea, whose fine wares were designed for the wealthiest echelons of society, produced so little blue and white that only a handful of pieces, as few as seven or eight, have survived.

In the mid-eighteenth century, as the first English porcelain factories were establishing themselves, the competition was intense. Not only was there rivalry between the factories themselves but an additional threat existed in the form of the well-established delft and saltglaze potteries. The nature of the materials to some extent established their sphere of influence. The various soft-paste bodies used for earlier English porcelains were liable to warp and collapse during firing, and consequently dishes and plates were not produced in any quantity; tea wares and smaller items such as sauce boats and pickle dishes were more common. The one notable exception was the Bow pottery, where it was discovered that the addition of bone ash to the body gave much greater stability during firing. Conversely, the earthenware body of delft lent itself to the easy manufacture of flat wares such as plates and dishes. The Staffordshire saltglaze potteries, for all their charm, could not compete with the

novelty and beauty of porcelain and were finally superseded by the very cheap and easily produced creamware. Creamware was a more serious threat to the economic viability of blue and white porcelain, and eventually, under such great entrepreneurs as Wedgwood, creamware began to dominate domestic ceramics throughout Europe. However, from 1745-1765, in the first two decades of porcelain production, the greatest competition, and also the greatest influence, came from the vast quantities of tough hardpaste porcelain brought from China.

The shapes of the English blue and white porcelains were derived largely from silver forms and, to a lesser extent, from traditional pottery. The painting on blue and white porcelain was derived, for the most part, from Chinese sources. Exceptions to the overwhelming Chinese influence were designs based on the flower paintings of enameled wares, the stock patterns of floral borders copied from the French soft-paste factory of St. Cloud, and the relatively rare English genre scenes. More common than direct copies of Chinese patterns was a whimsical fusion of European rococo style and Chinese content, resulting in the delightful chinoiserie patterns that came to dominate blue and white decoration.

At their best, in the early years of production, blue and white wares were painted with such subtlety and vigour that they rival in beauty the more obviously splendid enameled wares, and cannot be considered in any way inferior to them. With the increase of pressure to expand production and cut costs the quality of work soon degenerated and by the 1760s

Bow Cylindrical Mug
Date: c 1750
Height: 3½in (9cm)

This mug depicts an unusual scene of a European lady and an oriental child in a fanciful gondola. The scene is painted in the characteristic bright blue of the early Bow wares and is unusually finely executed for a factory notable for vigorous, simple painting. Factory records seem to indicate that production at Bow exceeded that of Worcester in the early 1950's, but a much greater

quantity of Worcester porcelain has survived, a likely reason being the greater resilience of the latter.

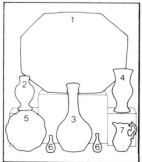

Collection: Gilbert Bradley

Group of Blue and White Wares

1. Liverpool octagonal dish, date: c 1765, length: 16½in (41.5cm). This dish was produced at Richard Chaffer's factory which was one of the larger manufactories that tended to specialize in blue and white.
2. Derby powder blue ground oviform vase, date: c 1765, height: 5in (12.5cm). Derby produced relatively little blue and white preferring enameled ornamental wares.
3. Lowestoft pear shaped

bottle, date: c 1765, height: 8¾in (22cm). Lowestoft produced delightful provincial wares for its local East Anglian market.
4. Liverpool swelling flared vase, date: c 1780, height: 6in (15cm). This vase was made at Seth Pennington's factory. Most of the wares produced there were rather clumsy and inferior; this piece is exceptional for the quality of the painting.
5. Bow stand for a finger bowl, date: c 1750, diameter: 5¾in (14.5cm). This rare

stand belongs to a small group known as the 'scratched R' group, which is attributed to Bow.
6. Two Liverpool miniature pear shaped bottles, date: c 1758, height: both about 2½in (6.5cm). These bottles are from a group of fairly primitive wares, tentatively attributed to William Reid's factory.
7. Worcester baluster cream jug, date: c 1754, height: 4¼in (11cm). This is typical of the finely painted early Worcester wares.

Lowestoft Bowl
Date: 1765-70
Diameter: 5½in (14cm)

Many Lowestoft wares were local commissions such as this bowl for Captain Osborn, inscribed 'Capt Osborn from Colchester'. Other wares were decorated with pictures of local churches, or local industries such as shipbuilding

Liverpool Cylindrical Mug
Date: c 1760
Height: 5¾in (14.5cm)

Produced by William Ball's factory, this mug belongs to a small group notable for its glassy glaze, rich, wet-looking blue and the quality of its painting.

much of the earlier care had given way to mechanical repetition of stock patterns. The introduction of underglaze blue printing around 1758 (which, in its earliest years showed considerable beauty in its own right) accelerated the decline, and by the 1770s mass production of indifferent wares was the norm. There are, fortunately, many exceptions to this trend, notable among them are the occasional charming pieces from the smaller, less fashionable, factories of Lowestoft and Liverpool.

Credit for the earliest production of blue and white porcelain in any quantity must go to the manufactory at Bow, usually dated from 1749. These early wares were heavily potted into simple shapes and boldly painted in a unique bright pale blue. They have a primitive character, but occasionally painting of a very superior quality and great charm can be found. In the middle period (1755-1763) the early blue was replaced by a darker blue and the painting, although of quite good quality, became more standardized with a range of stock patterns of Chinese origin. The porcelain of this period was often slightly underfired, making it porous and subject to staining. The later Bow productions, from 1764 up to the time of the factory's demise in 1776, were almost uniformly inferior. The earliest wares of Worcester and the rare productions of Lund's Bristol, Worcester's forerunner, are distinguished by the exceptional fineness of the potting and painting. The body was of a very different composition to that of Bow as soapstone, or steatite, was used in the paste. This had various advantages — ware virtually never stained and the tea and coffee pots could withstand boiling water, (an unresolved problem with the wares of other factories). The early Worcester pieces were painted in a delicate gray-blue and covered with a fine thin glaze which did not run; consequently the painting is always well defined. The most ambitious pieces were molded into shapes inspired by silver,

with scrolls, borders and cartouches in relief. As in other factories, the 1760s heralded a decline into mediocrity of form and decoration, but the quality of the paste and glaze was maintained until the end of the century.

An area of production that rewards the student and collector with constant surprise is the porcelain produced at the six or seven manufactories in Liverpool. The largest group of wares belongs to the factory owned in succession by Chaffers, Christians and Pennington. The finely potted early wares show a strong Worcester influence and are boldly painted. The later wares tend to decline in quality, but there are a few exceptionally well painted pieces. Of particular interest is a group of wares tentatively ascribed to William Reid's factory which existed from 1755-1761. The shapes are often derived from Bow originals and the paste is gray and primitive. The most striking feature of this group is the extraordinary quality of the European-style painting. Another Liverpool group with a strong individual style consists of pieces ascribed to William Ball's factory, which are painted in a deep, wet-looking blue under a particularly fine shiny glaze.

The last of the major producers of soft paste blue and white porcelain was Lowestoft. The wares of this factory, which were essentially produced for the local East Anglian market, possess a unique charm. They are provincial in character and sometimes decorated with local scenes, although more often with distinctive chinoiseries and floral patterns.

William Cookworthy discovered kaolin (China clay) and petuntse (China stone), the ingredients of true or 'hard-paste' porcelain, in Cornwall, and in 1768 began producing porcelain at Plymouth; this was later continued at Bristol. However it was not until the Newhall factory was started in 1782 that blue and white hard-paste porcelain began to be produced in any quantity in England.

Kaolin in Eng.

4

The Influence of Japan and the Kakiemon Style

Kakiemon holds a special place among ceramic decorative styles, for it withstood the long journey from Japan to Europe and being passed from one imitative hand to another on arrival, without losing its native charm, freshness and spontaneity. The Kakiemon style has continued to maintain its elegance and beauty, and is as attractive and sought-after today as it was three centuries ago.

The analysis of any kind of artistic inspiration is a difficult and slightly unhealthy exercise indulged in mainly by professional art critics, yet in the case of Kakiemon one is tempted to look for some special secret which can be responsible for its appeal.

The material itself is simple enough — a fine china clay which is treated to remove impurities and mixed with porcelain stone to produce the typical milky-white body. The shapes into which it is formed have diverse origins, but are usually well-proportioned, sometimes elegant, and the enamels employed in the decoration have generally an exceptional purity of color, particularly in the case of the blue.

The subject-matter of Kakiemon decoration is

Kakiemon Gourd-Shaped Vase
Date: 1661-1681 (Kanbun-Enpo period)
Height: 17¼in (43cm)

These high-waisted vases, often known as double gourd-shaped, derive their form from early Chinese types; these include vases with short, straight necks and wide waists of the Jiajing period (1522-66), and more sophisticated versions of the Transitional period (c 1640), from which this Kakiemon shape is copied almost exactly. The decoration comprises tree-peonies, chrysanthemums and other flowers and rocks in a natural arrangement, contrasting with a symmetrical design with looped stalks on the upper lobe, surmounted by a band of red stylized leaf design. Although at least twelve similar vases are known, this example is notable for the richness and clarity of the enamels, the extremely light and elegant way in which they have been applied, and the skillful use of black as an occasional strengthening accent rather than a rigid outline.

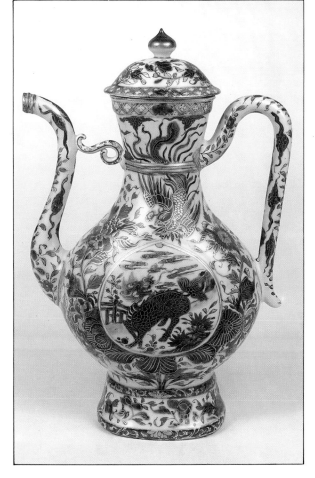

Chinese Imari Wine Ewer and Cover
Date: c 1730
Height: 13¼in (33.5cm)

While the palette of the Kakiemon potters had little influence on their Chinese equivalents, the so-called 'Imari' palette was more influential. This was a color combination of underglaze cobalt blue and iron-red enamel, with touches of gilding as the final detail. Early European collectors referred to versions of the Imari palette as 'Old Japan pattern'. The term 'Imari' is a later one, taken from the name of the port where the early, heavy coarse porcelains, intended for Europe, were packaged for shipment. However, the Imari palette was not entirely novel to the Chinese. During the sixteenth century, the same basic combinations, using underglaze blue and overglaze enamels enriched with gilding, had been applied to an earlier category of porcelain, known to Japanese collectors as 'Kinrande' (gold-brocaded) wares.

Bow Coffee Pot and Cover
Date: 1758
Height: 9½in (24cm)

Kakiemon decoration on English porcelain reached its zenith in the years 1750-1755, though Bow continued its use into the 1760s, still retaining much of the spirit of the Japanese decoration. Kakiemon decoration was also used at other factories, but tended to degenerate into dense panels far removed from the asymmetry and open space characteristic of the original.

Meissen Augustus Rex Vase
Date: 1730-35
Height: 12¼ (31cm)

This style of brilliant birds and floral decoration was evolved by J. G. Höroldt, and reached its peak in A.F. Von Löwenfinck who left Meissen in 1735. It still shows a clear debt to Kakiemon, but both the shape and the sheer opulence of the colors are totally original to Meissen.

fairly simple and was often copied with remarkable accuracy on European porcelain, being christened with whatever name seemed appropriate. For example, the 'flaming tortoise' is simply that Japanese symbol of longevity, the minogame, a freshwater tortoise of such a grand age that a long tail of pondweed has grown on its shell. The 'banded hedge' is the brushwood fence commonly seen in Japan, and the quite impossible 'pairs of phoenixes' are the equally mythical Japanese ho-ho birds which do appear in pairs, usually to herald matters of auspicious portent.

Other designs incorporate tigers with plum blossom or bamboo, quail with millet, various other birds such as doves and the long-tailed paradise fly-catcher, and flowers, especially *fuyo*, the Japanese hibiscus. The novelty of these Kakiemon designs, as far as eighteenth century Europe was concerned, probably lay in their asymmetry and in the large areas of the porcelain which were left without decoration. It would be difficult to conceive of any porcelain better suited to blend with the then popular rococo style.

One other design in the Kakiemon repertoire deserves mention, if only because it appears so frequently on the small dishes as to seem almost an obsession with the decorators. This is the story of the eleventh century Chinese statesman Shiba Onko

who, while still an infant, displayed a talent for what would today be called 'lateral thinking'. The tale is simple: Onko and his tiny companions climbed up the sides of a huge water jar to watch some goldfish inside; one boy, leaning too far, lost his balance and fell in. Unable to get him out again, his playmates ran off in terror, all save Onko, who, seizing a rock, smashed a hole in the side of the jar and removed the water, therefore saving the boy from drowning. In Europe the subject was something of a mystery, and acquired the title 'Hob in the Well', after a popular eighteenth century play. A misconception of the story in Arita led to the production of strange versions when the story was copied by the Meissen and Chantilly manufacturers.

However, accuracy of subject matters little: it is the splendid style of Kakiemon that counts. It is a style that delighted eighteenth century Europe and brought with it all the mystery of the Orient — that romantic paradise which so stirred the imagination of western man. In those days, its pure white body and enchanting decoration brightened many a dark corner in royal palace and country house alike. Today, in spite of much scrutiny and still more discussion, Kakiemon still appeals; it seems to be nothing so much as the delightful result of an inspired, but always lighthearted, labor of love.

Kakiemon Bowl
Date: Early 18th century
Diameter: 12¼ in (31cm)

The bowl is decorated with a Karashishi and a branch of tree-peony. The Karashishi or 'Chinese Lion' was undoubtedly based on a dog rather like the modern pekinese. Said to exemplify the power of the Good Law of Buddha, Karashishi are often shown among rocks and peonies. With its superb white body and elegantly placed and restrained decoration, the bowl demonstrates the classic Kakiemon style. The chocolate-brown rim was copied from Chinese porcelain, where the color had the practical function of

concealing small defects in the rim which sometimes occurred during firing; in Kakiemon, however, the brown rim was purely decorative.

Detail of Kakiemon Bowl *This detail shows the light, delicate way in which the bright enamel colors have been applied, almost as in a watercolor painting The black outline is used sparingly, more as an occasional strengthening accent, and does not appear at all around the flower. In some later Kakiemon pieces a more rigid black outline is found, closely filled with color, which inevitably produces a less lively effect.*

Japanese Kakiemon-de: the Style of the Kakiemons

The Kakiemon style of enameled porcelain delighted the West and provided a lasting influence.

Kakiemon, or *Kakiemon-de* (Kakiemon-style), is the name used for a type of fine white-bodied Imari porcelain. It is decorated over the glaze in red, green, yellow and blue enamels with elegantly spaced and uncrowded designs derived mostly from China, the Chinese-influenced Kano school of painting, or the native Tosa school. Further types of Kakiemon porcelain have enamel decoration adapted from Dutch *chinoiserie* designs, overglaze enameling combined with underglaze blue and pieces with underglaze blue decoration alone, although these are considered less typical. The name derives from Sakaida Kakiemon, regarded as one of Japan's greatest geniuses of ceramic decoration and credited with the creation of overglaze enamel wares towards the end of the Kanei period (1624-1644), at Nangawara near the town of Arita in Hizen province.

Hizen, besides being a great ceramic center was, in the seventeenth century, the home of the famous Tadayoshi school of swordsmiths and the Saga Kaneiye family of metalworkers. Saga was the capital town of Hizen, but the names of three other places there are more familiar to western ears: Arita, Imari and Nagasaki. Arita lies near the middle of the province, in a valley surrounded by high mountains. It was ideally suited to the production of porcelain, partly due to the abundant quantities of Arita-ishi (Arita stone, the best kind being almost pure kaolin) quarried nearby, and partly to the local pine forests which fueled its kilns. Some eight miles to the north was the small port and market-town of Imari, where porcelain made in the Arita district was gathered to be sold and shipped to the much larger port of Nagasaki in southern Kyushu. From here it was exported either to Europe via the Dutch factory at Deshima, a tiny artificial island in the bay, or to Asia, or it was distributed to other parts of Japan.

'Arita' is the term generally used in Europe to describe most Hizen porcelain; the name 'Imari' is reserved for the elaborately decorated polychrome enameled pieces known in Japan as *nishiki-de* or 'brocade-pattern'. The Japanese, however, prefer to use 'Imari' as the name for all Arita wares, unless writing for, or speaking to, foreigners, when politeness, or the fear of being misunderstood, impels them to follow the Western method. 'Kakiemon Imari' is thus a Japanese rather than a western nomenclature.

Overglaze enamels, or polychrome enamels, are known in Japan as *aka-e* or *iro-e* and in China as *wu-tsai*. They were produced at the Cheng-te-chen kilns in Kiangsi from the Yuan dynasty (1280-1368) onwards, and gained popularity during the Ming period (1368-1644). According to Professor Tsugio Mikami, these decorated Chinese wares were imported into Japan through the port of Nagasaki as early as the Muromachi period (1394-1573), and

Kakiemon Bowl
(opposite) The outside of the bowl is decorated in colored enamels with chrysanthemums and a mountain dove on a branch of a weeping willow tree. The combination of clear, bright color and economy of drawing produces a splendid effect. A large area of the bowl is left clear and the various elements of the design are superbly positioned, typical of the best Kakiemon decoration. An interesting feature is the way the design is continued on the foot-rim.

found favor with aristocrats, rich merchants and tea connoisseurs. But such pieces must have been rare, and it was Swatow ware (called in Japanese *gosu aka-e*) from Fukien and Wan Li wu-ts'ai which, reaching Japan in the seventeenth century, became the model for Japanese enameled porcelain. The technique of enameling on glazed porcelain is difficult, for the enamels do not always adhere properly, and precisely when and how the first pieces were produced in Japan is still controversial.

Tradition tells how a ceramics dealer of Imari, called Tojima Tokuzaemon, learned the process from a Chinese potter at Nagasaki and, with the object of establishing enameled porcelain manufacture in Japan, passed the information on to the potter Sakaida Kakiemon in Arita. There are still several points to be clarified concerning the Kakiemon style in its earliest years, although it is likely that the first designs were copies of Chinese wares. Similarly there are questions regarding the 11 generations of Kakiemon potters whose chronology is derived from records in the possession of the family. These cover the period of the first Kakiemon, traditionally 1596-1666, up to the eleventh Kakiemon, 1845-1917. Soame Jenyns, in his book *Japanese Porcelain*, discusses these questions at some length and suggests that the typical Kakiemon enamel style was probably not established until the time of the fourth or fifth generations (traditional dates 1641-1679 and 1660-1691). Tadanari Mitsuoka, taking a similar line, states that 'judging from the style, the tradition (that) Kakiemon I was the founder of *Kakiemon-de* ware cannot be believed, for in his works the influence of the late Ming enameled porcelain ought still to be seen, so that the *Kakiemon-de* should be attributed to his descendants a few generations later'. The solution may be, as suggested

by Soame Jenyns, that the early wares of the first three Kakiemons have been confused, in Europe and Japan, with Ko-Kutani wares.

Leaving these questions to one side, we can consider the typical forms and decoration of *Kakiemon-de*. The finest type of ware is a warm milk-white porcelain, popularly called *nigoshi-de* (opaque style), on which the enamels are delicately applied like watercolor, occasionally with a sensitively drawn black outline, but more often without it. Although bowls, dishes and bottles were thrown on the wheel, other shapes were molded — for example, the hexagonal jars with domed covers so popular in the west. In England they became known as 'Hampton Court' vases after the ones placed there by William and Mary at the time of their accession in 1689.

The similar pair illustrated opposite shows how precise were the measurements of these molded pieces. One of them has accidentally acquired a cover from a different vase and this contains more red and green in the color scheme. The mismatched cover is contemporary and an excellent fit, suggesting that these molded porcelain types were produced in some quantity by an elementary form of production line. The hexagonal vases are not typically Japanese in shape but were created for the overseas export trade in Kakiemon porcelain. This trading began about the middle of the seventeenth century, and owed its success to the internal disturbances in China caused by the collapse of the Ming dynasty. Chinese porcelain had always been in great demand in the West and in Asia, so that when production declined severely, the enterprising Dutch East India Company promoted the new Japanese porcelain in its place. The elegant designs on the sides of these vases are now purely Japanese, evolved from Chinese Song dynasty bird-and-flower paintings, a subject known in Japan as *kacho-e*. The flower is clearly recognizable

The map illustrates the kilns and ports of Hizen province, which forms the northwest part of Kyushu, Japan's southernmost island.

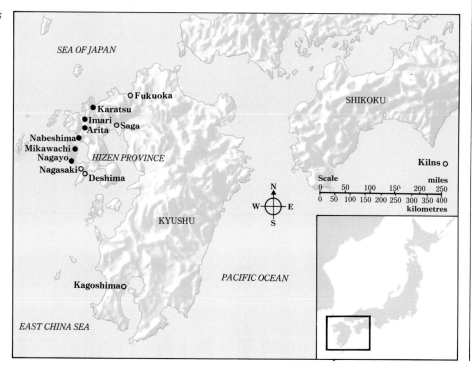

Pair of Hexagonal Jars and Covers
Date: 1673-1687 (Enpo-Jokyo period)
Height: 14¾in (37cm)

These jars are excellent examples of Kakiemon and are of historical interest. Resembling the pair at Hampton Court associated with William III and Mary, these jars originally belonged to William IV. Their earlier provenance remains a mystery, but it is possible that King William inherited them as part of his personal property from his great-grandmother Queen Caroline. Note the mismatched cover from a vase of similar shape and date but with a different color-scheme.

Kakiemon Baluster Jar
Date: 17th century
Height: 10⅛in (26cm)

This is a baluster jar of the type formerly known in the West as Ko-kutani, 'Old Kutani', but now considered to be early Kakiemon ware. Such pieces are usually rather coarsely potted compared with later works, and their enamel decoration, although always lively and charming, often covers the entire surface, as shown here. The designs are mainly copied from Chinese wares, based on Chinese paintings of the late Ming and early Qing dynasties, for these were imported into Japan, through the port of Nagasaki, from as early as the Muromachi period (1393-1573).

Oviform Jar and Cover
Date: Late 17th century
Height: 18½in (46.5cm)

This jar and cover were apparently copied from a chinoiserie design of Dutch origin. The directors of the Dutch East India Company ordered models for porcelain shapes in 1661. Whether any designs for decoration were sent with these models is unknown. However designs rather similar to that on this jar were ordered by the Company in 1734-1737 from the painter, Cornelis Pronk. This jar is earlier and the designs were probably by a Dutch predecessor of Pronk.

bowl in fact be late seventeenth century? Such finely potted pieces with the famous thinly glazed *nigoshi-de* body contrast with the many coarser types of Kakiemon where the ordinary Izumiyama clay was used, and there is a natural tendency to suppose that these elegant examples must be dated later.

Two of the best recorded, and datable, sources of information about *Kakiemon-de* in England are at Hampton Court Palace and Burghley House. There can be little doubt that the hexagonal vases at Hampton Court Palace are the 'colored jars of six squares' (facets) listed in the inventory of 1696. It seems likely that they were brought back with the Queen when she returned from Holland, where she is said to have wept copiously at her first meeting with King William of Orange. It would be pleasant to think that the charm and novelty of Kakiemon were effective in lifting her spirits. The Burghley House inventory predates the Hampton Court one by eight years, for it was made in 1688 by the fifth Earl of Exeter. Burghley is of great significance in the study and dating of Kakiemon because many pieces there can be identified in the inventory. It is a unique collection and it demonstrates very clearly the influence of Kakiemon on European taste, and the late Ming and Ching export wares.

Some of the most popular examples of Kakiemon are the figures of people and animals; for example, the rare and splendidly demonic model of a horse and the pair of highly imaginative tigers illustrated (opposite). These porcelain sculptures, or statuettes, are described by the Japanese as *katamono* or 'shaped articles'. The down-to-earth writings of the late Soame Jenyns on Kakiemon and other subjects suggest that many of these *katamono* were not made by the Kakiemon family at all, but came from neighboring kilns where the methods and distinctive color schemes of the Kakiemon family were copied. With this in mind, it is hardly accurate to call Kakiemon inimitable; rather it was influential, and was copied with great success at Meissen, Bow, Worcester, Chelsea and several other places. It seems ironic that it may never be possible to identify one piece of this enchanting porcelain as the work of an individual member of the family, particularly in the earlier years, but the name survives and will always stand for one of the world's great porcelain styles — *Kakiemon-de.*

as *fuyo* (hibiscus mutabilis) and the bird is probably a kind of long-tailed pheasant. These vases date from between 1673 and 1687. Splendid as they are, an even better example of the Kakiemon genius for design must be the bowl illustrated (page 98) decorated with a Karashishi, or Chinese 'lion dog', looking up at a branch of tree-peony.

The bowl is likely to be a little later than the vases, perhaps even early eighteenth century. This was a period of considerable elegance and sophistication in Kakiemon design and, if the Kakiemon family documents are to be accepted, it can presumably be associated with the fifth and sixth generations of the name. These record that Kakiemon V lived between 1660 and 1691, and Kakiemon VI between 1690 and 1735, but a student always faces the questionable accuracy and interpretation of the documents. Family histories hold an important place in Japanese life, especially when an aristocratic or artistic line is involved, and it may seem harsh to cast a cynical eye over them, but similar genealogies in the field of metalwork suggest that a sense of caution is necessary. Few serious students or collectors would now accept unreservedly the self-written family story of the Myochin armorers, or the multitude of attributions and certifications given to their forbears by the Goto family of sword-fitting makers. Could the

THE BURGHLEY HOUSE KAKIEMON

Kakiemon ware was made for export, and the unique porcelain collection at Burghley House is of immense importance to scholars. Two inventories were taken of it; a part of the first inventory, made for the Fifth Earl of Exeter, referring to 'My Lord's Dressing Roome' is illustrated below.

Kakiemon Model of Boy on Drum
Date: c 1680
Height: 5½in (14cm)

The last line of the first Burghley House inventory describes a pair of Kakiemon models of boys seated on drums holding large gourd-shaped bottles slung over their shoulders. They are described, very concisely, as '2 figures with Juggs at their backs'. They are still at Burghley, and one of the pair is illustrated (right). Their enamel decoration is in a

typical Kakiemon palette of turquoise, cerulean, red and black; dating from about 1680, they must have been quite new when acquired.

Pair of Kakiemon Tigers
Date: Late 17th/early 18th century
Height: 9½in (24cm)

Some of the most interesting and popular items in the Kakiemon potters' repertoire are models of people or animals, known in Japanese as Katamono. The pair of tigers illustrated (below) are typical examples. Since they are not indigenous to Japan, they were modeled, with great imagination, from paintings rather than life.

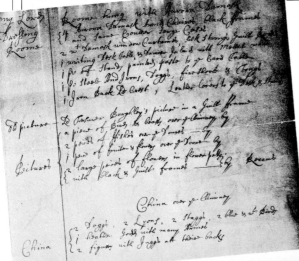

Kakiemon Model of a Stag
Date: Late 17th century
Length: 9in (23cm)

The sika, a small spotted deer, was once common in the forests of Japan, and is depicted here in a realistic and lifelike manner.

Kakiemon Model of a Horse
Date: Late 17th/early 18th century
Height: 17½in (44cm)

The horse is a rare model, since only three or four of this type are known.

Rose-Imari Baluster Jar and Cover
Date: c 1730
Height: 19¼in (48.5cm)

The unusually high and broad domed cover of this Chinese vase strongly recalls the characteristic proportions of a typical Japanese Arita porcelain vase of fifty years earlier. The horizontal flange above the in-sloping foot is also very unusual in Chinese porcelain ware, but not in a Japanese jar of these proportions. The 'baluster' shape is a staple of Chinese ceramic design, but proportions are critical in assessing the inspiration for a ceramic piece, and there is a definite Japanese 'feel' about the overall design of this pot.

The two details of the baluster vase show the enameled decoration. There were great technical innovations in overglaze enamels in the late seventeenth century, resulting in bold, rich, chemically created glazes.

The Japanese Effect on Chinese Ceramics

Without slavishly copying Japanese shapes and designs,
some Chinese potters subtly adapted their native ceramics in response to
new demands and ideas from the Japanese industry.

The effect of Japanese ceramic designs and shapes on the newly created European kilns in France, Germany and England is self-evident; the westerners who concentrated on producing low-fired tin-glazed earthenware and coarse stonewares readily plagiarized all the innovations of Japanese ceramics. The Chinese also took from the Japanese certain basic ideas, like the color palette of Imari, and the taste for garnitures. In both cases, the Chinese could see and copy the commercial success of the Japanese potters in selling these lines to westerners trading in the Far East, but the effect of Japan on China was more subtle than mere copying. Well before any significant trading existed with the West which influenced the production of ceramics, the Chinese potters were making and decorating vessels specifically to suit the taste of Japanese buyers. In important details taste was influenced by Zen Buddhism, the particular interpretation in Japan of Buddhist cults which varied throughout the Far East. But it also reflected Japanese domestic preferences and, even today, certain groups of Chinese Ming dynasty (1360-1644) wares are still regarded as typical 'Japanese market' Chinese ceramics.

The Japanese effect therefore had two forms. At an earlier date (1500-1640) the Chinese produced wares with unusual shapes and designs in response to specifically Japanese demands, at a time when the Japanese had no domestic porcelain industry. At a later date, the Chinese began to copy designs and shapes which the Japanese had sold with great success over many decades (1650-1720) to western merchants based at, and trading through, Hirado and Deshima in Japan, and Fort Zeelandia on Formosa. The first effect required a rather subtle treatment by the Chinese potters because of the Japanese preference for certain designs and shapes. A wide range of Chinese ceramics, for example, was produced for use in the Japanese tea ceremony. Broadly speaking, these ceramics were characterized by a 'spontaneous' simplicity. The Japanese tea masters valued freshness and artistic quality more highly than 'finish'.

The second effect of Japan on Chinese ceramics has always been considered rather more straightforward. A successful Japanese war against Korea (the so-called 'Potters War' in the late 1590s) resulted in a number of captured Korean potters being brought to Japan to inaugurate a more sophisticated domestic ceramic industry. A bitter civil war in China during the middle decades of the seventeenth century seriously disrupted trade with western merchants who bought ceramics. It also involved the burning of Jingdezhen, the ceramic-producing capital, which only returned to its previous vigor after 1683, when the major kilns were reorganized. During these disruptive decades, westerners found Japanese ceramics to be a convenient substitute for traditional Chinese ones. Enormous quantities were exported, primarily by the Dutch, from Hirado and Deshima to their entrepot in South Asia and Batavia, for transportation by ship to merchants bound for Amsterdam and London.

It was during these years, when Japanese export ceramics reached Europe in huge quantities, that the westerners developed a taste for the Imari palette — a striking combination of underglaze blue decoration with overglaze details enameled in iron-red and touched with gilding. In fact the palette derives from one of the Chinese color combinations most particularly associated with the 'Japanese taste' of the sixteenth century — the *Kinrande* palette: a combination of underglaze blue, a plain-colored glaze and overgliding in symmetrical brocade patterns. Kinrande pieces were small, elegant, and highly suitable for the tea ceremony. What was new about the Imari wares, potted and enameled at Arita, was their scale — sets of five large vases, big flower bowls and enormous dishes. Large and highly decorative, this Japanese export ware was perfect for palaces in Europe. European potters could adopt the patterns and palettes of Japanese export ceramics, but they were not able to pot large vessels for many years. The Chinese, however, were quite able to do so, and they could see how eager westerners were for these large, superbly decorated porcelain suites. For this reason the average size of Chinese ceramics, exported to the West after 1685, increased substantially. No longer were the Europeans satisfied with sets of small *Kraak* porcelain, blue and white dishes or bowls — the luxury Chinese porcelain of the early seventeenth century. They wanted massive jardinières and garnitures, decorative objects to accord with an increasingly grand style of life, and the Chinese provided an increasing amount as western trade with Japan declined during the early eighteenth century.

Few western historians of ceramics have really explored the years 1600-1700, when the effect of overseas trade stimulated demand for Far Eastern ceramics and gave its production a new orientation. It

105

Temmoku Jar
Date: c 960-1130
Height: 8½in (21cm)

Wares such as this magnificent black-glazed,

ribbed oviform jar epitomize the taste of Japanese collectors for stoneware which shows the potter's art.

is very probable that, contrary to generally accepted belief, this century saw a three-way, not a two-way effect on ceramic design — between China, Japan and Europe. It is usually claimed that in the seventeenth century Chinese wares were the only significant source of design for western potters. At the same time, however, contemporary European low-fired ceramics (tin-glazed earthenware) and higher fired stonewares certainly played a part in the development of a native Japanese porcelain industry. In turn, the designs and shapes of this new industry influenced the Chinese, primarily after the civil wars in the mid-seventeenth century that marked the end of the rule of the Ming dynasty. One incident in particular suggests the dissemination of this influence. In the early decades of the seventeenth century, the Dutch and English East India Companies 'dumped' relatively large quantities of European ceramics in Japan. Presumably they were reasonably cheap to ship and were used in the same way as Far Eastern ceramics going westwards — as a water-resistant, heavy layer to protect more delicate commodities higher up the hull. As a result, much of the blue and white porcelain believed to have been produced in Arita during the second half of the seventeenth century has the thick outlining, large washed-blue areas of design, and generously rounded contours of Dutch and English Delftware. Chinese porcelain of the Transitional period (*c* 1640-60) also incorporates a number of

shapes and characteristics which suggest the angular lines of German stonewares or the softness of tin-glazed earthenware, rather than the *Kraak* porcelain (blue and white ware) which preceded the Transitional period.

It is not easy to establish the exact chronology of these links, because much European knowledge and conventional dating of western chinoiserie ceramics assumes that European ones all derive from Chinese prototypes. In some cases, however, it is possible to distinguish which came first.

The jar and cover (page 104) is a remarkable example of a basically Japanese shape and design which was adopted by the Chinese, probably for their own export trade. The proportions are that of a straightforward Arita jar — the standard Japanese style normally found painted in blue and white or Imari. The foot recalls the Japanese version, sloping inwards from a flange, rather than the more normal vertical Chinese foot rim; it is a new type of shape which only appears in about 1720. During the Kangxi era (1662-1722), which was a time of great ceramic experimentation at Jingdezhen, a new enamel was developed which gave the effect of a lustrous black sheen. It was formed by firing a translucent lime-green glaze over a matt black pigment. There is no obvious Chinese prototype overglaze enameled ware of this period for what was an extremely rich and elaborate ground color, although the Chinese had long used a thin matt dark pigment to outline painted designs on ceramics. The Japanese did use it at a slightly earlier date (though not as a ground color) on the massive dishes of the Genroku period, which were painted with *bijin* (court ladies) who had rich black hair, and on the free-standing Imari figure models of the same date. The Chinese may well have developed the potential of this richly contrasting, alien new enamel combination from the Japanese. Certainly Europeans knew about, and appreciated, traditional Japanese representation of a *bijin*, but few historians have realized that the female figures which appear on the well-known designs were commissioned specifically from the Dutchman, Cornelis Pronk to be painted on Chinese porcelain in the 1730s, and that they are purely Japanese in taste. Nor are they isolated examples of a western designer using his interpretation of a purely Japanese figure on a Chinese dish. The *famille verte* dish, painted with the town arms of Limburg in Holland, has two bijin-like figures in alcoves flanking the large architectural feature at the center.

Further research is certain to amend, in many important details, the traditional view of the three-way relationship between Chinese, Japanese and early western ceramics. It is clear that Japan had a significant and direct impact on certain categories of ceramics produced in China during the sixteenth and early seventeenth centuries although the evident impact of Japan during the later seventeenth and eighteenth century has to be seen in the context, often ignored, of new European influences at work on Far Eastern ceramic production.

Rose-verte Armorial Dish (above)
Date: c 1730
Diameter: 19in (48cm)
Chinese Imari Plate
(left), 'La Dame au Parasol'
Date: c 1740
Diameter: 9¼in (23.5cm)

These two dishes indicate how far the standard conventions of Far Eastern design were muddled up in western minds. Both dishes are Chinese porcelain; both were painted in China, with designs taken directly from those supplied by European draughtsmen for reproduction on porcelain imported by the Dutch East India Company. However, in both cases, the standing ladies owe much to a Japanese 'standard' lady —

the type of elegant figure who appeared fifty years earlier, painted onto large Arita export flatwares and vases, or as a free-standing porcelain figure. During the seventeenth century, Japanese porcelain represented an enormous volume of the Dutch VOC South Asian bulk trade. It is not surpising, therefore, that this very striking figure painting should have influenced the designs of Dutch craftsmen. The the Cornelis Pronk design, known as 'La Dame au Parasol', is executed in the standard Imari palette, reinforcing the confusion over the origin of the design.

Meissen Kakiemon Circular Plate
Date: Early 18th century
Diameter: 9in (23cm)

The decoration on this plate is an imitation of the classic Japanese pattern, known in the West as 'Hob-in-the-Well'. While the brown rim on the Japanese ware was caused in the firing, the rim on the Meissen examples was painted in chocolate. The somewhat creamy body of this plate indicates that early or Böttger porcelain was used. In 1728 a new recipe for porcelain was introduced containing much more felspar and producing a harder, whiter effect.

The Kakiemon Style in Europe

*The presence in Saxony of quantities of fine Japanese wares gave an
impetus to their imitation at Meissen. At first, both
shapes and designs were copied faithfully, but gradually the Kakiemon theme was
blended with western subjects and deployed on western shapes.*

With the discovery by Vasco da Gama in 1497 of a sea route via the Cape of Good Hope, the Orient suddenly became more accessible. Previously the only western contact with the East had been by way of the silk route and its marketplace in Constantinople. At the end of the fifteenth century, however, the import of spices, silks and porcelain, (which had hitherto been rarely possessed), developed quickly. Vast quantities of oriental porcelain, including the wares of the Kakiemon family with their uncluttered and asymmetrical designs, came to be imported throughout the seventeenth and eighteenth centuries; it proved to be highly prized by European collectors, particularly as the secret of its manufacture remained hidden from the western potter until 1711.

Three important collectors of oriental porcelain wares quickly emerged; they were to have a significant influence on the tastes of the European nobility — the main buyers of this rare and new material. William of Orange (King William III of England) and his wife, Queen Mary, furnished their new home at Hampton Court with Kakiemon porcelain, which was brought to Holland through the Dutch East India Company towards the end of the seventeenth century. Augustus the Strong of Saxony so liked these Kakiemon wares that he bought a castle in 1717 to house his collection, and renamed it the Japanese Palace. In France, Louis-Henri de Bourbon, seventh Prince de Condé, also collected wares from the Arita province and furnished his chateau at Chantilly accordingly.

The Europeans were so thrilled by this new medium of porcelain that they tried to copy the productions both in paste and decoration. Johann Böttger was employed as an alchemist by the Elector of Saxony at Meissen in order to discover the secret of its manufacture, and when he finally succeeded in about 1711 his work closely followed oriental prototypes particularly in form. In Meissen, early decoration imitated the Japanese wares of the Arita province; so too in Chantilly, where potteries in the Japanese style were almost the sole production until 1740. The Japanese porcelains were at first slavishly copied, the same colors of iron-red, bluish-green, yellow and light blue being used, and sometimes the surface was enriched with gilding. Painted asymmetrical motifs of banded hedges, *Indianische Blumen* (flower sprays), quail and millet, flying squirrel and dragons made effective use of the white porcelain surface. The initial difficulties encountered by European porcelain manufacturers, both with the hard or true German porcelain and with soft paste porcelain in France, meant that shapes tended to be of square, hexagonal or octagonal section because they were less likely to suffer from kiln damage and distortions when fired.

Meissen Kakiemon Augustus Rex Vase and Cover
Date: 1730-1732
Height: 11in (28cm)

This closely follows examples made in Japan. There are, however, touches of pink that would not appear in a Japanese example, and the decoration is, as so often happens with copies, much more rigid and mechanical than in the original.

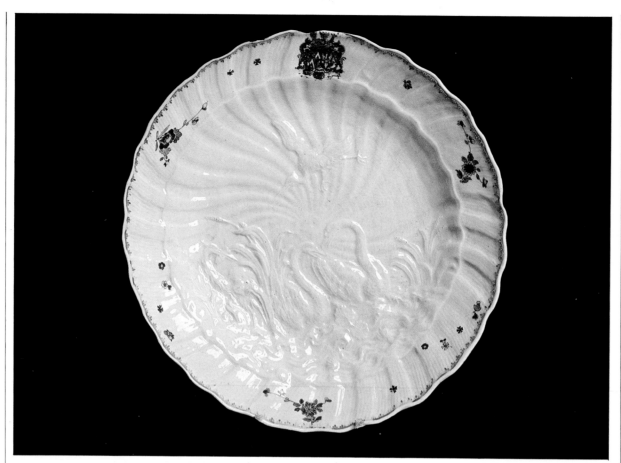

Meissen Plate from the Swan Service *(above)*
Date: 1775
Diameter: 13in (32.5cm)

Here the vestiges of Kakiemon floral decoration have persisted onto what is otherwise a wholly European concept. By this date the Kakiemon style at Meissen was definitely on the wane, and both European shapes and decoration were increasingly predominant.

Meissen Augustus Rex Chinoiserie Plate *(right)*
Diameter: 8¾in (22.5cm)

Floral decoration of Kakiemon inspiration is here combined with chinoiserie panels of the type evolved by the chief Meissen painter, Johann Gregorius Höroldt. The palette used on the floral decoration – a style of decoration introduced by Höroldt, known as Indianische Blumen (see detail far right), is far lusher than that used in the original Kakiemon decoration. The chinoiserie panels depict a European view of oriental life (see detail right).

Pieces from a Meissen Dinner Service
Date: 1740

Painted with fabulous beasts and flowering plants in a pseudo-Kakiemon palette, these wares are instances of an European extension of the range of decoration inspired by Japanese ceramics. The detail (below) shows the range of colors (wider than in original Kakiemon) used by the Meissen artist. The scattered flowers and insects are, however, a close copy of Japanese Kakiemon.

Representative of the European copies of Kakiemon wares is the so-called 'Hob-in-the-Well' pattern. Faithfully reproducing a Japanese original, the western artist failed to understand the Chinese legend upon which it was based. The painting represents the boyhood of Ssu Ma Kuang (1019-86), a Chinese sage of the Song dynasty, whose playmate fell into a large fishbowl and was in danger of drowning. In order to save his companion he smashed the bowl with a stone which let the water out. So impressed were the Chinese with the boy's quick thinking that the story became immortalized. The European porcelain decorator was, however, ignorant of the legend and depicted a vase half buried in the ground, smashed at the side, with Kuang pulling his companion through the top, which he could have done anyway, without breaking the vase.

The faithful reproduction of the Kakiemon originals was eventually to develop into decoration of a more European style. The Meissen decorators — Adam F. von Löwenfinck, J.E. Stadler, C.F. Herold, J.G. Herold, P.E. Schindler and the gilder Seuter — inspired by the Japanese and the Chinese porcelains, developed a style that combined both precise copying and fictional fantasy. *Indianische Blumen* in the Kakiemon palette was used extensively on forms derived from baroque Germany. The most important of all Meissen baroque dinner services, the Swan Service made for Count Bruhl, made effective use of *Indianische Blumen*,

lightly scattered over the wonderful molded surface. Stadler, Herold and Schindler developed this style of Kakiemon floral decoration by incorporating more colors and by using it to flank shaped panels of *chinoiseries*. The *chinoiseries* themselves, inspired by the Orient, depict European interpretations of the Chinese following various pursuits. On the whole these figures look European but have Chinese features and dress, and are depicted brewing tea or holding banners and bird lures on balustraded terraces.

The decorations on the prized Jersey Service, based on the engravings of the Dutch engraver, Petrus Schenk, epitomize the style of *fabeltiere*, or pictures of fantastic animals and birds. They are a combination of his own idiosyncratic interpretation of oriental taste and artistic palette. Fantastic animals and birds in both Kakiemon and *famille verte* enriched with the distinctive purple Böttger-luster provided a decoration indicative of the mystic East. Löwenfinck, who has always been associated with this type of decoration, presents both Chinese and Japanese ceramic decoration with a plainly European interpretation.

European efforts to produce their own porcelain were not purely based on artistic grounds. The huge trade deficit caused by commissioned imports from the Orient meant that too much wealth was leaving Europe and provided a need for European ceramic production in porcelain.

Chelsea Dish
Date: 1750-1752
Diameter: 11in (28cm)

This rare and splendid pattern has no Japanese prototype and is therefore thought to be an original Chelsea design in the Kakiemon style. The design is much more dense than an equivalent Japanese version, which would have larger areas undecorated and would have simpler prunus and bamboo branches. The richness of the design might have offended the Japanese eye, but would have appealed to the European taste for opulence. The 'banded hedge' is a common feature of Kakiemon designs and the contorted pose of the phoenixes is very characteristic. Kakiemon designs had been used in the preceding incised triangle period (1745-49), but achieved their greatest expression during the raised anchor period when this dish was made. Chelsea produced a glassy soft-paste porcelain of exceptional beauty (detail right); there is a tendency for the enamels to sink into the relatively thick glaze and fuse more completely than on the Japanese hard-paste porcelain where the enamels sit on the surface.

English Kakiemon

*This was the first oriental style of decoration that captured the hearts
and minds of early English porcelain manufacturers.*

In the early years of porcelain production in England it was natural that the entrepreneurs and craftsmen should look for inspiration to the Orient, where the production of porcelain was already an ancient craft. It is perhaps surprising that of all the different oriental styles then available the Kakiemon style should have become the most widely copied, in spite of its relative scarcity in comparison to the large quantities of *famille rose, famille verte* and blue and white then being imported by the East India companies.

There are several reasons for the popularity of the Kakiemon style. Firstly, the innate beauty of this mode of decoration and its suitability for porcelain made it irresistible. Having mastered the art of producing the fragile soft-paste bodies of the earliest porcelains, the potters required a form of decoration that would enhance and show off their material. The Kakiemon style, with its brilliant red, blue, green and yellow enamels and its judicious use of empty space proved to be a perfect foil. Secondly, the technique of Kakiemon decoration was relatively easy because of the small amount of readily available colors. It also lent itself to patterns that could be repeated and it did not require the painstaking attention to detail necessary for the popular European genre scenes. Thirdly, its introduction into England coincided with the arrival of rococo styles, and its asymmetry found a receptive audience eager for the novelty of this design.

Original pieces of Japanese Kakiemon were not common in England and it is likely that most English

Chelsea Vase and Cover
Date: c 1752 (red anchor period)
Height: 10½in (26.5cm)

A Chelsea hexagonal vase and cover painted with prunus, pine and bamboo, the 'three friends' of Chinese origin, divided by iron-red and turquoise panels. This vase is a close copy of a Japanese original in both decoration and shape, but the slight heaviness of the painting and the quality of the porcelain distinguish it from a true Kakiemon example.

Kakiemon designs were copied from Meissen. The Meissen porcelain wares themselves were often very accurately copied from the vast collection of oriental wares belonging to Augustus the Strong, Elector of Saxony; even the brown rim on dishes, bowls and plates, that was originally a technical device making it unnecessary to glaze the edges, was carefully copied. On the Japanese originals, however, it was high-fired with the porcelain; on the European copies it was simply an enamel color, low fired in a muffle kiln.

Kakiemon decoration on Chelsea porcelain seems to have started towards the end of the triangle period (1745-49), and was used mostly on the plainer wares. It was used extensively throughout the raised anchor period (1749-51) and into the early years of the red anchor period (1752-58) until about 1755, when it was partly replaced by the rather inferior Imari influenced brocade patterns, flower painting and scenes of European derivation. Although most of the patterns found on Chelsea ware were derived from Meissen, there are some for which there are no Meissen originals, such as the Lady in a Pavillion pattern, which suggests that they were copied directly from Japanese originals. One of the most splendid designs, found on three dishes, is of two glorious phoenixes between a banded hedge and a branch of prunus blossom; there is no known Japanese example and it is presumably an original Chelsea design. Particularly effective are the 'twisted dragons' copied from Meissen onto shapes, often of English silver design.

K akiemon wares at Bow were produced throughout most of the life of the factory. In the first half of the 1750s Kakiemon was the most widely used style of enameled decoration, and it was particularly popular at a later date for the large dinner services, most commonly with the 'quail' or 'partridge' pattern. Tea and coffee wares are less common in Kakiemon than in *famille rose* designs. Bow

Worcester Part Tea Service
Date: *c 1775*

This tea service is typical of the large production of the Worcester factory with designs derived from Kakiemon. While being of high quality and rather sumptuous the design is a far cry from the sparse beauty of the original Kakiemon designs; the dense panels of Kakiemon flowers leave little of the space that characterizes the prototype.

Kakiemon designs remained very faithful to the Japanese originals and varied little throughout the thirty years of the factory's output.

In the early period of Worcester, Kakiemon designs were never as popular as they were at Bow and Chelsea. Worcester favored designs of Chinese derivation in the *famille verte* or *famille rose* palette. Kakiemon designs appear on small hexagonal baluster vases which date from about 1753 and on some tea wares — the quail pattern was particularly favored on these. From the 1760s onwards, Worcester developed very popular patterns, such as the fan, mosaic and Imari patterns, which were based rather loosely on Japanese designs. The Kakiemon designs were a long way removed from the restrained originals and were densely painted with lavish use of gilding as in the 'Jabberwocky patterns'. The popular design of a 'Ho Ho' bird on a rock, often known as the 'Sir Joshua Reynolds' pattern, is exceptional in retaining some restraint. Tea wares with alternating panels of powder or scale blue and Kakiemon flowers were very popular and were produced in large quantities. Worcester generally decorated its finest later wares with styles of European derivation. Very little Derby porcelain was decorated in the Kakiemon style, except in imitation of the degenerate Worcester wares of the 1770s. Longton Hall produced tea wares with the quail pattern, but more often preferred European flowers or exotic birds. The Kakiemon influence was at its greatest in the heyday of English porcelain from about 1750 to 1755 and consequently, some of the finest of all English porcelains are in this style.

Bow Octagonal Plate
Date: c 1760
Diameter: 8½in (21.5cm)

This magnificent plate is a loose interpretation of Kakiemon, retaining much of the color scheme with a few additions and two exotic phoenix painted with great vigour. This exceptional plate, of a similar style to a bowl in the British Museum painted by Thomas Craft, cannot be considered typical as Bow usually copied the originals fairly faithfully. The design retains much of the spirit of Kakiemon with its dynamic asymmetry and use of the white background. The border flower swags (see detail) are a purely

European invention and the color scheme includes a rose enamel quite alien to the Kakiemon palette. The thick blue and rich gilding are typical of Bow. This plate is a rare example of the successful harmony of Kakiemon and European design.

5
The Observation of Nature

The reaction of the potter to his natural surroundings is a key theme that runs through the history of ceramics. In the East the motive force was the creation of funerary figures of the animals and attendants that had surrounded a deceased dignitary during his lifetime. Classic examples of these are the camels and horses of the Tang dynasty which were also the first serious attempt by potters to depict the animals that surrounded them in a more than schematic fashion. During this period potters consciously began to observe their fellow men and the fauna around them and attempted to portray them as individuals rather than as types. Even though human figures, horses and camels were produced in large numbers by the Tang potters, they are quite evidently the product of close study and an understanding of how they moved and worked as distinct from a stylized representation of what the potter imagined they looked like.

The wide gap that divides the Tang potter from the porcelain manufacturers of eighteenth century Europe is not simply a question of 1000 years and a distant culture. The destination of the product was entirely different. The wares of the European porcelain factory were intended for the living quarters of the quick, rather than the last repose of the dead. The eighteenth century was an age in which the boundaries of knowledge were being steadily

Meissen White Porcelain Jug
Date: c 1731
Height: 20in (50.5cm)

This is one of the major pieces modeled by J.G. Kirchner (and later Kändler) for Augustus the Strong's Japanese palace in Dresden. It is called in German an 'untier' (monster jug). In fact it is a strangely contradictory object since its juggish nature is in contrast with its animal form, and its animal form is vitiated by its ostensible purpose. The jug is, of course, incapable of fulfilling this purpose – an example of a typical eighteenth-century conceit.

Collection: Mr and Mrs Edmund M. Pflueger, New York

Large Brown-Glazed Standing Stallion
Date: Late 7th/early 8th century
Width: 1ft 11in (60cm)

The largest pottery animals and figures of this period often lack the movement and elegant balance of smaller objects which were easier to fire in one piece without warping or collapsing. This perhaps explains why this heavily potted Ferghana stallion appears less alert, less full of character than most stallions of its breed.

Unglazed Pottery Standing Lady
Date: Late 7th/Early 8th century (Tang)
Height: 14½in (36.5cm)

This Tang pottery figure of a lady, serene and rather hieratic in conception, illustrates clearly the contrast between the early wares of China and the mobile expressive figures of the eighteenth century. The Ansbach Harlequin (far right), small though it is, seems, thanks to its stance, to be in the process of movement. The Tang figure, by contrast, is frozen in eternity.

Meissen Figure of the Scowling Harlequin
(below left)
Date: c 1740
Height: 7¼in (18.5cm)

Meissen Figure of the Greeting Harlequin
(below)
Date: c 1740
Height: 6in (15cm)

Both these figures were modeled by J.J. Kändler and are part of the series of comedy figures that he created in rapid succession between 1735 and 1742. Each figure is self-sufficient and the strong colors are carefully used to offset the white surface of the porcelain itself. Undoubtedly the master modeler kept a tight control on how his figures were decorated.

Chelsea Botanical Plate
Date: c 1755
Diameter: 9½in (24cm)

Botanically accurate painting of this type is a peculiarly English invention. Known as 'Hans Sloane' plates after the patron of the Physic garden in Chelsea, they are copied from the prints and drawings of the great botanist, George Ehret. To eyes accustomed to the usual decorative flower painting of the eighteenth century, it is surprising to see such humble vegetables as turnips and carrots decorating plates that were destined for the tables of the wealthy clients of Chelsea. This type of painting, which continued until at least 1760, can also be found on Bow porcelain.

pushed back; man's natural curiosity was at its highest peak and direct observation and recording of the natural world was at its keenest. At the same time rococo, the style which dominated the middle decades of the century, was imbued with a spirit of fantasy. This led to some strange and original results. The porcelain manufactories and the faience potteries of the day produced bowls, teapots and jugs which were superficially very accurate depictions of fruit, vegetables, monkeys and squirrels, boar's heads and hens on the nest. This lifelike treatment of the articles contradicted their functional purpose. It is almost certain, however, that pieces such as a monkey jug and squirrel teapots, although in theory of practical use, were not seriously intended to be used and were merely examples of the eighteenth century passion for conceits.

Parallel to the making of botanical and animal forms were the wares depicting botanical, zoological and ornithological specimens. These benefited from the stream of illustrated books, such as Miller's *Figures of Plants* and de Buffon's *Birds*, which were part of the eighteenth century passion for classification, and which were available to the manufacturers, either in their published form or, as at Chelsea, as preparatory drawings for publication. Classification

also influenced the depiction of homo sapiens, and in this case too the engraved image was a rich source of inspiration.

The art of François Boucher, which was swiftly disseminated by engravers such as Nilssen, was to have a dynamic influence on the porcelain manufacturers of the 1750s, 1760s and 1770s. His ideas were transmitted both as decorative subjects, painted on the surface of wares, and as actual figure subjects in biscuit and in glazed and colored porcelain. Typical of this style of engraving is de Ferriol's *100 Nations du Levant* which depicted the national costumes of the Near East. These were transformed into porcelain figures by Kändler and Reinicke at Meissen and were in turn imitated more or less directly at other German factories, and at Chelsea and Bow in England.

The most interesting and successful depiction of man on the ceramics of the period was, without doubt, the Italian comedy. Here the passion for a series of related figures is manifest, although this is a minor aspect of the whole conception. It is the relationships between a group of humans that count, and the whole Italian comedy is but a theatrical satire on those very relationships which were to be crystallized in the porcelain of the day.

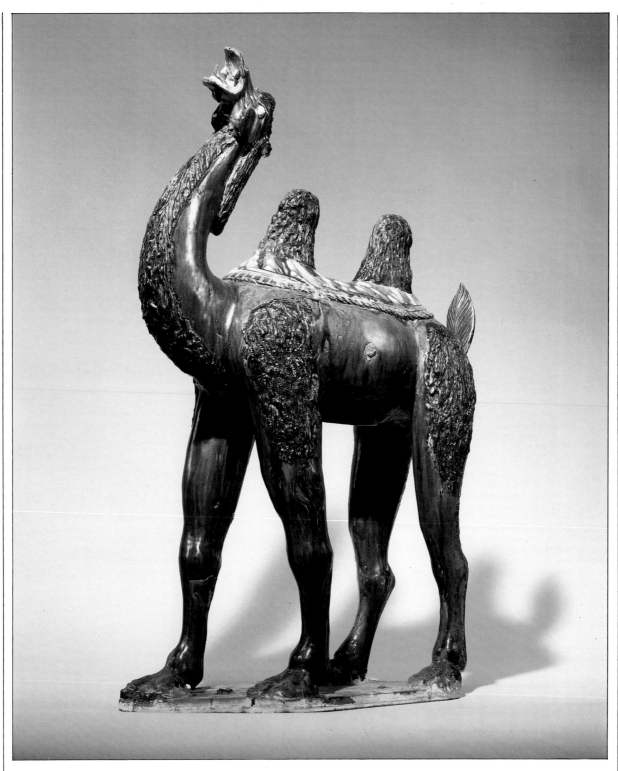

Sancai Pottery Model, Bactrian Camel
Date: Early 8th century
Height: 2ft 7in (79.5cm)

The term sancai (three color) refers to the combination of three different mineral colors in the glaze, deliberately run together in a standard but rich and harmonious palette.

This model was one of the many funerary figures buried with the Chinese emperors. The funerary figures were almost invariably assembled from elements molded separately by pressing into master molds, and 'sticking' (luting) together with a dab of liquid clay slip. This technique (called 'repairing') gave the early

potter an opportunity to model very complex figure groups, or even models of buildings. However, inevitably it limited the scope of postures or the number of models that could be created in the Tang potteries specializing in these objects, which were created specifically as tomb goods.

The Animal World of the Tang Potter

Pottery sculpture, imitating everyday objects, was required to adorn tombs, and early Chinese potters were inspired to produce realistic models of both exotic and domestic animals for this purpose.

The natural world fascinated the Chinese, at every level, from the august Emperor poring over hereditary treasures to the humble potter sketching in mineral pigments onto a piece of Cizhou stoneware. The misty mountain peaks of the south, the harsher ranges of the north, were constant subjects for scholar-painters, and these were mastered by repetition and the close study of treasured versions from early masters. Like the medieval European monarchs, the Chinese Emperor kept a menagerie of strange animals, which was a constant source of fascination to the court. These exotic breeds were often gifts from tribute bearers who visited from far outposts. The nomadic tradition gave the Chinese a knowledge of, and affection for, horses and equestrian skills were maintained and perfected by long hunting expeditions in which, on occasion, the entire imperial retinue would participate.

Chinese draftsmen may have used a different method to portray perspective from European Renaissance artists, but they often managed to create as convincing and homogeneous a vision of figures and animals in nature as any western master of the vanishing point, whether it was a mountain range, a horse or a group of feeding quail. The Chinese did not merely portray with realism what

Detail of Bactrian Camel *(right) The rich glaze colors of Tang funerary pottery must have made a tomb, full of newly potted figures and vessels, a very bright and luxurious sight. Often the glaze has survived in excellent condition, though acid or alkaline soils in different areas of China can cause a degradation to the surface which gives a shiny iridescent look. This camel has, however, not been affected, and the glaze is in rich, and apparently almost original condition.*

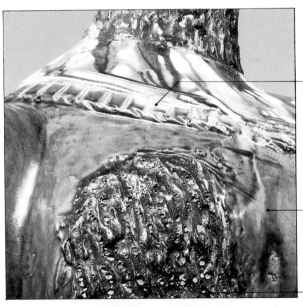

The dappled pattern around the base of the hump has been deliberately mottled to distinguish the harness fittings from the brown hide of the animal.

Most common of all the colored glazes found on Tang funerary figures, brown tones shade from the palest color to a rich dark chocolate. Collectors prefer a bright chestnut tone such as this one, especially if the glaze has retained its original sheen.

The roughened surface under a matt dark thin brown glaze suggests fibrous tufts of course hair, and contrasts with the smooth, richly glazed body.

Detail of Genuine Crackle Glaze on Sancai Figure *A useful rule of thumb for collectors is that the Tang pottery crackle is normally very small, while that on fakes appears as much larger fragments of glaze. Crackle is caused by the ceramic body cooling at a different rate from the glaze, causing it to pull apart through internal tension.*

Detail of Fake Crackle Glaze on Sancai Figure *In this twentieth century, probably post 1949, fake, the crackle is much too wide for the figure. Fakes of early glazed (and unglazed) funerary figures apparently first appeared on the international art market shortly after the First World War, although the railway excavations in China (often carried out under European supervision), which produced enormous quantities of genuine examples, had begun two decades earlier.*

Two Sancai Equestrian Figures
Date: Late 7th/early 8th century (Tang)
Height: 15in (37.5cm)

One figure holds a small bird, possibly representing a bird of prey used for hunting. It is very common to find the head of a rider left unglazed, even when the remainder of the figure has elaborate glaze decoration. The pale color of the horse's head on the left is due to degradation of the straw glaze, which will often develop an iridescent sheen and, at worst, flake off if buried in an atmosphere of acid or alkaline humidity. The other common glaze colors less often degrade, although the rarer blue shades often acquire an iridescent surface.

they observed around them. While western religious (and classical) iconography is primarily concerned with depicting humans — animals being symbolic appendages (St. Jerome's lion, St. John's eagle) — Buddhism and Taoism gave the Chinese an animal pantheon for inspiration and the figures appear in a variety of forms, from sculpture to paintings on ceramics.

Funerary rights gave the early Chinese potter the greatest opportunity to transfer this acute perception of animal and human form into sculpture. Initially, the burial of an important dignitary required human sacrifice and the provision of full-scale accoutrements in order to provide him with the accustomed pomp in the next life. But by the reign of the first Qin Emperor, Qin Shi Huangdi, clay figures were acceptable as substitutes, although these figures, of which there are enormous quantitites buried with him, were life size and laboriously modeled from life. From the Han period to the late Tang (very roughly, the first millenium AD), tombs were filled with a bewildering variety of ceramic, bronze and wood figures, representing the elements of everyday life. The ceramic sculpture reached its most elaborate during the early years of the Tang dynasty and lasted until the internal An-lu Shan rebellion in 756. The subsequent invasion by the Tibetans in 763 disrupted the prosperity and security which had provided the Sui and Tang court with an appearance of unprecedented luxury for a century

and a half. The richness of court life and culture is mirrored in the ornately glazed ceramic tomb sculptures discovered in metropolitan China, and particularly in the area around the Tang capital Chang'an. Most have been recovered through graverobbing, random excavation and railway-building in the early decades of this century. Only in recent years have systematic excavations of dated tombs provided a clearer chronology for these remarkable ceramic figures and animals. The chronology indicates clearly that the finest examples were indeed products of an earlier luxurious era at the center of a rich culture (the most sophisticated in Asia) and that their production ceased quickly when the prosperity declined, so that by the end of the eighth century there were no longer massive tombs full of superb glazed models.

This 'substitute sculpture' included, at different times over the centuries, models of servants, merchants, concubines, mythical tomb guardians, warriors and officials; houses, farms, pigsties, granaries and massive military watchtowers. Animals of all kinds occur, both real and mythical, including camels, elephants, zodiac figures, dogs, felines, unicorns, and a whole range of domestic farmyard stock and poultry. Horses are by far the most common animal models, and they come in a limited range of poses and sizes, but are saved from repetition by the wide variety of glaze decorations, harness trappings and riders which include archers, dignitaries, polo players, warriors, drummers and even provincial officials wearing peculiar wide-rimmed hats. The accuracy is remarkable, making it possible to trace the interbreeding of different equine stock. Produced in enormous quantities, the models were assembled from press-molds and often glazed over a white slip background which the Tang potters had found helpful in assisting adhesion of the glaze. This enabled the full richness of the mineral inclusions to appear in the firing, after green, brown, straw or blue glazes were poured, splashed or more carefully applied to the surface, often in combination.

The camel exemplifies the internationalism of China under the early Tang emperors, during the seventh century and first half of the eighth century, due to the fact that it was the only animal on the silk-route caravans. It is hard to comprehend the immense tedium, fatigue and boredom that a caravan procession experienced during the long marches across the wastes of Chinese Turkestan, the marshes of Lop Nor and the mountain ranges at the far western end, called the Pamirs. It also required courage because the isolated outposts of the Empire provided travelers with litte protection against tribes of marauders, and none at all against the blistering sandstorms, bitter cold and unhealthy conditions. The British archaeologist Sir Aurel Stein has left a fascinating record of the punishing nature of his journeys during the early excavations west of the policed imperial frontiers. His book *On Central Asian Tracts* is both a survival guide, giving information on how to prevent blisters on camels and how to eradicate insects, and a description of an archaelogist's treasure hunt among deserted, sand-covered oases for remarkably well-preserved textiles, manuscripts and artefacts — the debris of the silk route settlements fueled from the east. The Dunhuang grottoes at the eastern end of the route bear witness, in the richness of the fresco designs and other evidence of wealth, to the charitable donations lavished on the terminal oasis by fearful or grateful long-distance travelers.

The camels depicted on Tang ceramics are of two kinds; the Bactrian camel, two-humped, and the dromedary, with a single hump. It was primarily the Bactrian camel which carried expensive trade wares westwards and eastwards. Cargo such as bales of silk and canisters of spices were transported overland to the entrepots west of the Himalayas and Pamirs and on to Samarkand and Tashkent, ending up ultimately (in the medieval period) at Venice. From there it was shipped across the Mediterranean to a European destination, just as the Romans had done previously. Some of the largest and rarest glazed models of camels are shown carrying merchants on their backs; many are laden with containers, relief-molded with ferocious demon masks to scare off the opposition. One remarkable example, excavated in China, is unexpectedly laden with a band of musicians. The camels and their accompanying grooms or merchants, many modeled with non-Chinese facial features, document and illustrate an adventurous, efficient and opulent era of early Chinese history.

Glazed Pottery Miniature Elephant
Date: late 7th century
Width: 2½in (6.5cm)

It is rare to find miniature models of elephants. The elephant was probably extinct in China by the medieval period.

Courtesy of Messrs. Spink & Son, London

Painted Pottery Polo Player
Date: late 7th century
Length: 14½in (36.5cm)

This figure is probably female; it is unusual to have a woman represented in action. Polo was popular in metropolitan China.

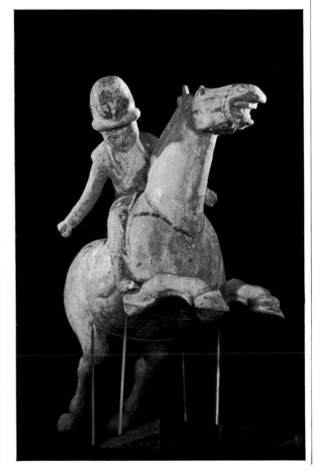

Meissen White Figure of a Parrot *(avara)*
Height: 4ft (121cm)
Date: c 1731

In eighteenth century Germany these figures were called avara ware. Kändler was working on this model in the latter half of 1731. It is one of the earliest pieces in which his full naturalistic style is evident. The bird is caught in a 'snapshot' of movement which clearly demonstrates a close observation of the species. These birds originally cost over 100 thalers each.

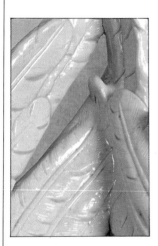

Detail of feathers and head *The lifelike rendering of the head and feathers emphasizes Kändler's close observation of the living bird.*

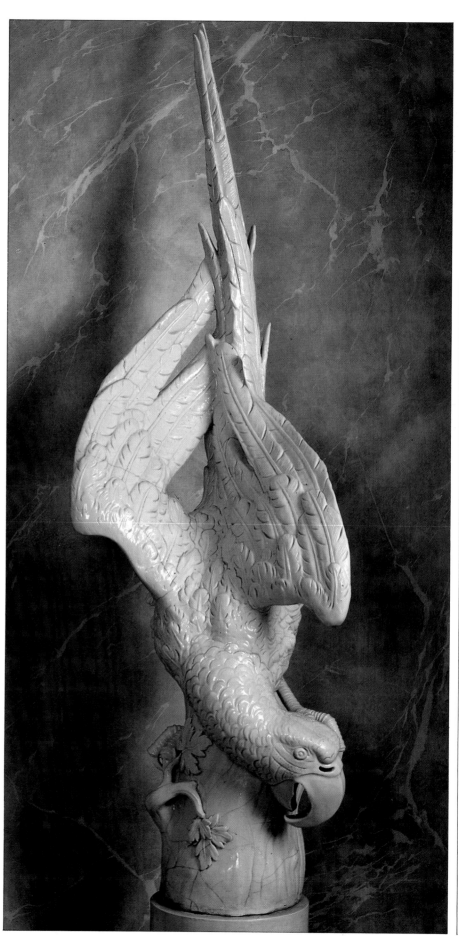

The Meissen Menagerie

*The naturalistic modeling of animals in porcelain
at Meissen was one of the greatest achievements in the history of ceramics. Largely
due to one man, Johann Joachim Kändler, it was to have a great
influence throughout Europe and on the English factories.*

A gap of just under a thousand years elapsed between the collapse of the Tang kilns and the next period in which the portrayal of animals and birds was to occupy the potter's mind seriously. It was at Meissen, some little way outside Dresden, the capital of Saxony, that another remarkable creative phase was witnessed between 1730 and 1733; fortunately, this period of production was well documented. A rich, powerful and determined patron, Augustus the Strong, Elector of Saxony, owned the Meissen porcelain factory at this time. He had also acquired a new palace which he resolved to fill with the products of his manufactory. Augustus conceived everything on a grand scale and he determined to fill his magnificent Japanese-style palace with a monumental series of vases and animal figures. However, before this splendid plan could be realized, there was a series of major technical obstacles which had to be overcome. Augustus was under the mistaken impression that porcelain was a material which had a similar scope to marble, and that his factory would therefore be able to create ceramic pieces which would rival those sculptured in stone. However, nobody had ever successfully fired a massive piece of porcelain, or indeed pottery, on a scale approaching the proportions of Augustus' plan. Indeed no-one had even conceived of such figures before. In the first instance Augustus employed Johann Gottlieb Kirchner as his modeler. Kirchner's products were limited by his blinkered and conservative approach to the subjects he was commissioned to depict; the earliest animals therefore were static in rendition and regressive in spirit. They include a rhinoceros, inspired by early German woodcuts in the Dürer tradition, but more reminiscent of an armadillo, and an elephant bearing little resemblance to the beast it was attempting to represent. Owing to the lack of technical experience in producing and firing pieces on this scale, Kirchner was also unable to be progressive in his compositions. He had to avoid modeling features onto his animals since these were liable to collapse in the kiln. Indeed, the difficulty of

**Meissen White Figure
of a Falcon**
Date: 1731
Height: 22in (55cm)

This is another of the models on which Kändler was working in 1731. It was evidently quite popular as 18 examples were produced. The extensive cracking on the body of the bird is the result not of breakage, but of problems in the actual firing of the piece in the kiln.

Collection: Mr and Mrs Edward M. Pflueger, New York

Base of the Falcon *This picture of the underside of the bird shows the cracks caused in the firing. It also shows the coarse and gritty nature of the body.*

Pair of Meissen Figures of Bears
Date: c 1745
Width: 7¼in (18.5cm)

These bears are clearly described by Kändler in the 'Taxa', a manuscript record he kept of his work between 1740 and 1744. The bright naturalistic colors of the animals are set off by the white base with its colored leaves and flowers. On the back of the bases are the blue crossed swords marks of the Meissen factory.

Pair of Bow figures of Dismal Hounds
Date: c 1758
Height: 3in (7.5cm)

Although these quite clearly show the influence of Kändler at Meissen, they are not derived from a Meissen model. The talented modeler responsible for these, and other Bow animals, is as yet unidentified.

Collection: Winifred Williams Ltd.

firing the pieces dogged their creation from beginning to end. Their size made it essential for them to be massively potted and this created further problems. The thick body was, as a result, rather coarse and gray in appearance and it tended to collapse in the kiln due to the sheer weight. The thickness of the article was another source of difficulty, causing cracking as the moisture was driven out in the firing.

Augustus' original intention was to have all the figures decorated in colored enamels, but this idea was abandoned due to the many problems and defects encountered during the early stages of firing. There were constant attempts — from 1730 to 1733 — to improve both the ceramic body used and the kilns in which the pieces were fired. However, to judge from the pieces that have survived, these were only relatively successful. In 1731 Kirchner was joined in his work by Johann Joachim Kändler, who had trained as a sculptor. Kändler had spent the years 1723-30 in the workshop of the sculptor Thomae, and he had achieved his mastership in the latter year. Although he contributed his own ideas to the solution of the technical problems at Meissen, he did not manage to eradicate them altogether. He did, however, entirely change the basis on which the animals were conceived. In-

stead of modeling an elephant as he though it looked, (as Kirchner had done), Kändler went to the Royal menagerie to see for himself what the birds and beasts looked like. He studied their attitudes and their movements, and the figures he produced are redolent of his careful observation of the animals in the flesh. What he saw is recorded in his 'Taxa' — a record he kept of his activities, which is confirmed by contemporary records of the kinds of animals that were in the Royal collection. The results of his close observation of the animal kingdom are astounding, particularly when we remember the static and unrealistic nature of the early attempts by Kirchner and the long years of emptiness which preceded them. Almost overnight Kändler produced lifelike representations in the round which actually resembled the beasts they were depicting.

He created a great many of these figures, the sum total of his output being around 70 pieces. However, the scale on which they were conceived hindered the creation of a technically sound product. Production was constantly delayed and completion prevented due to problems with the firing. Almost every figure that has survived shows faults in the firing in some degree or other, and many more must have been lost during the manufacturing process. The defective condition of the models, after the initial stages of production, effectively prevented the addition of fired colored decoration, although some examples were decorated in cold colors. Perhaps fortunately, this form of decoration has disappeared with the passage of time. Cold decoration, while initially quite bright, quickly faded and chipped off, leaving the article looking dirty. At the height of the work on his great design, Augustus the Strong died, but his son Augustus III decreed that work on his father's scheme was not to be interrupted. However, as the driving force behind it was removed, no new figures were added to those already conceived, and as the work in production was gradually finished, the project came to an end, never to be resumed on a serious basis or on the scale previously attempted. On the face of it, this was a sad ending to a great plan, but it was to prove a boon to Meissen and to the porcelain manufacturers that imitated and drew inspiration from the factory over the next three decades. Although he was no longer under pressure to design large figures on a scale that defeated technical capacity, Kändler did not lose his interest or ability to create animal figures. His newly acquired freedom to reduce them in scale meant that the problems caused in firing the porcelain could be eliminated and, as a result, he found it possible to decorate the animals in natural colors. The impressively lifelike figures which Kändler had already produced in white had been denied the ultimate touch of verisimilitude by the technical inability to color them. In the case of the smaller figures executed later, natural scale had to be sacrificed to technical necessity, but these enjoyed the benefit of color. Kändler's later porcelain figures, therefore, proved to be a perfect compromise in which the scale, decoration and the materials used were in perfect harmony. Augustus' 'grand design', although itself unsuccessful, had given rise to some magnificent byproducts. In the decade from 1735 to 1745 Kändler produced a continual flow of animals and birds at his atelier. This was an immense achievement, considering the wide range of other figures and wares that he was responsible for at the same time. The 1740s also saw the establishment of many of the great second-generation porcelain factories. The majority of them reflect the influence of Meissen to some extent but, with the animal figures in particular, the effect of the Meissen tradition is paramount.

Vincennes, which in its early years reflects Meissen in many aspects of its production, turned out animals clearly inspired by the German factory. They did however go on to make a few models which were entirely of their own design. Chelsea also derived the idea of animal figures from Meissen and the coloring used is imbued with the tonality of Kändler's figures.

The birds and beasts of Bow, Longton Hall and Derby are all, in their different ways, 'provincial' interpretations of the theme already followed successfully by Kändler. This was not the case generally in Germany, and it may be due both to the proximity of Meissen and the remarkable solution offered by Kändler to the problematical creation of animal figures that other manufacturers were effectively discouraged from producing similar objects. Consequently, all the animal and bird figures produced by the rival factories scattered across Germany were not equal to the output at Meissen, and Kändler's animal figures still reign supreme in their domain.

Pair of Chelsea Figures of Parakeets
Date: c 1752
Height: 5in (12.5cm)

The Chelsea modelers, unfortunately still anonymous, did not follow the style of Kändler's models, nor did they apply direct observation of nature. Their bird figures were almost all derived from the illustrations found in 'A Natural History of Uncommon Birds' by George Edwards. Because of the two-dimensional source, the Chelsea birds usually suffer from having only one viewpoint and are therefore pale echoes of the innovatory three-dimensional figures of the Meissen factory. The illustration (right) is from George Edward's 'A Natural History of Uncommon Birds' (plate 6, vol.1), which was published in London between 1743 and 1747. The flat image depicted here was transmitted to the porcelain birds.

Derby Tureen, Cover and Stand
Date: c 1800
Width: 19in (48cm)

This beautiful tureen was painted by William Pegg, the Quaker. The superb white paste and soft glaze produced by Derby at this period provide the perfect canvas for Pegg's botanical painting. The style of Pegg's flower painting is very individual. His flowers are extremely lifelike and vivid and cover almost the entire surface that he was decorating. The tulip (detail right) is clearly painted from life.

English Botanical Ware

The peculiarly English form of floral decoration of botanically accurate specimens, was pioneered at Chelsea and Derby.

Flower painting has been a mainstay of the ceramic decorator's art since the earliest Chinese porcelains and throughout the European tradition, and certainly a great many pieces of decorated porcelain do have some floral or botanical designs. Flowers clearly lend themselves well to the medium; their beauty and fragility are complemented by the porcelain and their bright colors can be closely matched with ceramic enamels.

Flower painting on early English porcelain derived both from the stylized oriental forms of Kakiemon and *famille rose* and, more importantly, from the great naturalistic prototypes of Meissen and Vincennes. By the 1740s in Europe flower painting had developed into a very sophisticated art. The intention was not to reproduce nature too exactly, although painters were capable of this, but rather to paint decorative bouquets of real or imaginary flowers. The notion of painting botanically accurate single flowers was peculiarly English, although the idea came originally from Germany. It was first undertaken at Chelsea during the red anchor period in about 1755.

The Chelsea botanical plates have become known as 'Sir Hans Sloane's plates'. Sir Hans Sloane was one of the great figures of the day; he was an eminent doctor, collector and botanist and his personal collection formed the nucleus of the British Museum collection. He was also patron of the 'Physic Garden' at Chelsea. His name has been associated with the Chelsea plates due to an advertisement in 'Faulkner's Dublin Journal' of 1758 stating that they were enameled from his plants. However, credit should rightly go to the botanical artist, George Ehret, who came to London from Heidelberg with a letter of introduction to Sir Hans Sloane and was employed to illustrate specimens from his collection. Ehret is the only artist whose name has been traced to Chelsea botanical designs, and indeed botanical decoration was foreshadowed in some Meissen

Pegg's recently discovered sketchbook, along with various loose sketches, illustrate clearly that he painted from life. It also confirms the attribution of many pieces, such as the tureen (opposite), to his hand. These sketches were painted in 1813 on Pegg's return to Derby from his self-imposed exile. Pegg had previously burnt most of his drawings and books in 1801 in a fit of religious zeal.

**Chelsea Botanical
Lobed Saucer Dish**
Date: c 1755
Diameter: 8½in (21.5cm)

*The earliest botanical
painting on English
porcelain is that of Chelsea.
A wide variety of botanical
subjects were used ranging
from exotic flowers to such
mundane vegetables as
turnips. Many
plants have been attributed
to the drawings and
paintings of George Ehret,
the German botanical artist.
One of his prints — an
auricula with a speckled
wood butterfly and a
fritillary — is illustrated
(right).*

wares of the previous decade, based upon Ehret's designs before he came to England.

Chelsea plates frequently include butterflies and insects, which can also be found on Ehret's original prints. The Chelsea artists took considerable care to copy designs accurately but were not above grafting on extra leaves, often from quite different plants, to suit the composition. Unlike most floral decoration, which concentrated on pretty and exotic flowers, the Chelsea botanical plates were often decorated with paintings of common English plants, with the roots showing. Sometimes just the fruit and leaves of a gooseberry, hazelnut or other superficially dull plant are shown. However the effect is very pleasing and a refreshing contrast to the prettiness of most flower painting. Botanical painting at Chelsea continued well into the gold anchor period, perhaps until 1765.

Botanical plates in a very similar style were produced at Bow from about 1756 and it is possible that they were executed by painters from Chelsea who are known to have worked at Bow during this period. While they are not uncommon, they are rarer than the Chelsea examples and are among the earliest non-oriental styles of decoration produced at Bow.

Botanical painting reached its zenith at Derby in the late eighteenth and early nineteenth centuries,

Chelsea Oval Dish
Date: c 1755 (red anchor)
Diameter: 11½in (29cm)

This finely painted dish is typical of the naturalistic but nonbotanical flower painting found on Chelsea porcelain and derived from Meissen. Although the individual plants are often identifiable, there is no real attempt to produce botanically accurate flowers, the purpose is simply to paint an attractive bouquet. This style of painting was the most widely used on Chelsea porcelain and can be found as decoration on wares of all shapes.

Bow Octagonal Plate
Date: c 1755
Diameter: 8½in (21.5cm)

Botanical wares were produced at Bow from about 1755 in the Chelsea tradition and, at their best, were of comparable quality; but for the most part they were cruder, although still pleasing. Painters from Chelsea are thought to have worked at Bow during the years 1757 and 1758 when Chelsea production was reduced during Nicholas Sprimont's illness, and presumably much of the production of botanical wares can be attributed to these painters.

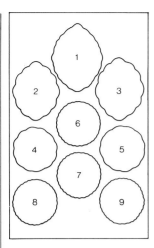

Part of a Derby Botanical Dessert-Service
Date: c 1790

This fine service is typical of the work of John Brewer; each piece is named in English and Latin on the back.
1. Star anemone
2. Common passion flower
3. Lilium Martagon
4. Stalk crane's bill
5. Yellow day lily
6. Wood night shade
7. Double lilac primrose
8. Rosa Eglanteria
9. Common tulip tree

Derby Lozenge Shaped Dish
Date: c 1800
Diameter: 10½in (26.5cm)

This dish is similar to the famous 'thistle dish' in the Derby City Museum and Art Gallery, England that 'Quaker' Pegg is recorded to have painted from a lady thistle gathered by him one Ascension holiday; until the discovery of Pegg's sketch book this was the most important evidence for attributing this style of painting to Pegg.

after two decades of neglect. The quality of non-botanical flower painting was also excellent. William Billingsley, who was apprenticed to Edward Withers in 1774 and succeeded him in about 1790, was perhaps the greatest English porcelain painter in this style. He painted roses and other English garden flowers in bouquets and as border patterns in a very naturalistic style, probably painting directly from nature rather than botanical prints, as had previously been the style.

Billingsley left Derby in 1796 to go to Pinxton. The flower painting was carried on by John Brewer and William Pegg. Brewer painted flowers in the style of Billingsley and also undertook the botanical painting. He often painted foreign and exotic flowers, which would have been taken from prints found in books such as 'Curtises Botanical Journals', known to have been sent to Derby in 1792. William 'Quaker' Pegg was perhaps the greatest of all botanical painters on porcelain and one of the most colorful characters to grace the history of English ceramics. He was from a humble background and was brought up a strict Calvinist. Throughout his life he was burdened with a tormented conscience. He started work at the age of ten in the Staffordshire potteries and went to Derby as a painter in 1796. However he could not reconcile himself to so seemingly trivial an art as flower painting and in a turmoil or religious fervor and guilt became a Quaker in 1800. He then left the Derby works for a job in a stocking factory making silk stockings. Even this was too luxurious so he turned to making cotton stockings. He pleaded with his employer to spare him the agony of ornamenting such humble clothes and was consequently allowed to make plain ones. His conscience abated sufficiently to allow him to resume his work at Derby in 1813 and a year later he married. He lost the sight of an eye in 1817 and after much soul-searching became convinced that this was a terrible judgement on him. He left in 1820 to open up a small shop in Derby where he died in 1851.

William Pegg always painted from life as can be seen from his sketch books. His flowers are generally lifesize and cover the whole surface of a dish with great vigour and abandon, as if they have been tossed carelessly across it. The gilding of the borders of Pegg's plates is very restrained, usually a simple narrow band. It is fortunate that Pegg's first term of employment, and the beginning of his second, coincided with the production of a particularly attractive porcelain body at Derby, which gave a fine surface for painting.

The botanical tradition of painting continued intermittently throughout the nineteenth century, but never again did it attain the heights reached in its early years.

Pair of Nymphenburg Italian Comedy Figures
(Columbine and Scaramouche)
Date: c 1760
Height: 8in (20.5cm)

Modeled by Bustelli, each figure has an impressed Bavarian shield mark in blue and white, with gilt surround and incised with the figure 2. The flattened surfaces so typical in wood-carving are plainly visible in the figure of Columbine. The sophisticated decoration, carefully related to the plastic conception of the figures, is designed to enhance the modeling. The painting of the face serves to emphasize the vitality with which all Bustelli's figures are imbued. He was also able to depict the human form and its spiritual essence in a fashion without parallel among porcelain modelers. The delightful details (see right), such as the patch on her temple echoed on the mask in her hand, bear witness to the skill of the unknown painter who decorated her. Obviously the cooperation between modeler and decorator was particularly close.

The Italian Comedy

*The theater, a well-known feature of life in
eighteenth-century Europe, proved a fecund source of inspiration for the European
porcelain manufacturers and gave rise to their most successful
creations.*

Throughout the eighteenth century, in a vast proportion of the European porcelain factories and at a few potteries, there runs a strong, constant and above all successful theme: the *Commedia dell'Arte* — the characters of the Italian comedy. This subject had an appeal at all levels of society and was also totally free of national boundaries. It was widely disseminated, both by the printmakers whose images were dispersed among the libraries of the rich and powerful, and by itinerant players who were the forerunners of *I Pagliacci*, the opera clowns. The production of sets of figures on a thematic basis was at the same time a symptom of the late Baroque and the Rococo. This popular style was frequently expressed in series depicting the continents, the seasons or the senses. However each series was limited by the very nature of the subjects, to four or five figures. This quite obviously did not offer much scope for variation, either in interpretation or display.

These artistic limitations did not apply to the Italian comedy. Firstly, and essentially, it involved a greater number of characters and was more elastic. The precise number of persons involved in a given drama was a matter of interpretation, and was always subject to the whim of the individual artist or factory. This led to a wide range of variations among the many factories producing figures of this kind. Some made only a few figures, as at Bow, Ansbach, Strasbourg, Kelsterbach and the Cozzi factory in Venice. At Meissen in 1744, on the other hand,

**The Nymphenburg
Commedia dell'Arte**
approx. 8in (19.5cm)
1. *Capitano Spavento*
2. *Leda*
3. *The Abbé*
4. *Corine*
5. *Harlequin*
6. *Lalage*
7. *Scaramouche*
8. *Columbine*
9. *Donna Martina*

10. *Il Dottore*
11. *Julia*
12. *Pantalone*
13. *Lucinda*
14. *Pierrot*
15. *Isabella*
16. *Ottavio*
*The sixteen figures that
make up Bustelli's comedy
series arranged in the pairs
by which his scheme was
orchestrated. The only
complete set of these figures
that is still extant is in the
Bayerisches National
Museum*

MEISSEN FIGURES AND THEIR INFLUENCE

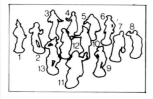

The Meissen Commedia dell'arte
Date: c 1745
Size: approx 7in (18cm)

Modeled for the Duke of Weissenfels by J.J. Kändler and P. Reinicke
1. Giangogulo
2. Mezzetin
3. Hanswurst
4. Scaramouche
5. Dr. Boloardo
6. Isabella
7. Columbine
8. Narcisino Malalbergo
9. Beltrame
10. Harlequin
11. Capitano Spavento
12. Scapin
13. Avvocato
Compared with Bustelli's comedy, made some 15 years later, these figures are static and do not relate positively to each other.

Chelsea figure of Scapin
Date: c 1752
Height: 4½in (11.5cm)

This was molded directly from one of the Meissen figures procured in Dresden in 1751 by Sir Charles Hanbury-Williams for Sir Everard Fawkener, a patron of the Chelsea factory. The illustration is from Riccoboni's 'Histoire du Theatre Italien' (below) which inspired the Meissen Scapin and through it the similar Chelsea figure.

HABIT DE SCAPIN

Johann Joachim Kändler and Peter Reinicke made the Duke of Weissenfels series which consisted of between fifteen and twenty figures. These were derived in the main from the engraved illustrations by Francois Joullain for *Riccoboni's Histoire du Theatre Italien*, which had been published in Paris some seventeen years earlier. Although conceived as a series the individual figures were not designed to relate to each other in any specific way. This of course meant that they could be arranged at will by their owners, but it also meant that there was no meaningful link between them. Prior to this, Meissen had produced splendid comedy figures in stoneware in the early 1720s and Kändler himself had created a succession of simple Italian comedy figures and groups between 1735 and 1740. These were in the true spirit of the late Baroque, strongly modeled and brightly colored. They tend to express a fierce and menacing rather than a kindly humor and are individual works of art of great originality and power. However, as each figure is conceived on its own the question of relating it to others does not arise. In fact, all the porcelain figures of the period, even those conceived in pairs, only have a very static relationship with one another in which mutual reaction is minimal.

When, in 1755 or thereabouts, Franz Anton Bustelli began the creation of his comedy figures at the Nymphenburg factory, his approach to the problem was entirely different and this is evident in the uniqueness of the final result. At Meissen, and subsequently at all the other manufactories, the porcelain figure was produced from a master model executed in clay. Bavaria, where Bustelli was working, was the homeland of a long-standing and excellent tradition of carving in wood. So, unlike his colleagues elsewhere, he used wood as the material for producing his master models, and carved rather than modeled them. Thus the first, and most visible, difference between Bustelli's figures and the 'common herd' is the planiform surfaces in which they are conceived. Although the molds were taken from the master model in the conventional fashion, and the figures were otherwise produced in the same way as all others, the woody nature of the original material stands out clearly.

Bustelli's figures are also anomalous because, unlike the Weissenfels series or Wenzel Neu's later series from Kloster Vielsdorf which are derived from an engraved source, they seem to be purely the inventions of his imagination and do not derive from any previous images. There does exist a drawing of figures curiously similar to his creations, but its exact relationship with them remains to be defined. Bustelli's comedy also diversifies from all others in its dramatis personae. There are sixteen figures, eight of which are common to all comedy series — Harlequin, Colombine, il Dottore, Isabella, Pierrot, Scaramouche, Pantalone and Capitano Spavento. The remaining eight — Ottavio, Corine, the Abbé (or Anselmo), Julia, Leda, Lalage, Lucinda and Donna Martina — are peculiarly Bustelli's. These sixteen figures are 'orchestrated' in parts and the eight pairs interact and combine to enact a drama. For a long time the true key to the pairings, and so to the artistic and dramatic relationship between the figures, was lost, but the correct pairings have been agreed upon and their order within the whole series has been established. Thus Harlequin is matched with Lalage, il Dottore with Donna Martina, Pierrot with Lucinda, the Abbé (an insipid family-confessor) with Corine who is reading him a letter she has had from her lover Leandro. Scaramouche is with Columbine, the captain is dashing towards Leda, who stands to protect the next pair, Ottavio and Isabella, and Julia and Pantalone form the last couple.

These pairings are by no means the conventional ones, but this is not what constitutes their chief point of interest which lies more particularly in the interaction between each pair of personalities. The pose of any single figure is only explicable when he or she is set beside a true companion. The Abbé's obsequious listening stance is only relevant in relation to Corine, who is reading her letter to him, and her attitude is only made clear by reference to him. Each pairing expresses the interplay between the characters. However, perhaps the most interesting element in each of the compositions created by these pairs of figures is the empty space between them and across which they gaze. In a strange way, Bustelli succeeded in focusing attention on the way in which his characters interact, rather than merely the expressions on their faces.

In terms of their decoration too, the Bustelli figures are equally remarkable. Already at Meissen, Kaendler had exercised a strict control over the way in which his models were decorated. In the Nymphenburg figures, the decoration seems to be even more closely linked to the modeling. We do not know who the decorators responsible for the actual painting of the figures were, although there is one group which can convincingly be attributed to the same hand. However, the anonymous people responsible obviously worked in close collaboration with Bustelli, because colored and gilt decoration appear to be part and parcel of the whole figure. The inventiveness of the modeling is matched only by the daring of the decoration. The *moiré* and embroidered decoration, and the details of hair and complexion are the products of consummate skill. Although the figures are best seen and interpreted in their pairs, each one is conceived as a satisfactory separate entity to be seen and appreciated from every angle.

It may, at first sight, appear strange that such a successful creation should have apparently had little or no effect on subsequent efforts in the same field. This is perhaps due primarily to the very individual technical approach that Bustelli adopted to their creation. A second critical factor must have been the relatively small numbers in which the figures were made, providing them with limited potential as a source of inspiration or imitation. However the most vital reason for the lack of imitation is that Bustelli's interpretation exhausted all possibilities in the particular direction he had elected to take.

6
The Debt to Metalwork

The craft of pottery long predates that of metalwork, and earthenware vessels are among some of the earliest artifacts that have survived. These early vessels are nearly always of circular cross-section which was a natural ceramic shape even before the introduction of the potter's wheel, as a plastic material such as clay does not readily lend itself to sharp angles. The technology required to reach temperatures necessary for the production of metals was probably derived from pottery kilns but these crafts separated early on and developed independently. Metal vessels, which in the earliest periods were bronze, were formed by casting and beating out and were sometimes joined together from sections. Ceramic vessels were formed by hand and, in later periods, thrown on a wheel, pressed into molds or joined together from sections; later still slip-casting was introduced, which consists of pouring a liquid suspension of clay into a porous mold.

The differences in materials and construction between metal and pottery vessels naturally generated different forms. Ceramic vessels in particular had to be of sound construction to avoid warping and collapsing during the firing process.

In China as early as the twelth century BC during the Shang dynasty, fine stoneware copies of the much more expensive and highly prized bronzes appeared; this started a tradition that continued into succeeding dynasties. In the Tang dynasty (AD 618-906) the fine silver wares were copied in pottery, and flasks derived from leather prototypes were made. Most of the greatest wares of the Song dynasty (AD 960-1279), which are considered by many people to be the finest stonewares and porcelains ever produced, were of purely ceramic form, but under the influence of the contemporary scholarly courts ceramic copies of archaic bronze ritual vessels were made to satisfy their veneration for times past. The shapes of the great im-

Famille Verte Kendi
Date: c 1700
Height: 8¾in (22cm)

The kendi (water sprinkler) was long reproduced in porcelain, but this relatively late example is a very close copy of a Middle Eastern metal one; this is particularly noticeable in the grooved sides recessed to resemble punched flutes.

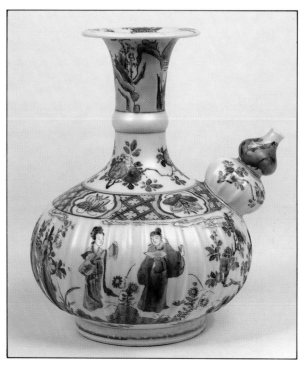

Underglaze Red Cupstand
Date: c 1350-75
Diameter: 7¾in (19.5cm)

Tea drinking was popular under the Song Dynasty, and cupstands are commonly found in lacquer, metal and monochrome glazed wares. As with so many copper-red painted wares from the Yuan and early Ming periods, the mineral has not fired properly and in this case has a grayish tint — a shame since the stand is particularly crisply press-molded and finished.

Meissen Beaker
Date: c 1725
Height: 3¼in (8cm)

The shape of this beaker is copied directly from silver, the gadrooned foot is a particularly silver feature. These early wares, which were produced some twenty years before the first porcelain was made in England, are of baroque form, which was shortly to be superseded by the flowing curves and the asymmetry of the rococo style. Romanticized harbor scenes with exotic figures and cargoes were a favorite form of decoration in this period of expanding trade and exploration.
The molding on the base of this porcelain beaker is almost identical to its silver original, as can be seen above.

Bow Silver Shaped Sauceboat
Date: 1750
Width: 9in (23cm)

Bow produced a large range of wares that were left undecorated or had only gilt decoration. Many white wares were copied or influenced by Chinese 'Blanc de Chine' wares from Fukien; this sauceboat is of pure English silver form and is similar to others made at Worcester. The elaborate scrolls of the handle and the relief festoons are typical silver features that lend themselves well to porcelain.

perial blue and white wares of the Ming dynasty (1368-1644) were frequently copied from Persian metalware, notable among these were ewers with their characteristic long elegant spouts. In China domestic ceramics were cheaper than their metal counterparts, but the finer porcelain wares were prized above all except those in precious metals.

In Europe in the fifteenth and sixteenth centuries pottery vessels were generally considered inferior to the works of the gold- and silversmiths, but the finest Italian Maiolica pieces of the sixteenth century were given a place of honor in the households of the upper classes; these wares were mostly of purely ceramic form relying on their range of colors and quality of painting for their appeal. The more humble domestic pottery of Europe, on the other hand, competed with and frequently derived their shapes from pewter and other base metal wares in common use.

The advent of porcelain in eighteenth century Europe coincided with the widespread popularity of tea drinking, so many early porcelain wares were designed for this purpose. Tea-bowls were adapted from Chinese prototypes, but the teapots and coffeepots were often based on silver counterparts, as were many items in dinner services such as sauce boats, salts and tureens. The interchange of ideas between ceramics and metalwork has worked in both directions throughout the centuries and both crafts have been enriched by the cross-fertilization.

Pair of Chelsea Silver-Shaped Plates
Date: c 1753 (red anchor period)
Diameter:

Plates and oval dishes of this type were copied from silver originals made by Nicholas Sprimont, the Huguenot silversmith who became the proprietor of the Chelsea factory. Silver prototypes exist hallmarked with the date letter for 1746/47. Few types of decoration are more sought after than these painted scenes from Aesop's Fables that are attributed to J.H. O'Neale, the great Irish painter.

Blue and White Ewer
Date: Early 15th century
Height: 13in (32.5cm)

The ewer exemplifies all the qualities of the finest early Ming porcelain which combines domestic potting ability with foreign metalwork inspiration. The spout is softly squared and set at an unexpected angle, the handle rounded and the body a 'metal' cylinder, transformed into a ceramic version. Chinese potters derived their metalwork shapes from objects such as the Khorasan (Middle Eastern) copper bronze baluster ewer (below). The intricate decoration on the porcelain ewer — misty blue cobalt scrolling lotus — loses some detail in the very slightly blue, lustrous translucent glaze, minutely dimpled to the eye. On the top of the spout is a later collection inventory mark, a name incised into the glaze and filled with black pigment. It records a 'silk route' provenance for the piece which is an appropriate commentary on a vessel with cosmopolitan origins. Almost certainly created at Jingdezhen, the ewer combines non-Chinese elements in its shape, derived from metalwork, and a non-native mineral (ground cobalt) in its design. Yet the unique Chinese flair for assimilating ideas has produced a superb Chinese vessel.

Metalwork and Chinese Ceramics

*Seeking constant novelty in their ceramic designs and shapes,
Chinese potters incorporated the angular forms and linear designs of
foreign metalwork into their work.*

The wide respect for the inspiration that Chinese ceramics have given to the world's potters can sometimes obscure a basic fact. Chinese potters also owe much of their art to other cultures which have provided them with novel shapes, decorations and pigments. At three different times in history, during the Tang, Ming and Qing dynasties, Chinese ceramics have been dramatically and directly influenced by alien cultures introducing, for example, unprecedented angularity, discordant color schemes, an asymmetric quality and an emphasis on surface decoration at the expense of the ceramic medium. These contacts with non-Chinese cultures, usually arising during periods of domestic prosperity and settled political circumstances, gave rise to remarkable disparities of color, shape and taste which were accentuated by the great technical changes in Chinese ceramics.

Under the Tang dynasty the unprecedented luxury of court life attracted envoys from far and wide, particularly during the seventh and early eighth centuries. The glazed stonewares of the period include wide-ranging design elements from diverse Near and Middle Eastern sources. These are visible in molded details, such as the rosettes on funerary figures, or in the non-Chinese character of slender-lobed oval bowls shaped after silver vessels to resemble half fruit, or phoenix-headed ewers with relief-molded designs of equestrian archers firing backwards (the so-called 'Parthian shot' ewers). The overlapping sources are imprecise, but there is no mistaking the cosmopolitan nature of the Tang pottery. Ideas were absorbed and transmitted by the import of Sasanian silver vessels, and the legacy of Hellenistic design, exemplified in subjects engraved on metalwork of foreign origin, recently found in China.

While the traditional elements of relief-molded Chinese ceramic decoration survived to some extent, (for example, hunting scenes and cloud pattern designs), new and distinctively Near or Middle Eastern decorative elements are also evident. Pairs of animals and birds appear repeatedly; there is no clear Chinese precedent for these, nor for the Western half-palmette scrolls which were integrated

THE DESIGN OF THE EWER

Both these ewers have bodies modeled as pears, with broad lower sections and tapering necks. But these two ewers differ in date by half a century, and the proportions subtly reflect the difference. In the earlier ewer, painted in underglaze red, the potter has not yet quite established the proportions that the stretcher and spout require to avoid an unbalanced form. By contrast the proportions of the blue and white ewer are almost entirely harmonious; the body is more slender and the applied handle and spout more sinuous. Moreover the painted design on the blue and white ewer is spacious and confident while the panels on the red ewer specifically recall the linear designs of Islamic metalwork.

Blue and White Ewer *(left)*
Date: early 15th century
Height: 13in (32.5cm)

Underglaze Red Ewer
(above)
Date: mid-14th century
Height: 12in (31cm)

Yingqing Stem Cup
*Date: 13th/early 14th
century*
Height: 3½in (9cm)

*Yingqing is a generic name
for pale-glazed stonewares,
which are only occasionally
as sophisticated as other
early monochrome
stonewares. This crisply
potted cup has an unusually
fine translucent glaze, with
a distinctive blue tint. The
barbed rim, lobed well and
applied bands of beads all
recall features of metal
vessels.*

**Yueyao Green-Glazed
Stoneware Candlestick**
Date: Sui/Tang Dynasty
Height: 6¾in (17cm)

*The grooved bands, crisp
overlapping leaves above the
larger drip-pan and the
general proportions show
that elaborate early
imitations of metal forms
were particularly effective in
high-fired stoneware.*

with native patterns to form elaborate running floral bands. As Rawson has shown ('The ornament on Chinese silver of the Tang Dynasty', *British Museum Occasional Paper No. 40, 1982*), a new corpus of designs evolved which could be easily engraved or punched onto silver vessels, the most luxurious vehicles for carrying elaborate decoration under the early Tang dynasty. Both flat and relief-molded decorations can therefore be found which exhibit Western influence, while the new range of shapes in Tang silver vessels themselves came to influence ceramic production during this extraordinarily creative period, especially in the case of yue yao (pale green glazed stonewares) and ding yao (ivory glazed porcellaneous stonewares).

The Ming period is the second era of cross-cultural creativity. The early Ming emperors, products of a dynasty descended from native Chinese stock, were great internationalists. On land the Ming emperors were not keen to increase their territorial holdings; like their Han predecessors, they were content to systematically organize the enormous bleak areas of Chinese Turkestan, protecting the eastward sections of the camel routes around the Gobi desert. And along these routes, in the late fourteenth and fifteenth centuries, came new types of metal vessels, introducing novel designs and shapes which the Chinese were not slow to paint with the underglaze blue and red ground-mineral pigments to create the magnificent bold and inventive vessels that characterize the era.

The exact prototypes of these new shapes are not known, and it is difficult to be precise about the speed of assimilation because this era saw the development of underglaze painting which revolutionized ceramic design and production. The process was probably a long one, however; during the later Yuan decades (1280-1360) Chinese potters began to exhibit a remarkable technical ability to throw and fire large underglaze decorated porcelain vessels. Paradoxically, the effect of such techniques can only be seen when the earliest of these vessels returned along the trade routes to the West; the Chinese Imperial collections, now largely housed in Taiwan, are notably weak. The Chinese regarded them as coarse, especially the large vessels which are associated with the Near Eastern shrines where they have survived in quantity.

Massive dishes have sharply barbed rims and densely painted, symmetrically arranged patterns, of birds, mythical animals, fish (especially large carp) and a narrow range of flowering foliage. Heavily potted vases and jars sometimes have strangely faceted bodies; |very|occasionally| they are elaborately pierced with two layers to the body, the inner one solid, the outer with reticulated floral trelliswork. Often, in the West, they are fitted with Near Eastern metalwork rims, collars and necks, the porcelain necks having been removed either deliberately or after damage. Pear-shaped ewers have sharp curved stretchers supporting the long serpentine spouts, and equally long upright handles. Later the Moslem communities in China gained a political ascendancy and penetrated the highest ranks of the Imperial Court; the process is directly visible in the ceramics. The Emperor Zhengde lived the life of a dissolute Near Eastern Imperial potentate; his ceramics are often inscribed with edifying Koranic proverbs and improving maxims, either for export or for the use of the Moslem communities.

The seaborne eastward exploration by the Portuguese, Dutch and latterly the English, introduced the third epoch during which native taste was diverted by imported metalwork and alien crafts. This time the process was accompanied by such economic and military aggression that China suffered irreversible social changes. From 1700, for 150 years, the ceramics were, in large part, reduced to a mundane quality, appropriate enough to sell to entrepreneurs who had forced the Chinese nation into widespread opium addiction to aid the European and American balance of payments. The Chinese previously only took silver bullion in payment for goods, but opium from British colonial territory became an excellent substitute for bullion. Nevertheless, during the late seventeenth, and more particularly, the eighteenth centuries, when the English East India Company in effect controlled the Canton entrepot, the Chinese potting tradition adapted to cope with peculiar European demands. Chinese pot-

ters copied Dutch brass candlesticks in Transitional blue and white porcelain, plaster models of Dutch ladies and gentlemen in *famille verte* and English pewter inksets in *famille rose*. Also they transferred armorial bookplate designs onto partially blank dinner services shaped like European silver, and the fanciful designs of the Dutch draughtsman Cornelis Pronk onto water cisterns and trencher salts.

The difference between the exotic creations of these years and the results of the two earlier eras of Western 'inspiration' was that almost all of these were returned to Europe immediately, as commercial commissions. The imperial kilns at Jingdezhen and private kilns working on domestic commissions could produce the most exquisite indigenous Chinese porcelain at the same time as a neighboring kiln could produce the domestic paraphernalia for a London dinner party. The two styles were produced for two distinct markets. Although there is no question that European baroque and rococo provided far less inspiration for Chinese ceramicists than Soghdian silverwork, the canons and terminology were probably assimilated. Post-medieval European technical designs such as clocks, enamels and glassware, and also scientific literature, had been given an amused reception in Chinese official circles when introduced by Jesuit luminaries, but the Manchu emperors never allowed them to overwhelm the native cultural traditions. Indeed, the Manchu emperors were keen to emulate and recreate the domestic wares of the early Ming period, the underglaze blue and monochrome glazed wares.

Blue and White Pilgrim Bottle
Date: Early 15th century
Height: 12¼in (31cm)

The shape is based closely on bottles made in metal used for containing liquids, rather than on the softer, less rounded ones simulating leather which appear in Tang and Liao ceramics. The two handles were used to secure the bottle tightly beside the large panniers of goods either side of the camel's humps. The bottles can be seen in place on the pottery models of camels.

Blue and White Pen Box
Date: Early 16th century
Width: 12½in (32cm)

A precise copy in porcelain of an Islamic 'qalamdan' or pen and ink holder, originally found both in metal and lacquer. The influence of Moslems at the court of the Emperor Zhengde (1506-23) resulted in a new range of porcelain shapes, many with pious Islamic inscriptions.

Johann F. Böttger was the alchemist employed by Augustus the Strong at Meissen at the beginning of the eighteenth century. Using the earlier research of von Tschirnhaus, Böttger developed the first European porcelain in about 1709. He barely lived to see its successful production.

Pair of Böttger Stoneware Candlesticks
Date: c 1711
Height: 7½in (19cm)

A comparison between these candlesticks, modeled by Johann Jacob Irminger, and an almost contemporary silver pair (right) shows *clearly how little the Meissen examples had departed from their metalwork forerunners. The form of this silver pair, with minor variations, had wide currency in Germany at the time. The similarity to metalwork is emphasized by the polished areas.*

The Influence of the Silversmith on European Porcelain

*The discovery of porcelain in Europe created a need for
a whole new range of forms. Initially these were supplied by the silversmith; the
development of a compromise, between shapes designed for metal
and those for the new material, took some years.*

The discovery of porcelain in Europe, although it solved a mystery, also posed a great problem for the manufacturers. What form were their wares to take and where were they to turn for ideas? Many of the new porcelain wares were required to hold hot liquids such as tea, coffee and chocolate, which were all relatively new and fashionable beverages. This had not been within the compass of the faience makers as their wares could not hold almost boiling liquid. Therefore a whole new range of pieces had to be designed in the new material.

Many potteries and porcelain manufactories drew on ideas imported from the Far East. At Meissen the Far Eastern influence can be seen in the shapes of saucers and tea and coffee cups. Slop-bowls, which are only larger versions of the tea-bowl, and some sugar bowls also show clear Chinese influence; the court silversmith, Johann Irminger was called on to supply designs for the remainder of the factory's range of wares. It is therefore not surprising that much of the early products of the factory, both in stoneware and porcelain, have a heavy debt to the world of metalwork. This influence was to dictate the forms of many pieces and, through their forms, the

Pair of Meissen Armorial Altar Candlesticks
Height: 18in (45.5cm)

These were part of an altar garniture ordered by Augustus III of Saxony for his mother-in-law, the Empress Dowager of Austria. Since such things had previously only been produced in brass, copper or silver, the Meissen factory had perforce to rely on a basically metal model. The decoration, which is restricted to gilding, is reminiscent of the engraved ornament that might be found on a metal piece.

Meissen Armorial Candlestick
Date: 1738-1740
Height: 8in (20cm)

This candlestick belongs to the great Swan Service modeled by Johann Joachim Kändler for Heinrich Graf V. Brühl. The Swan Service was the first really huge porcelain service to be produced in any European factory, and it set the standard for the later products of Sèvres and elsewhere. Artistically too it represents a watershed – the shapes and designs of the wares not simply borrowed from the silversmith, but instead created with porcelain in mind. Although a debt to a French silver original is quite evident in this piece, the end result is definitely a totally resolved piece of porcelain. No longer is it a silver design masquerading as a product of the porcelain manufacturer's skill.

nature of the decoration of the wares.

The candlestick is a classic instance of this — the example in Böttger stoneware is only shortly removed from its silver prototype; its decoration is to all intents the same as would appear on a silver example, the only significant difference being the variations of surface that were achieved by polishing the stoneware. As stoneware gave way to porcelain the candlestick did not significantly change. Its many small surfaces afforded little opportunity for the decorator to display his art, and so the basic form remained that of a piece of metalwork.

Stoneware and porcelain table wares suffered a different fate. The metal beaker was used throughout aristocratic Europe for the consumption of wine and spirits. Its surface was generally plain, and all molded ornament was concentrated on the foot, which was raised off the ground on an ornamented rim to prevent the cold metal from marking surfaces with condensation. In the porcelain version the original silver shape was slavishly copied to the extent of reproducing the fine molded detail under the foot, a wholly gratuitous feature. Where it differs from the candlestick is that the remaining flat surface offered a large, uninterrupted and continuous area for the decorator to display his skills. This was also a conspicuous feature of all the teawares of the period. The molded decoration was confined to handles, spouts and finials, therefore producing extensive flat surfaces for very elaborate and brightly colored decoration.

The shape of the teapot, coffee pot and slop bowl was generally rounded in the true potter's tradition. However the tea-caddy and the earliest forms of the sugar box were rectilinear in construction, and are further examples of a direct translation of a metal design into stoneware, and then porcelain. Rectangular objects are most ill suited to the potter's art as their flat sides tend to warp in the firing and the angles tend to split. The earliest rectangular tea-caddies even had sliding lids copied from their silver equivalents.

Metalwork shapes dominated the design of porcelain and stoneware pieces at Meissen until the 1730s; only then, when the modelers, Kändler and Eberlein, were working on the Swan Service, did coherent shapes and decoration evolve which were totally expressive of the medium for which they were conceived.

Meissen Oblong Octagonal Sugar Box and Cover
Date: c 1724
Height: 4in (10cm)

The sugar basins at Meissen, both in stoneware and porcelain, were initially of this shape, which was so closely based on a metal prototype that it proved very inconvenient to decorate. As a result, it was eventually replaced by the round covered shape that has survived to this day.

Meissen Beaker and Cover
Date: 1723
Height: 6in (15cm)

Modeled for the Meissen factory by Irminger, this beaker and cover bear further witness to the immense debt of Meissen forms to silver. The relief elements, the stiff leaves and tassels and the baluster finial have made little or no concession to the new medium in which they have been expressed.

Böttger Red Stonewear Tea-Caddy
Date: 1710-1715
Height: 5in (12.5cm)

The box shape of this tea-caddy clearly reveals its silver origin. The engraved decoration is another feature that is usually associated with the work of the silversmith rather than that of the potter. This particular form was to survive until at least 1740 although it was to acquire a short neck and a shallow cylindrical cover.

Chelsea Goat and Bee Jug
Date: 1745-49 (triangle period)
Height: 4¼in (10.6cm)

Goat and bee jugs are among the earliest English porcelains — a number of examples have the word 'Chelsea' and the date 1745 incised in the base. The jugs are believed to have been designed by Nicholas Sprimont. The fine naturalistic modeling and glassy white paste are characteristic of the earliest Chelsea porcelain, as is the sensitivity and restraint of the enameling. The delight that the early producers of porcelain took in the beautiful and novel material itself is shown by the large areas of the body left undecorated.

The bee, formed separately, was added to the unfired jug before glazing.

The enamels were painted onto the glazed and fired surface and fired on in a muffle kiln. The enamels tend to sink into the glassy glaze to give a soft effect while in hard-paste porcelain they tend to sit on the surface of the glaze.

Silver Shape in English Porcelain

The birth of English porcelain is closely connected to the work of silversmiths and this is clearly evident in the form of the pieces.

The history of early English porcelain is intimately connected with that of silver. Indeed some of the most illustrious of the early porcelain entrepreneurs were silversmiths. In the middle of the eighteenth century porcelain began to fulfill many of the functions for which silver was being used, and grew to be in direct competition with it. At first porcelain tea and table wares were just copies of, or at least influenced by, the silver originals, but later in the neo-classical period the direction of influence is less easy to trace.

Nicholas Sprimont, who became the proprietor of the Chelsea factory, was born in 1716 in Liège where his father was a silversmith. The latter was probably a French Huguenot who had moved north to escape religious persecution. Sprimont came to London and registered as a silversmith in 1742. In the same year Thomas Briand, another Huguenot silversmith, read a paper on the manufacture of porcelain to the Royal Society and displayed a fine white ware which he claimed was as good as Chinese porcelain. These two young silversmiths, both enthralled by the idea of making porcelain, approached Charles Gouyn, a prosperous Huguenot silversmith, to fund the venture. The Chelsea factory was thus formed by men whose manufacturing experience was in silver, so it is not surprising that the early years at Chelsea were dominated by wares strongly influenced by silver forms. Briand and Gouyn both left the Chelsea enterprise in its early years and Nicholas Sprimont became the proprietor.

Nicholas Sprimont silver is very rare — only a handful of pieces are recorded. A few pieces were made as late as 1747, two years after the founding of the Chelsea factory which was in production by 1745. A number of 'Goat and bee' jugs, dated 1745, still exist and were almost certainly designed by Sprimont, although most of the existing silver prototypes have proved to be fakes. There is also a remarkable silver centerpiece by Sprimont in the Victoria and Albert Museum, which incorporates goats into the design in a very similar way.

Sprimont's work was predominantly in the rococo style and he was fond of using realistic forms from nature, such as those seen in the crayfish and shell salts mounted on a base of naturalistic rocks and shells shown below. There exists two silver prototypes of these in the Royal Collection at Windsor Castle, England. Many tea wares of the triangle period at Chelsea (1745-1749), were formed in relief from acanthus leaf and tea plant patterns which echo

Large Silver Centerpiece
Date: 1747-48

this large centerpiece is one of the very few surviving pieces of Nicholas Sprimont silver. The goats supporting the basket are similar to those on the Goat and Bee jug (opposite), which tends to confirm the authorship of the jug.

Pair of Chelsea Crayfish Salts
Date: 1745-49
Width: 4½in (11.5cm)

This pair of silver prototypes form part of a service made for Frederick Prince of Wales. The very naturalistic modeling and use of rock work and shells is typical of the rococo style. The shape owes nothing to the ceramic tradition.

THE STYLE OF THE TEAPOT

The growth of tea drinking as a custom opened a large market for teawares; silver competed with porcelain for teapots, milk jugs and sugar-bowls, but porcelain monopolized the production of tea-bowls and saucers. Teapots of beauty and elegance were required as tea drinking was a social habit cultivated by the rich and civilized. Although the overall shape of a teapot is a Chinese innovation, the form was soon adopted into the repertory of English craftsmen who created many different styles in both ceramics and silver.

Chelsea Fable Decorated Teapot and Cover (top)
Date: c 1752 (red anchor)
Width: 7¼in (18.5cm)

This fine teapot, decorated by Jefferyes Hamett O'Neale, the greatest of early Chelsea decorators, is molded with strawberry leaves, buds and flowers reminiscent of silverwork in the early rococo style.

Chelsea Teapot and Cover (middle)
Date: c 1765 (gold anchor)

This opulent teapot reflects the taste for richly decorated wares, often inspired by Sèvres porcelain which became fashionable in the gold anchor period (1758-69). The extravagant form of the pierced spout and handle and the dense decoration are a far cry from the earlier restraint when areas of porcelain were left undecorated. The design, however, still retains a certain elegance.

Coalport Ornithological Teapot and Cover (bottom)
Date: c 1805

The clean elegance of this neoclassical teapot came as a reaction to the excesses of the rococo. Similar shapes can be found in silver.

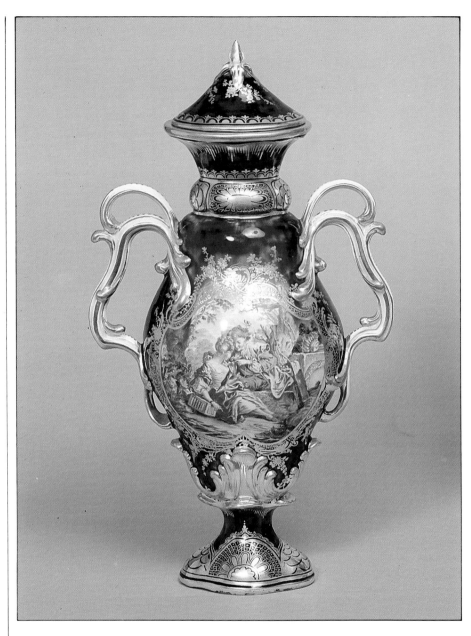

Chelsea Vase
Date: 1765 (gold anchor)
Height: 12¼in (31cm)

One of a garniture of three vases decorated by John Donaldson, this vase is typical of the outrageous excess of the high rococo at Chelsea. Inspired by increasingly lavish decoration at Sèvres, Chelsea sought to emulate it, sometimes with dubious results. The applied molding around the base and the eccentric convoluted handles owe nothing to the potter's craft and have more in common with contemporary silverwork. The proportions of this vase are hardly worthy of the quality of decoration. Before the Second World War vases of this type were considered among the greatest works of Chelsea and greatly sought after; taste has changed and the earlier, simpler wares are now generally preferred.

closely the *repoussé* work then popular on silverware.

Between the years 1750 and 1755, shapes that were more convenient for potters were increasingly adopted at Chelsea, many of them derived from Japan. These new ceramic shapes tended not to have relief decoration and were either faceted or shapes of circular cross-section that could be thrown on a wheel. However silver shapes were still a strong influence throughout the red anchor period (1752-58), as can be seen from the teapot decorated with fable subjects by Jeffreyes Hammett O'Neale, and in plates with shell-molded borders decorated by the same artist. Silver forms continued into the gold anchor period (1758-69) and are seen in the rococo extravanganzas, such as the ornate garniture of vases painted by Donaldson.

An awareness during the eighteenth century of the influence of silver forms is shown in the catalogue of Chelsea porcelain sold by Ford in 1755 in which 38 lots are described as being 'of silver shape'. These shapes formed an important part of the repertory of the other English porcelain factories, although they did not dominate the wares to the same extent as they had dominated early Chelsea porcelain. Andrew Planche of Derby was a goldsmith and Samuel Bradley, a partner at Worcester in 1751, was a silversmith. Early sauceboats, particularly from Bow and Worcester, frequently show a strong silver influence. The workforce of these factories was mainly drawn from the existing delft and saltglaze potteries which had themselves been influenced to some extent by silver and other metal forms.

Towards the end of the eighteenth and into the early nineteenth century the neoclassical style came to dominate both porcelain and silver designs. Many of the shapes lent themselves equally well to both mediums, as can be seen in the clean lines of the teapot (opposite) from Coalport and similar productions of other factories of that period.

7
The Revival of Craft Pottery

Towards the end of the nineteenth century certain artists and thinkers in Britain began to speak out against what they considered to be the decadent taste of the day. John Ruskin, and in particular William Morris, whose words were to have far reaching repercussions, called for a reappraisal of the arts within the whole of society.

Some artists responded directly to this plea. William de Morgan, the potter, inspired by Persian ceramics, designed tiles and pots which showed that he adhered to the view Morris advocated. Others working in different materials, notably some furniture makers and weavers, tried to get back to earlier traditions. This radical thinking did bear fruit and, by the end of the nineteenth century, the Arts and Crafts Movement had emerged in Britain and Art Nouveau was an international art style.

Within the pottery industry of the day there were those who sought to raise standards and turn away from the over-embellishment of the high Victorian era. The outcome of this was 'art-ware', some made by newly created departments within the factory system itself, others by the smaller art-studios that arose in response to the demands of a clientele stimulated by the Arts and Crafts Movement. A wide range of work resulted and, although much more restraint was exercised, many art-ware pieces were highly decorated. One example of this style is the colored luster ware, made for the Pilkington factory by Forsyth and Mycock.

The monochrome tradition, inspired by Chinese wares, also found favor with many art-potters at the start of the twentieth century. Bernard Moore's high-fired monochrome glazes, particularly the flambés, stand out in this exacting genre, Reginald Wells also did notable work with simple glazes while the Martin Brothers, working in saltglazed stoneware, produced a succession of interesting pieces ranging from simple, organically-inspired forms to bizarre bird and animal pots with grotesque modeling All of these potters worked within the industrial limits of the age; this meant that they used refined clays and materials together with the glaze technology and forming methods provided by industrial expertize.

More relevant still when considering the main changes which occurred in the years which followed, was the fact that these potters were designers who were not necessarily the makers of the pots and were

Black Raku Tea-Bowl
Date: Late 17th century
Diameter: 4½in (11.5cm)

This Raku tea-bowl, with mixed black and brown glaze, is an excellent example of the style originally developed by Chojiro. The glaze, rich in iron and manganese, had a tendency to change from black to reddish-brown if not cooled quickly, and the effect has been used here to produce an attractive chestnut-colored blush. A single gold lacquer repair has been strengthened with two small rivets, one gold and one silver, and adds greatly to the charm of this ware.

Crackle-Glazed Square Vase *(right)*
Date: 1735-1795 (Qianlong period)
Height: 11½in (29.5cm)

This eighteenth century monochrome decoration, consciously imitating the famed Guanyo glaze of the Song dynasty, is treasured above all other palettes by Chinese scholar-conoisseurs.

Song Oviform Jar
Date: 960-1130 (Northern Song)
Height: 8¼in (21cm)

This dark brown glazed jar (below) shows the effect obtained by firing a plain glaze very thinly on the vertical ribs.

Stoneware Vase
by Bernard Leach
Date: c 1959
Height: 14½in (36.5cm)

This example of Leach's mature work (right) shows the fine effect of the Japanese temmoku dark brown and rust glaze, together with the combined influence of the Song wares and Japanese decoration on Leach's art.

not therefore responsible for the complete process from clay to fired article. The execution was left to artisans whose job it was to interpret the designs. Even the Martin Brothers who, quite rightly, have been called the first of Britain's studio-potters, worked by division of labor — one brother doing the throwing, two other brothers handling the modeling and glazing, and the fourth running the business.

Any real change in this way of working could only come from a new source of inspiration, from someone outside the industrialized system. Such a person was Bernard Leach who, ironically, knew of William Morris through the Japanese philosopher Yanagi. Leach's work fitted admirably into certain aspects of the Arts and Crafts Movement, especially the quietist and more anonymous-seeking ideals of those craftsmen. Leach had been introduced to pottery through a now famous garden-party in Japan where he first painted on pots that were being prepared for a raku firing. These wares were traditionally associated with the tea-ceremony which played such a vital part in Japanese arts. The choice of simple pieces for the ritual of tea drinking was much to Leach's liking and from this time onward he set about learning the potter's art from his Japanese teacher, Kenzan. In 1920 Leach returned to England from Japan to set up a studio at St Ives in Cornwall, near to the local materials he needed for his work. With him was the young Japanese potter, Shoji Hamada, and within a year or two a small band of potter pupils had gathered at the Leach pottery. One of these, Michael Cardew, had been taught to throw pots by the country potter, Fishley Holland. Through this association he became interested in the preindustrial tradition of English pottery — the lead-glazed, slip-decorated earthenware. In the 1920s he and Leach rediscovered this style and, for a brief time, between the two world wars, Cardew revived the galena-glazed slipware at his pottery at Winchcombe in Gloucestershire.

Much has been written about Bernard Leach's philosophy and the ideals of the group of potters who worked closely with him. His book, *A Potter's Book*, written at Dartington in 1939, explains his belief in the potter as a craftsman, concerned with every aspect of making, from the selection and digging of clays to the final firing of the pots in kilns designed and made with his own hands. Many potters today work in the way he propounded, producing simple functional pots by traditional methods.

However, Leach also believed that some potters could be artists and in this he was in accord with several other artist-potters working in Britain and Europe after the First World War. The most influential of these in this country was William Staite Murray who, in 1925, became head of the ceramics department at the Royal College of Art in London. Murray believed that pots could be every bit as expressive as painting or sculpture and that the potter's art was in fact a fine art. From his department, during the 1930s, came a number of students who, after the Second World War, became key figures in the educational revival of ceramics in Britain. Educational reform which slowly evolved throughout the first half of the century gathered pace after the war and any appraisal of the revival of studio-pottery must take account of the work of the Colleges of Art in Great Britain from this time onwards.

Many notable potters have influenced the course of events by the example of their work, or directly through their teaching in the schools of art. Of these, two stand out because of the effect they have had on the younger potters working today. They are Lucie Rie and Hans Coper. Unlike Leach who aspired to marry certain Far Eastern traditions with the medieval English style, or Cardew who believed uncompromisingly in pottery as a functional art, Lucie Rie and Hans Coper looked to different sources of inspiration for their work. In the case of Lucie Rie, who trained in pre-war Austria, it was classical Greek and Roman pottery while Coper, undoubtedly the most original potter of his time, turned to more ancient mediterranean cultures and looked to contemporary sculpture as a source for his monumental work. The future may show that the revival of studio pottery needs the wide base that these many varied potters have provided if it is to continue to grow.

Symmetrical Pot
Date: 1974
Height: 13½in (34cm)

During the last stage of his career, in Somerset, Coper made many pots with symmetrical paired dints in their sides, effectively turning radial symmetry of the wheel into the bi-symmetry of many living creatures, including man.

White Glazed Stemcup
(above)
Date: 1403-1424
Diameter: 6in (15cm)

White Glazed Stemcup
(right)
Date:Late 14th/early 15th century
Diameter: 5½in (14cm)

These two stemcups are deliberately shown from different angles to accentuate the differences in proportion which are easily missed. They are indeed closely similar. Both were made using molds as well as the potter's wheel; the rough unglazed shapes were left to dry to a leather-hardness, at which point they could be shaved with a potter's knife until they became almost paperthin. The cylindrical stems, made separately, were similarly shaved, and then luted to the base of the bowls with a dash of liquid slip. Still a matt clay color, these raw vessels were dipped into clear glaze flux and fired to fuse the glaze and body. Some white stemcups have a hidden design barely engraved in the body of the bowl, or a reign mark at the centre of the interior. Both of these are filled with glaze so that the surface appears to be completely smooth. White wares of this kind are not pieces for a western museum showcase, to be admired for the size, the decorative quality and bold colors. They are created and carefully weighted for handling by a connoisseur, the carved 'an hua' (secret decoration) being the highlight.

The Monochrome Tradition

*Many connoisseurs are of the opinion that no product of the
potter's art more closely approaches their ideal than a well-potted functional vessel,
covered in a fine glaze, suffused with a single mineral color.*

No nation of potters has taken the production of ceramic forms, decorated with a single-color glaze, to a more refined level than the Chinese. Western potters traditionally regard a vessel's biscuit or glazed surface as a canvas, an area to be decorated cosmetically. However, a few twentieth century studio potters have been directly influenced by the Orient. Chinese and Japanese connoisseurs have always seen virtue in the plain surface and have always taken pleasure in the texture and form of the vessel, and the hue of the integral glaze. It is an approach and a taste very remote from that of the Europeans. Few early monochromes in the Chinese style have ever come to Europe, apart from early freaks like the Fonthill-Gagnieres yingqing ewer which made an immensely tortuous journey along the Silk routes, as a gift to Near Eastern courts during the medieval period. The only exception is the early celadon-glazed wares which traveled to the Near East and Egypt on both overland and sea routes in the early medieval period; especially the massively potted barbed-rim dishes, yanyan vases and fluted deep bowls of the Yuan and Ming periods.

There is a widely-held belief that the finest single-color wares ever produced in China (or anywhere for that matter) were the glazed stonewares and early porcelains of the Northern and Southern Song dynasty, and particularly of the former, before 1127. Kiln sites, widely scattered, produced a great variety of bodies and glazes. The bodies were normally fired black, brown, oatmeal-colored or gray. The glaze hues were exceptionally diverse, often obtained from different ground metallic oxide inclusions — the rich lavender, purple and green of jun, the pale ivory of ding, the faint blue of yingqing (known to earlier collectors as qingbai), the streaky or mottled rust and 'chocolate' glaze effects on Jian, Jizhou and Henan wares. Only a few of these were further embellished with overglaze decoration, and then it was only rarely painted in enamels. More often it has a darker oxide spray of flowers, a leaf-shaped paper cut-out, burnt black into the surface. Frequently the biscuit surface was decorated before glazing and a molded or carved design was added when the unfired vessel had dried to leather-hard in the sun and would not warp if pressed or incised. Designs were usually symmetrically ordered — scrolls of leafy lotus and peony blossoms, dragons coiled into a roundel, a curling single spray of flowerheads, sketchily outlined like a Chinese character, as though by a calligrapher, a

pair of fish lazily swimming, forming an oval medallion, emblematic of marital bliss. The translucent but faintly tinted glazes enhance the pattern, pooling in the deeper recesses of the carved decoration, and firing richer or darker the deeper the recess. The plain shapes and natural ceramic forms focus attention, but unlike western equivalents they are integral to the vessel, not mere vehicles for the pattern.

Superb as these wares are, they do not provide a contrast with other ceramics of the period, as the Ming monochromes do. The Song potters may, latterly, have experimented with the two underglaze pigments — cobalt-blue and copper-red — which their successors learnt to handle spectacularly under the Yuan and early Ming. But there is little evidence at this early date of the precious, effete quality that gives a homogeneous character to the monochrome wares of the Ming and Qing dynasty; a character of deliberate and expert skill, unlike anything the West has ever produced. The white stemcup illustrated (opposite) exemplifies this; an exceptional command of throwing has produced a vessel perfectly balanced and modeled, utilitarian yet of classic refinement. A rich, lustrous, clear glaze enhances the pure white porcelain body, precisely knife-pared to such thinness that the vessel feels as if it is formed of glaze alone.

The yellow glazed wares of the fifteenth and early sixteenth century are in the same style. Yellow was the imperial color, but as a glaze on porcelain, it was extremely hard to control in the kiln. The large numbers of yellow monochrome ('Imperial Yellow') saucer dishes that survive from the reigns of Chenghua (1465-1487), Hongxi (1488-1505) and Zhengde (1506-1521) suggest considerable efforts were made to master the technique, and the yellow glaze was also applied over the magnificent blue and white wares during the century, to give a spectacular color contrast. However the phase was shortlived. The later Ming potters preferred darker monochromes — aubergine, iron-red, violet blue — but above all they enjoyed combinations of enamels and glaze washes, as in the Fahua wares of the sixteenth century and the later bold, elaborate underglaze blue and overenameled wares of the Wanli period (1573-1619).

The Qing emperors, the Manchu usurpers from the north who supplanted the native Ming dynasty, enjoyed a classic taste for monochromes. Their new

Dingyao Hexafoil Saucer-dish *(right)*
Date: AD 960-1130
Diameter: 9½in (24cm)

The slightly indented rim frames two unrelated, but perfectly balanced designs, shallowly incised in the unglazed body. A running band of peony flowers and leafy foliage surrounds the border; a baby dragon is sinuously coiled in the interior. The metal strip around the rim is a common feature of early monochromes, particularly during the Song period. Many vessels have an unglazed band which was intended to be fitted with a collar of copper, silver or (sometimes) gold. The technique seems to have arisen because of the smallness of many foot-rims. One purpose of the foot-rim was to keep the glazed surfaces clear of the floor when being fired in a kiln, otherwise dirt would adhere to the fusing surface. When the foot-rim was particularly short, it was probably easier to fire the vessel upside down on its rim. A decorative metal collar could then be fitted, which would provide a protection for the very thin crisp rim.

Three 'Chrysanthemum' Saucer-Dishes
Date: 18th century
Diameter: all approx 6in (15cm)

The eighteenth century saw the introduction of brilliant new glazes including these three: ruby-red, rust-brown and lime-green.

technical potting abilities, in conjunction with the advice of Jesuits based at the Chinese Court on new ways of chemically creating enamel colors, gave a particularly rich and luscious quality. But the monochrome revival of the very late seventeenth and eighteenth century coincided with an archaizing phase under the Manchus — a phase of literary revival and a new interest in the early excavated bronzes readily found in the Imperial Chinese collections at Beijing. Many single-color glazes therefore appear on Qing dynasty vessels, influenced by earlier metalwork. These were often angular and far removed from the simple lines of the Song and early Ming ceramics.

For the first time however, one class of contemporary monochromes found favor in Europe and was exported there in large quantities. Shipping lists indicate a strong western market for the white porcelain wares of Dehua in Fujian province on the southeast coast, especially for the figure models. Vessels are much less commonly mentioned. The Buddhist Goddess of Mercy, Guanyin, appears early in European inventories. She is modeled carrying a child, and bears an uncanny resemblance to the Madonna, causing reflection on how early Portuguese Catholic images traveled inland from Fujian ports. Other exported models include animals, especially dogs, cockerels and Buddhistic lions or 'Dogs of Fo' formed as joss stick holders. Some were obviously inspired by specifically European originals — Dutch topers on barrels, a European family group at table — even pulpits. These white figures were only occasionally embellished with precious metal mounts, the earlier treatment for treasured and rare Chinese porcelain in Europe. This was a little surprising, because by this time the French (Parisian)

Peach-Bloom Glazed Brush-Washer *(below)*
Date: 1662-1722 (Kangxi)
Diameter: 5in (12.5cm)

One of the eight prescribed shapes for containers used by a scholar at his writing desk, this beehive brush-washer is incised with three roundels of dragons in archaistic taste, visible under a speckled copper glaze (see detail bottom). Frequently fired imprecisely, the color *should appear as rich pink, but can vary widely, sometimes firing a bright apple-green. The pink color results from firing a glaze containing ground copper oxide in a reducing atmosphere. It is a shade which occurs only on small vessels.*

Longquan Celadon-Glazed Vase and Cover
Date: c 1300
Height: 9½in (24cm)

This monochrome is notable for the rich, almost turquoise glaze. Stoneware of this quality and richness were recovered in the 1970s from a vessel which sank off the coast of Korea in the early fourteenth century.

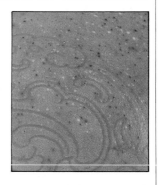

orfevriers and marchand-merciers had discovered a strong market for plain Chinese monochromes, lavishly mounted in ormolu, a western refinement which complemented the luxurious ormolu-mounted European furniture. The merchants took whatever plain Chinese porcelain they could find, to judge from the examples extant. It was the contrast between plain-colored porcelain and rich, elaborately-chased ormolu which mattered rather than the date, quality or origin of the porcelain.

The monochrome tradition has given rise to the most consistently satisfactory and sophisticated range of Chinese ceramics. The glazes are normally of fine and even quality. Even when accidentally misfired, the aesthetic approach is such that the result can be appreciated as a novel version of a regular glaze. Peachbloom wares of the Kangxi period (1662-1722), the 'eight prescribed shapes' made for the scholar's desk, were preserved even when the copper glaze underfired to a mottled apple green, rather than a rich, even peachy pink. The body of these wares is generally fine, as fine as any molded or thrown in that particular era. It was crisply cut with a knife, shaved to an exceptional thinness, carefully fired to avoid distortion or warping (though the vessels for handling are rarely big enough to distort in firing). The incised decoration under the early dynasties was fresh and immediate. During the Ming and Qing it was delicate and much more precisely controlled (in the latter case, often drawn from fully-finished archaistic designs). Unlike any other ceramics potted by the Chinese, appreciation of the best monochromes demands the concentration of a scholar, and requires the experience, the judgement and the unerring eye of a connoisseur.

Korean Ido Bowl *(left)*
Date: *c 1550-1600*
Height: *5½in (14cm)*

Of all imported pieces the most valued by the Japanese were the Ido bowls, and some teamasters preferred them even to Raku ware. Many Korean bowls were the work of peasant potters and were used for eating rice as well as for drinking tea. The Koreans cared little for them, preferring the beautiful Koryo celadons which were made for the court and the upper classes. Now scarce in their country of origin, many were brought to Japan by Hideyoshi's armies at the end of the sixteenth century. The name Ido may have originated from a person who collected them, or from a place called Ido near Keisonando in Korea.

Raku Mizusashi *(water jar) (middle)*
Date: *18th/19th century*
Diameter: *5¾in (14.5cm)*

This mizusashi (water jar) is of an unusual ocher color. It was used to contain clean water for refilling the kettle and rinsing the tea-bowl.

Black Ichinyu Raku Tea-bowl *(right)*
Date: *c 1640-1696*
Height: *4in (10cm)*

This tea-bowl is attributed to Raku IV, generally known as Ichinyu, the name he adopted on becoming a priest in 1691. He died in 1696, aged 59, and is said to have made pottery at the Baiko temple at Yamada near Kyoto. This bowl shows the vermilion glazing over black; the glazing was Raku IV's speciality and was especially beautiful when wet.

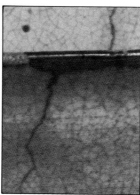

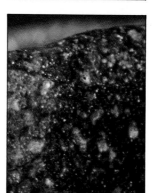

Detail of Korean Ido bowl *This detail shows the several small gold lacquer repairs where the glaze has chipped at the rim. This type of bowl was copied at the Hagi kiln in western Japan, founded by Korean potters.*

Detail of Ichinyu Raku Tea-bowl *This illustration shows the strongly textured body produced by mixing in pulverised burnt clay or 'grog', known in Japan as shamotto.*

The Influence of the Tea Ceremony on the Japanese Potter

The complex Japanese tea ceremony created an appreciation for a range of unsophisticated ceramics with simple yet strong shapes.

Tea, which is native to Southern China, was used by the Taoists in the hope of achieving immortality, and by the Buddhists to prevent drowsiness during meditation. The Chinese monks of the Ch'an sect of Buddhism, precursors of Zen, developed the practice of a formal gathering before an image of Bodhidharma at which they drank tea from a single bowl. From this simple ritual was derived Cho-no-yu, the Japanese Tea Ceremony, for the spread of Zen philosophy carried the tea ritual of Song China to Japan. Although tea was known in Japan before the Kamakura era (1185-1338), its extensive propagation there is usually ascribed to the Zen teacher Eisai (1141-1215).

Pottery also has an ancient history in Japan, and probably reflects the national character more truly than porcelain, which was, for the most part, made and decorated in a style which would make it attractive to foreigners. Although excavated fragments suggest that Japanese ceramic history may have begun as early as 2000 BC, Japanese ceramic art, as we know it today, was established early in the thirteenth century, at Seto in Owari province.

According to legend, the potter Kato Shirozaemon, also known as Toshiro, settled there after a visit to China, and found suitable clay for making a Chinese-style brown-glazed ware. Seto became the pottery center of Japan, and Toshiro was described as the 'father of pottery'. Although the practice of glazing earthenware can be traced to the eighth century, it was Toshiro who made it into a fine art. His few remaining pieces, or rather those attributed to him — mostly tea jars — are highly prized as 'Old Seto', and the name Setomono, 'things from Seto', became a generic term for pottery throughout eastern Japan.

However Seto was not the only center where Japanese pottery developed. During the Kamakura period (1185-1333) there were six active ceramic-producing areas in Japan, known as the 'Six old kilns'. They were Seto (which can claim to be the most ancient), Tokoname, Shigaraki, Tamba, Bizen and Echizen. Early productions at Seto developed under the strong influence of porcelain of the Chinese Southern Song and Yuan dynasties, but the later development of Japanese pottery owes a great debt to the Koreans. The powerful Daimyo, who took part in Toyotomi Hideyoshi's Korean invasions at the end of the sixteenth century, brought so many potters back to strengthen their local pottery industries that the campaigns have been christened 'The Pottery

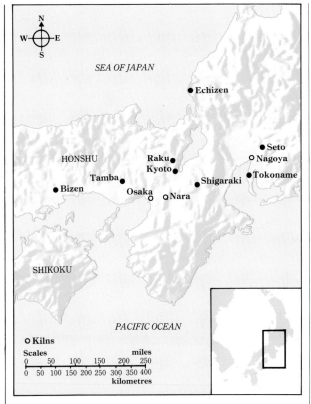

Japanese Tea Company *This illustration shows a group of women taking part in a Japanese tea ceremony (cha-no-yu) – a complex ceremony, orchestrated by a highly skilled tea master.*

The map shows the kilns active in Japan during the Kamakura period (118-133).

Wars'. China however, through the tea ceremony, was to exert a great influence on Japanese pottery styles. By the fifteenth century the ceremony had become an independent secular performance, patronized by the Ashikaga Shogun Yoshimasa and the Kyoto aristocracy; their aesthetic advisers were Zen monks from the Kyoto monasteries, men of scholarship and taste such as Murata Juko (1422-1502).

Juko recommended this form of tea-drinking, with its spirit of harmony and tranquillity, as a way in which Yoshimasa might use his Chinese treasures — the precious celadons, Temmoku wares and Song dynasty paintings. Later tea masters, notably Takeno Jo-o (1502-1555) and Sen no Rikyu (1521-1591), emphasized gentleness of spirit and the Zen ideal of a simple, frugal life. It was such men who set the standards of the tea ceremony by favoring the unpretentious items of daily life, finding in them a profound, unassuming and tranquil feeling, defined in Japanese by the word 'wabi'.

At first, tea-bowls and other utensils were selected from the everyday products of Japanese rural kilns, but by Rikyu's time it became customary for tea masters to commission them from selected artisans. Their individual qualities were used to demonstrate the master's aesthetic ideas, and outstanding pieces became known as the 'meibutsu' or 'objects of fame', often with their own names, histories and provenances.

The belief that Japanese ceramics could be as fine as the Chinese, and that beauty might be found in simple, even imperfect objects, was a revolutionary one, for ever since the Yayoi period (400BC-AD100) Japanese pottery had developed along lines set by China and Korea. Interest in these wares grew as the tea ceremony became increasingly personal and profound under the influence of successive tea masters and developed in the Japanese people an appreciation of honest and straightforward pottery that has made their ceramic tradition world famous.

One of the best examples of the deliberately simple or 'aesthetic' style created by a tea master is Raku ware, named after the sixteenth century potter Chojiro Raku who, under Rikyu's direction, established the original Raku kiln in Kyoto for the express purpose of making tea bowls. Raku bowls, low-fired and soft-bodied with a lead glaze, are often considered the best suited of all to the requirements of the tea ceremony, and were later produced at a number of kilns throughout Japan. They are handformed, and made either by coil-building or by turning up and pinching into shape a circular slab of clay, without the use of a wheel.

Raku tea bowls must be thick-walled so that they can be held comfortably. The body of the ware is formed from a high-temperature clay with about 25 percent of pulverized burnt clay added; this enables them to withstand the sudden changes of temperature to which all Raku ware is subjected during manufacture. The glazes are applied thickly,

Red Raku Tea-Bowl
Date: Early 17th century
Diameter: 4¾in (12cm)

This red Raku tea-bowl, in the style of Honami Koetsu, is covered with a pinkish-gray, heavily-pitted and crackled glaze; it has several gold lacquer repairs known as naoshi.

Shidoro Tea Container
(right)
Date: c 1568-1614
Height: 10in (26cm)

Shidoro is a variety of stoneware that closely resembles Seto ware, although the body is usually a darker grey and the pieces tend to be heavier and thicker. This Shidoro tea container (chatsubo) has a streaked brown glaze.

Black Lacquer Container *(left)*
Date: 19th century
Height: 2¾in (7cm)

This black lacquer container *(Natsume)* is decorated with a stylized chrysanthemum in gold lacquer. Natsume are used for usucha or thin tea (powdered tea). The name derives from the shape which resembles the natsume or jujube berry.

Ceramic Tea Container *(middle)*
Date: Probably 18th century
Height: 2¼in (5.8cm)

This tea container *(cha-ire)* is Zeze or Seto ware; it is used for koicha, or thick tea, and has a turned ivory lid.

Takatori Jar *(right)*
Date: 17th century
Diameter: 5½in (14cm)

This jar is of low baluster shape, decorated with dark brown splashes on a red ocher glaze. The Takatori kilns were established in 1600 under the direction of a Korean potter and were active until the Meiji period (1868-1912).

sometimes in several coats, and fired in a muffle in the form of a cylindrical fireclay sagger. Crazing, an important feature of the Raku glaze, is obtained by removing the bowl from the kiln with tongs and immersing it in lukewarm water; certain tea masters considered that bowls with an uncrazed glaze produced a harsh sound when the powdered tea was beaten in them with a bamboo whisk, disturbing the tranquil atmosphere of the tea room.

Free use is made of a bamboo knife *(takebera)* or a metal trimming tool *(kanna)* in the final shaping of Raku tea-bowls, and the marks made by these simple instruments are prized because the individuality of the maker is said to be easily understood through them. Where the coil-building method is used, a slight suggestion of the coils is usually left to form a part of the decorative effect. The bowls are never perfectly round, for they must fit comfortably into the hands, and the rims, which instead of flaring out bend inwards very slightly, are made with an undulating curve so that they feel pleasant and yielding to the mouth.

The thick and lustrous lead-oxide glazes of Raku produce simple colors of black, brown, green and white, but the wares are usually divided into black Raku *(kuroraku)*, red *(akaraku)* and white *(shiroraku)*, sometimes called incense burner ware (kororakuyaki). When a Raku bowl is filled with green tea its color should blend with the glaze, and when picked up and put down it should give a feeling of steadiness. Even the highly regarded Ido bowls from Korea cannot match Raku in this respect.

All these points were carefully studied by Rikyu, who directed the shape and texture until he was satisfied. Apart from the Raku family, the great calligrapher and sword appraiser Honami Koetsu (1588-1637) was noted for his tea bowls. They belong to the Raku tradition started by Chojiro, but also reflect the taste of a later age, with distortions in their shape and a strongly marked sense of external decoration. His pieces vary considerably, but nearly all show a great richness of form which demonstrate Koetsu's individualism.

Bernard Leach (self-portrait, left) was a great admirer of Medieval pottery and English slipware. In the seventeenth and eighteenth centuries slipware was in common use for domestic purposes — mugs, jugs, pitchers and basins were thrown on a wheel and oven dishes were pressed over molds. Leach explored and developed this tradition.

Slipware Dish
Date: 1950, St Ives
Size: 14 x 11in (35 x 28cm)

Slipware is a low-fired earthenware decorated with slip. Traditionally slipware is glazed with a thin coat of galena (lead sulphide), producing a coat of honey-colored glass over white slip and a rich brick color over the red clays. The dish (above) was made on a hump mold. Yellow ocher slip was poured over the inside when the clay was leather-hard and the surface was combed with a notched kidney rubber.

Rectangular Stoneware Dish
Date: 1960, St Ives
Size: 8 x 5in (20.5 x 12.5cm)

The dish (left) was made without using a mold. It was covered with a pale celadon glaze, over combed white slip on the inside and black temmoku on the outside. The dish is a good example of adapting the technique of slipware to stoneware.

Bernard Leach

*Leach set out to build a bridge between East and West –
delighted by what he learned in rural Japan, he achieved a revolution in taste in
the West with his gracious domestic pots.*

Bernard Leach was, above all, an artist who later became a potter. His lifelong fascination with the Far East, and his recognition of the beauty and simplicty of the lifestyle and philosophy of its people; refelcted in their crafts, made him a major contributor to the revival of pottery as a craft in the West. It was the meeting of East and West in his work that made him a leader of the avant-garde movement of his day — a revolt by cultured people against the garishness of factorymade pottery. Leach set out to make beautiful domestic pots that people could afford, so enriching their daily lives. His ability to draw enabled him to develop his inborn talents as a decorator and, his skill in design and his subtle use of color has continued to be an inspiration to artist potters in the West.

Leach was born in Hong Kong in 1887 and was taken, as a child, to Japan. He was educated in England and studied drawing under Henry Tonks at the Slade School of Art in London. He learned etching from Frank Brangwyn and returned to Japan in 1909 to teach there. He became interested in pottery after making his first piece of Raku ware at a tea party in 1911, and he went on to study pottery under Ogata Kenzan VI, a descendant of the tea-masters. It was from his friends in Japan — Dr Yanagi, Hamada, Tomimoto and Kawai among them — that he learned the profound philosophy of life and art which sustained the vigor and beauty of the everyday objects still in·use in Japan at this time.

Leach became known in Japan for his etchings, his lively brushwork drawing and his pottery, and it was through these media that he, in turn, influenced his Japanese teachers. A working potter from the West was a new phenomenon for the Japanese and his work was much sought after in a land where pots were collected by discerning people who owed their principles to the Tea Masters — men of piety, learning and vision who cultivated 'the seeing eye'.

In 1915 he moved to Peking with his family, living in part of a temple, but a year later he moved back to Japan to built a workshop on Dr Yanagi's estate at Abiko. It was Leach's stay in China which enabled him to expand his views on ceramics and, in particular, the wares of the Song dynasty opened up for him a whole new world of ideas on form and decoration. His visit to Korea in 1918, with his mentor Dr Yanagi, also nourished his sense of that imaginative beauty which is manifested in the pottery of that country. Yanagi was instrumental in drawing

**Stoneware Beaker:
'Fish Banners'**
*Date: c 1931
Height: 4in (10cm)*

Leach's lively drawings in sepia ink are spontaneous records of what he saw in the passing moment. The drawing of a fish kite (left) is a good example of the source material he used when decorating pots. The sensitive brush drawing on the stoneware beaker (above) shows how he fitted the design to the form.

Leach's attention to the incense burners of the Han period, the bisqued figures of the Six Dynasties, the pottery of the Song, blue and white Imari ware, Yi dynasty and white porcelain pieces, and painted Seto plates.

At Abiko Leach endeavored to make English eighteenth century slipware, using the Raku method. He was making pots in an alien land and this was his first attempt to plant his feet firmly on the soil of the English Tradition. In 1920 Leach returned to England with Hamada, a young research chemist who, inspired by Leach, had decided to become a potter. Together they built the first two-chambered oriental climbing kiln in the West, on the sloping ground behind St Ives in Cornwall. They set up a workshop along the lines of those Leach had become accustomed to in Japan. Japanese rural potteries made inexpensive wares for domestic use, selecting from regular production any pieces of unusual quality for exhibitions. Leach had a vision of his workshop making pots for for every man's use, but he was also an artist who never made the same thing twice and he continued to make exhibition pieces.

Hamada and Leach were eager to find the roots of Western pottery in England and they began to look for clues. They found fragments of feathered dishes in the newly plowed fields of Cornwall and Hamada discovered, when spreading cream on blackberry jam, how to make a feathered pattern. An up-draft kiln was built for firing galena glazes and some of Leach's warmest and gentlest pots were made using this medium. Yanagi, on seeing these pots in Japan, wrote: 'Leach's stoneware we admire, but his slip-ware we love. It is born, not made'.

In 1923 Hamada returned to Japan. Leach, with Michael Cardew, his first pupil, further developed slip-decorated earthenware. By 1927, however, he was coming to the conclusion that slipware was not suited to modern life since it was not durable enough for everyday use, and he eventually abandoned it in favor of stoneware and porcelain.

At St Ives Leach was supported by a loyal team. It was his son, David, and wife Janet who brought stability to the workshop by managing the production of the domestic ware. Although it was Bernard Leach who designed the tableware, to his own high standards, David Leach put the designs into production. Unaccustomed as people were to such unassuming pottery for use in the home, in time, the Leach Pottery 'Standard Ware' became very popular.

Over the years Leach regularly exhibited and traveled in Japan and together with Yanagi and Hamada, he visited Scandinavia and lectured in the United States. His declared mission was to build a bridge between East and West and he sustained his effort with determination, setting an example and clearing a path for later generations of potters. He was, first and foremost, a practicing potter and craftsman, with a creative spark illuminating his thoughts and his work. Hamada said of him: 'Never losing the fresh outlook of the beginner, he cultivated his art for over half a century and still retained the wonderful qualities of the amateur. Leach came by these qualities through rigorous self-discipline and desisted from undertaking what did not suit his temperament. He sought no greater skill than he found necessary'.

DECORATING TILES

Drawing with a brush on the absorbent surface of tiles was akin to drawing with ink on absorbent paper. Leach became a master of this technique, as can be seen from the countless drawings he made of the things he observed every day during his travels in Japan. He used the ancient symbol of 'the Tree of Life' for decorating tiles and jars (below left). For many years decorative tiles for fireplace surrounds (below right) were made at

St Ives. Fireclay tiles were washed over with a thin slip; the motifs and patterns were painted with a brush, using iron and modified cobalt pigments; details were often drawn in line, through the iron pigment, with either a sharpened bamboo or metal stylo to reveal the white background - a combination of brushwork and sgraffito.

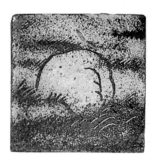

Porcelain Plate
Date: c 1965, St Ives
Diameter: 7½in (19cm)

*In the West we expect
porcelain to be thin, white
and translucent, but in the
East it is not so. Korean
porcelain is heavier and
quieter, more like jade or
marble. The porcelain Leach
made at St Ives lies between
Korean and early Chinese.
The glaze is pale green,
containing a fraction of iron,
and the firing is done in a
reducing atmosphere. The
plate (above) was thrown and
turned, the pattern incised
into the surface, then
brushed over with a weak
wash of black cobalt oxide
and raw ocher. The effect*

*derived from etching and
pen and wash drawing can
be compared with English
scratch blue. The marks on
the underside of the dish
show Bernard Leach's
signature (top right) and the
St Ives Pottery mark (bottom
right).*

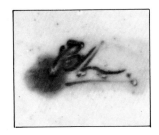

Onion Pot
Date: 1970
Height: 12½in (32cm)

A late and slender 'onion' pot, made for an exhibition in Nottingham in 1970, and now in the collection of William Ismay. The pot was made in two parts and joined where the throat is narrowest. Brushmarks show on the outside (see detail) — the inside is glazed black.

*All Coper pots are stamped with a seal **(right)**, combining his initials and the image of a bowl on a wheelhead. The seals vary in size from ½-1in (1-3cm) and sometimes they are square. In one late seal the letter 'C' is rectilinear in form.*

Hans Coper

*The German-born potter who represents the influence of Europe and the
Modern Movement, and whose creative horizons
stretch beyond conventional pottery to embrace sculpture and the whole
of three-dimensional design.*

Hans Coper's pottery is unique in modern ceramics. Made between 1947 and 1977 it does not follow any tradition, and although it is often described as sculptural or pioneering it is in fact neither — the artist simply developed an original range of pottery shapes and surfaces and it was not his intention to lead a movement away from traditional pottery. Put a Hans Coper pot in among a hundred other examples of modern ceramic work, however, and it will stand apart, perhaps aloof, with quiet dignity, commanding respect and attention.

Hans Coper arrived in Britain as a refugee from Nazism in 1939, and with minimal formal training as a potter but a natural grasp of visual design, he became an assistant to Lucie Rie in her post-war ceramic button studio. Applying rigorous standards of design which, like the Bauhaus of his native Saxony, went back to first principles and eschewed the purely ornamental, he assisted Lucie Rie in the shaping of tableware, and put the designs into practice using considerable self-taught skill on the wheel as a thrower. As early as 1951 he was making his own stoneware pottery, mainly globular pots and tall bulbous jugs, decorated with strong sgraffito designs in black and white, reminiscent both of African contour-carving and the abstract expressionism he had left behind on the continent of Europe.

He continued to work with Lucie Rie until 1958, when he set up his own studio in Hertfordshire, dividing his time between the development of composite ceramic forms and industrial design work in the field of ceramic tiles, bricks and exhibition design. His work at this time was massive, blunt and ungracious, as if made in reaction to the luscious traditional work of Leach and Cardew, for which he had little regard. He pursued a series of themes, almost all of which depended on the inter-relationship of two or more contrasting forms — a bowl-shape on edge intersected with a column, a tall but spreading shape bisected by a disc, a bulb-shape surmounted by a drum. Using the wheel as his principle source of form he was rarely, by the mid-1950s, content to leave a wheelmade shape intact, but preferred to squeeze it, turn it on its edge or combine it with other forms, making the final work the combination of several thrown units. This self-justifying exercise kept his work within the realm of pottery, as opposed to sculpture, but gave rise to anthropomorphic interpretations. In less sensitive hands these wheelmade components could easily have become

**Egg-shaped and
Cylindrical Vessel**
*Date: c 1974
Height: 12¼in (31cm)*

*An interesting combination
of an egg-shape and a
squeezed cylinder; the
resulting form is anchored to
its base with a fine steel
dowel. Hans Coper made a
great many pots with
separately thrown bases in
the later part of his career.
In each instance, the base
was thrown specifically for
the pot it was to support. The
detail shows the surface
texture of the pot.*

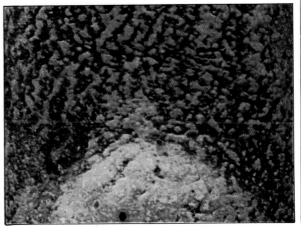

Pottery forms
Date: 1960
Height: 8in (20.5cm)

This pot is from the Hertfordshire studio and is seen in front of a plaster cast of a clay bas-relief showing overlapping pottery forms. The pot is made from three thrown units and blackened with iron oxide and manganese dioxide. The bas-relief was the only one Coper ever made, but it puts into a permanent form his habit of sketching out pottery shapes in clay and indicates his interest in the spatial shapes created between adjacent forms.

clumsy, banal or repetitive. Hans Coper's highly self-critical approach prevented any descent into repetition or any teetering into the precious. He certainly respected the precision of the engineer above the inspiration of the aesthete, and tried to accomplish in clay a predictable and precise result, aesthetically pleasing and functional, but not, in Bauhaus terms, beautiful because it is functional. The combination of contrasting forms allowed endless variation of proportions. Hosts of pots made at this time show a family likeness, a genetic history, but he never made two pots alike.

Coper set up another studio in London in 1964, at which time his reputation as a potter had become international and his services were sought as a teacher. Working with Lucie Rie for a major exhibition in Rotterdam in 1967, he produced mature work of the highest standard, and from this time onwards no inferior or questionable pot ever left his workshop. Apart from certain architectural commissions, including the candlesticks for Coventry Cathedral and work at Sussex University, Coper was now working exclusively on individual pots which were all made from a single clay body, and coated either with manganese dioxide to make a graphite-like black sheen or a series of white slip layers which gave a waxy, cream-colored surface often roughened with a texture like the 'tooth' of a canvas. The pots were carefully fired once only in an electric kiln (in an oxidizing atmosphere), and the glaze that he sometimes used on the insides of his pots to make them impervious was applied at the same time as the slip, so that a single encounter with the kiln achieved the desired result, and the likelihood of chance effects was minimized.

After 1967 Coper moved to the country, establishing a studio and a home for his family in Somerset. His best work was produced here until a debilitating disease restricted his output from 1975. During the early 1970s he developed a series of simple slender vertical forms in the shape of a cross — so fine at their base they required cementing to a plinth for stability. These, and the egg-shaped forms he made about the same time, represent the most refined stage of his work and the embodiment of the principle he borrowed from Mies Van der Rohe: 'less means more'. Certainly the work has a density out of proportion to its weight and size. Although the pots made late in his life are much smaller than the early heavy work they have as much technical dexterity and inventiveness and a great deal more power. Many find that they are spiritual works which evoke an emotional response. They are pots, not sculpture, but they bear a resemblance to the spare, stylized votive figures of the Cycladic Islands from the pre-Classical period. Coper enjoyed the feeling of contact with anonymous craftsmen of the past through such permanent artefacts, but in the twentieth century his greatest mentors were Giacometti and Brancusi. He traveled to Paris to see the latter in 1957.

The difficulties and hardships of his personal life and his tragic death at the age of 61 undoubtedly reduced the output of this creative artist, but he managed to pack into his career of thirty years more work and variety of pots than any of his contemporaries. In stature, as a European potter of his age, he stands alone, unrivalled.

Group of pots
Date: 1968
Height: 10-14in (25-35cm)

The spade shape, made from two cylinders, one flattened and inserted into the other, was developed after 1965. The grooved ovoid pot on the left is a very early example of a favorite late form. All the pots shown here are coated in white slip.

Cycladic form
Date: 1972
Height: 11½in (29cm)

The main form is made from two thrown elements, carefully combined, and with a textured surface emphasized by brown manganese and iron oxide underpainting which shows through the slip. The base is black.

173

8

Wares: Useful and Decorative

All vessels in ceramics, whether they are hollow or flat, started with a functional purpose. However many of them, and particularly those prized by collectors, have had their functional intent subordinated to a decorative purpose and this often contradicts their practical role. A classic example is the Italian *Istoriato* dish in which the flat surface became simply another canvas for the skills of the painter. It is unlikely that these dishes were ever used for food, and many contemporary pictures show them on display on walls and side-tables. In the eighteenth century much of the colored and gilded porcelain wares, though again overtly useful, had delicate decoration which would barely have withstood the rigors of daily use — metal implements scratching the surface and constant washing abrading the gilding. Equally, the expense of many of these products must also have precluded their regular use.

A constant output of decidedly functional wares has, however, continued throughout the years of production. Many centers which produced wares of quality that tended to escape use also made simpler, more functional pieces, but these have often failed to survive the wear and tear of everyday use.

Most functional items have varied little in shape over the centuries. The plate is the prime instance of this — the only changes being in depth, width and border shape. Decoration provides the main cultural stamp and clearly reflects the fashion of the time and place of production. This varies considerably on ceramics from small sprays of flowers on Japanese wares of the Kakiemon family, to the opulent baroque and rococo wares of Meissen. Containers such as tureens and bowls, tea-caddies and sugar boxes have also varied little in basic form. In fact, the simpler their form, the more practical they were to use.

However the eighteenth century tureen, which was the vehicle of flights of fancy in both porcelain and faience, was frequently so smothered in molded and painted ornament that it could only be used with the greatest care. It is evident that the practical purpose of this piece took a very minor place when it became the basis for a decorative tour-de-force.

The detail from Botticelli's 'Wedding Feast', was painted for the Pucci family in 1483. It shows the fashion in which maiolica vases and dishes were used as decoration on top of 'cassoni' (chests). Thus even at this early date the finest products of the Italian potter were destined not for practical use, but as a means towards splendid decoration.

Series of Meissen Thimbles
Date: c 1740
Height: each approx. 1in (2.5cm)

Meissen had quite a large output of these small objects, and no grand sewing box was complete without one. At least 200 have survived. The unworn gilt interior of almost every surviving example lends support to the probability that few of them were ever used.

Meissen Chamber Pot
(left)
Date: c 1725
Width: 7¾in (19.5cm)

Meissen Bourdalou
(right)
Date: c 1725
Width: 7½in (19cm)

Rarely have two such functional objects been so richly decorated. The quality of the decoration is extremely good, and is treated in a very adventurous way because of the temptingly large surface afforded to the painters. Even the interiors are painted and gilded, leading one to doubt whether they were ever intended for use. The subjects on pieces of this type, although disguised as chinoiserie scenes, are frequently explicitly coarse but this appealed to the humor of the day.

Details of Chamber Pot and Bourdalou
This detail from the chamber pot (right) shows a man smoking a pipe; the panels on the reverse depict a child using a chamber pot, and other figures peeping through a screen at a man undressing in order to join a woman in bed. These amusing subjects, set within Böttger's pink-lustre surround and the gilder's baroque decoration, illustrate clearly the peak that the porcelain decorators' skills had reached at this period. The detail of the bourdalou's decoration (top right) shows a scantily clad woman bathing, another subject which obviously appealed to the humor of the day.

Wares for the Toilette

*The course of daily life in the houses of the wealthy demanded many
useful objects in pottery and porcelain, from wigstands to
chamber pots, pots for pomade and patches. Some of these were conceived so
luxuriously as to make them almost too lavish for use.*

Prior to European discovery of porcelain manufacture, tin-glazed pottery objects were used by the wealthy for various toiletry needs, including washing bowls with water ewers, shaving bowls and bleeding bowls. In the eighteenth century the development of the toilette reached heights of sophistication, never before experienced. The range of toiletry requirements dictated by prevailing fashions provided the porcelain potter with the need to create many new forms. For example, the fashion for wigs created a demand for a stand on which the wig could be placed at night. The wearing of patches, considered an enhancement to beauty, also provided a convenient cover-up for the unsightly blotches left from small-pox. It led to the potter being commissioned to produce a suitable receptacle for the black silk and court plaster patches.

The more basic toilette needs were made more convenient in the eighteenth century by the use of portable china receptacles such as chamber pots and bourdaloues. The latter objects derive their name from the preacher Père Louis Bourdaloue (1632-1704) who arrived at the French court in 1675 to preach the Lenten sermons. His sermons were weighty and profound and had considerable impact upon his audiences, not only because of their profundity, but also due to the length of his dissertations. Women who were not certain of being able to hold out for the duration, particularly after a bumpy carriage trip, used to arrive at the chapel with a small china receptacle which they concealed under their skirts and which became known as a bourdalou. By the mid-eighteenth century porcelain bourdaloues were common productions of both French and German potteries. They were basically all of the same shape, designed to fit comfortably between the legs of the user.

The natural progression of this useful object was the chamber pot for night time use. Bathrooms were scarce in eighteenth and nineteenth century houses, and being a guest in a large manor house could mean a long walk in order to relieve yourself. The chamber pot solved this problem and could easily be stored under the bed or in a cupboard. By the nineteenth century it was a common feature in most houses.

Bourdaloues and chamber pots provided the foundations of ceramic use in toiletry, a feature which is now taken for granted in contemporary bathrooms.

One of a Pair of Nevers Faience Wigstands
Date: 1750
Height: 12in (30.5cm)

The gentry removed their wigs before going to bed and placed them on stands. These were generally of wood and rather dull when unoccupied. Pottery examples such as these combined their practical function with a decorative one when not in use

Staffordshire Jug
Date: c 1800
Height: 16in (40cm)

This fine jug, modeled as Falstaff, reflects the growing interest of the period in theatre and other arts, and it illustrates how this subject matter was increasingly used as decoration for jugs. Another jug modeled as Paul Pry, for example, is dated 1825, when John Poole's play of the same name was published. The turn of the century was quite late for the production of Toby jugs, but they were still at the peak of their popularity. By this date, the potter's modeling skills had improved dramatically, as had the range of colors available to him.

Yorkshire Martha Gunn Toby Jug *(left)*
Date: c 1800
Height: 6½in (16.5cm)

The considerable success of the Toby was not confined to Staffordshire, and many Northern potteries made jugs of this type around the turn of the century. This example has fine facial modelling and 'autumnal' coloring. It provides a good contrast to the earlier Staffordshire Toby jug (c 1750) where the colors are limited and the facial features crudely picked out (right).

Drinking Vessels

The provision of vessels for beer and, to a lesser extent, wine was a constant activity of potters and, later, porcelain manufacturers throughout northern Europe.

Drinking vessels have provided a great deal of scope for variety in form. In the East, where the tea ceremony played such an important role in society, craftsmen produced a range of objects for drinking and pouring. In the West, drinking vessels for alcoholic beverages, along with flasks for the transportation of liquids, provided the main source of inspiration. The latter included items such as the pilgrim bottle with its strap handles through which thongs were fed so that it could be slung easily from the shoulder. The former included drinking receptacles for wine, cider, ale and beer of differing shapes and materials, varying according to the wealth and tastes of the consumer.

Prior to the discovery of porcelain manufacture by Johann Böttger (1708-9) in Germany, glazed pottery dominated utilitarian productions and throughout the eighteenth century it continued to provide the bulk of domestic wares. It was only the commercialization of porcelain manufacture in the nineteenth century that made it accessible to less wealthy people. The development of the tankard, a predominantly German production, used for the consumption of beer and ale, illustrates clearly its increasing accessibility.

The shape of tankards varied little from the cylindrical and the baluster. Sometimes, however, novel melon and vegetable tureens appeared. Decoration, on the other hand, varied enormously from simple flowers and landscape vignettes to intricate paintings, religious subject matter, coat-of-arms and regional symbolism. The majority of pottery tankards had pewter hinged covers and pewter foot rims — the cover serving to protect the contents and the foot rim to prevent damage to the pottery. Porcelain tankards, on the other hand, rarely used pewter for the mounts, but rather silver, silver-gilt and gold.

Public-house drinking in inns and taverns gave rise to other tavern amusements which in turn inspired a

Liverpool Delft Blue and White Puzzle Jug
Date: c 1750
Height: 7¼in (18.5cm)

This trick jug was used in a tavern sport played not only in Britain, but also in France and Holland. Made in tin-glazed earthenware, the jug bears a challenging legend in regional dialect: 'Here Gentlemen come try your skill/Ile hold a wager if you will/That you don't Drink this liquor all/Without you spill or lett sume fall'.

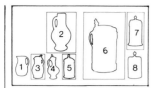

Cross-section of Tankards

These illustrations show some of the different forms, materials and decorations of tankards. The earlier tankards are of baluster form while the later ones are cylindrical. The most variation appears in the decoration which includes armorials, chinoiseries, royal portrait busts, regional symbols and religious subject matter.

1. English mediaeval earthenware jug, date: late 14th century, height: 7½in (19cm).
2. Hamburg faience blue and white armorial jug, date: c 1660, height: 8¼in (21cm).
3. Nuremberg faience tankard painted in black monochrome, date: 1670, height: 8¾in (22.5cm).
4. Nuremberg faience blue and white enghalskrug, date: first half eighteenth century, height: 10¼in (26cm).
5. Nuremberg faience blue and white tankard, date: c 1730, height: 6¾in (17.5cm).
6. Meissen gilt chinoiserie tankard, date: 1725/30, height: approx 9in (23cm).
7. Berlin faience yellow ground tankard with a portrait of the King of Prussia, date: c 1750, height: 9¼in (23.5cm).
8. Brunswick faience powdered-purple ground tankard, date: c 1725, height: 8¼in (21cm).

variety of quirky features on tankards. The puzzle jug, originating from the sixteenth century, is a good example. Usually these jugs are of baluster form with cylindrical pierced necks. The rims have three or four barbs which in fact, are spouts. The innocent participant in the game is asked to drink from a full jug without spilling a drop, a task that seems impossible because of the pierced neck. The trick is achieved because the handle is hollow and leads from the bottom of the jug to the rim, from which the spouts protrude. By sucking through one and blocking the others, you can solve the puzzle.

In England in the eighteenth century, the wit and sarcasm of the literary and artistic world clearly influenced pottery productions. The Toby jug is a good example of this social trend. In 1761, the Reverend Francis Hawkes published his *Original Poems and Translations* in which he included a poem by the Italian poet, Geronimo Amalteo, entitled 'Metamorphosis', and which Hawkes subtitled 'Toby Reduced'. The poem tells of the life and death of Toby Fillpot, a genial toper. The last verse runs:

'His body, when long in the ground it had lain,
And time into Clay had resolv'd again,
A Potter found out in its Covert so snug
And with part of fat Toby he form'd this brown jug.'

The translation was so successful that Carrington Bowles decided to publish an engraving after a

design by Robert Dighton which showed Toby in characteristic pose with his pipe in one hand and full tankard in the other. In turn, Ralph Wood, the early Staffordshire potter, was undoubtedly inspired by the engraving to produce the now well-known character-jug. The model was obviously a great success and inspired many variations on the theme, both from Wood and other Staffordshire potters. Other characters are the Thin Man, the Hearty Good Fellow, the Night Watchman, the Snuff-Taker, the Parson and the Convict. It is not certain whether all these figures were based on actual characters, although some certainly were. The Prince of Wales appears in a jug called Prince Hal or Bluff King Hal, where he is depicted in fancy dress, supposedly worn at a Brighton fancy dress ball. His supposed consort,

Martha Gunn the Brighton bathing attendant, was also a popular subject. Depicted in tricorn hat with the Prince of Wales feathers, she sits in a similar fashion to Toby and holds two flasks.

Tobys were also made in a less sardonic and amusing manner. Several national heroes were depicted, including Lord Howe of the 'Glorious First of June' fame, Admiral Vernon, hero of Portobello in 1739 (although it has been suggested that his appearance on a tankard had more to do with his introduction of the rum ration than his victory), and even the Preacher John Wesley. Ralph Woods' original translation from print to pottery continued to inspire the production of character jugs and tankards throughout the nineteenth Century and into the present century.

**Princess Maria
Josepha Snuff Box**
Date: c 1752
Size: 3¼ x 2¼ in (8 x 6cm)

The eighteenth-century
artist, Bernardo Bellotto, a
nephew of Canaletto, spent
much of his later life in
Dresden, Vienna and
Warsaw, painting views of
the cities. The etching
(right), which is a copy after
one of Bellotto's Dresden

river views, almost certainly
provided the source for the
painting on the Princess
Maria Josepha Box; they are
almost identical.

The Princess Maria Josepha
Box (above) was undoubtedly
designed to be carried upon
her person. It is painted with
views familiar to her: views
of Dresden and of royal
castles. It is possible to trace
some of the views directly to
contemporary paintings by
Bellotto. Typical features of
the Meissen productions of
about 1745 were the
elaborate chased gold
mounts and thumb-pieces
further decorated with
colored stones. The interior
of the base of the box (right)
has an all-over fleur-de-lys
pattern which was generally
used by the monarchy to
mark their possessions.

182

Smoking and Snuff

The arrival of tobacco in Europe created a demand for a wide range of utensils for its consumption and storage. The potter and the porcelain manufacturer were quick to meet the demand thus created.

The introduction of tobacco to Europe provided ceramics, and other decorative arts, with the impetus to create new objects for both storage and use. Romano Pane, who accompanied Colombus on his voyage in 1492, recorded the strange Indian custom of grinding a golden leaf and sniffing the resultant powder. At first considered by Europeans to be a barbaric custom, it became a well-established ritual by the mid-sixteenth century. Pipe smoking and the chewing of tobacco were predominantly a lower-class activity, but the partaking of snuff grew to be a socially accepted practice among the courts of European nobility, particularly by the middle of the eighteenth century. However aristocratic acceptance throughout Europe was by no means universal. Tsar Michael regarded snuff-taking as a disgusting habit and decreed that persons convicted should have their noses cut off upon a second offence. James I of England similarly detested its use and it even inspired him to write in 1604: 'A Counter Blaste to Tobacco', a wonderful piece of violent propaganda. Even though these two were by no means alone in their dislike of the substance, all efforts to abolish the use of tobacco failed. Governments of Europe were quick to realise the revenue-raising possibilities of the trade and policy balanced precariously between attempted prohibition and half-hearted encouragement, and finally compromised by making the leaf expensive through heavy taxation.

The plague, a constant worry for our ancestors, was probably responsible for securing complete social acceptance of tobacco. Doctors started recommending smoking, chewing and sniffing for its disinfectant qualities, and by the middle of the eighteenth century, snuff-boxes and associated utensils were being made in the finest available materials for ruling monarchs and the nobility. The peak of skill achieved in galanterie production is clearly illustrated by the snuff box made at Meissen in Germany, presumably in connection with the marriage of Princess Maria Josepha of Saxony to the Dauphin, elder son of Louis XV and father of Louis XVI, in 1749.

It is perhaps not surprising that the best porcelain boxes should have come from Meissen in Saxony, considering the Prussian and Saxon passion for tobacco and the fact that porcelain manufacture was first discovered in Meissen. Snuff boxes designed to fit upon your person were most common. Frederick the Great of Prussia even had a leather-lined pocket to protect his precious boxes. Meissen boxes varied in form but were mostly rectangular with slightly domed covers, and were fitted with gold, silver or gilt metal hinged mounts, according to the quality of the object or the client's wishes. A characteristic shared by many of these Meissen boxes is that their bases are also slightly domed; this means that the painted surfaces on the bases of the boxes are protected, as only the corners of the boxes touch the surface on which they are resting.

Thanks to social acceptance of tobacco in the eighteenth century there developed a whole range of smokers' porcelain accessories for the wealthy. These included pipes, pipe-stands, pipe tampers, tobacco storage jars, snuff storage jars and snuff boxes for tables and pockets. The spittoon for tobacco chewers also appeared in porcelain. This cuspidor (spittoon) acted as a recipient for the waste of one of the less salubrious and hygenic habits of tobacco users. Not a particularly common object to be found in porcelain, its form derived directly from contemporary metal shapes with bulbous body, wide rim, narrow orifice and strap handle.

Dutch Delft Blue and White Snuff or Tobacco Jar
Date: mid-eighteenth century
Height: 10½in (26.5cm)

There was a massive production of this type of jar in Delft. The jars were usually painted with the name of their contents in a conventional cartouche and were fitted with a brass cover.

Glossary

Alumina: Oxide of aluminium; an important ingredient of potter's clay and of many glazes.

Armorial ware: Any ceramic ware decorated with a coat of arms.

Augustus Rex ware: Vases and other ware commissioned by Augustus the Strong, Elector of Saxony, or his son Augustus III, from Meissen. Often monogrammed AR on base.

Baluster: Tall, swelling shape, of vase or other item, resembling the uprights in a balustrade.

Banded hedge: Decorative motif on Kakiemon porcelain, showing a hedgerow tied with parallel bands.

Barbed rim: Rim of vessel, with oblique projecting points.

Bentonite: Highly plastic clay, mainly formed from montmorillionite. Added to difficult clay bodies in small amounts, to increase their plasticity.

Bianco-sopra-bianco: (Italian, 'white on white'.) Opaque white decoration on slightly bluish-white background. Used on Italian maiolica from sixteenth century.

Biscuit firing: First firing, at a relatively low temperature, before glazing.

Biscuit ware: Ware that is left unglazed.

Blanc de Chine: (French, 'Chinese white'.) Eighteenth-century term to describe translucent Chinese porcelain from Fukien province, exported unpainted.

Bleu céleste: (French, 'celestial blue'.) Turquoise blue ground color introduced at Sèvres in 1753.

Böttger porcelain: First European true porcelain, developed by J.F. Böttger at Meissen by 1711.

Böttger stoneware: Hard red stoneware made by Böttger from about 1705.

Brocade pattern: Japanese decorative pattern, imitative of woven brocades. Copied by many European factories.

Brown rim: Dark edge color on certain Japanese bowls and other pieces; caused by a thin layer of copper deposited when the ware is fired standing on its rim.

Carrack (kraak) porcelain: Thin, mass-produced Chinese blue and white porcelain handled by Portuguese East India Company and Dutch VOC during sixteenth and early seventeenth centuries.

Cartouche: Shield or tablet in a scrolled frame, bearing an inscription, arms or other device.

Celadon: Glaze, originating on Chinese stoneware, obtained from iron fired in a reducing atmosphere. From very pale green to near-turquoise.

Charger: Large plate for serving meat.

Chased: Silversmithing term for decoration indented from the front — opposite of repoussé.

Chinoiserie: Eighteenth-century European style, involving fanciful use of Chinese ornament and motifs.

Cobalt blue: Blue obtained from cobalt oxide, which can be used in both oxidizing and reducing atmospheres, and at the full range of firing temperatures.

Crackle: Deliberate crazing effect on a glaze, caused by different cooling rates of glaze and body, which pull apart slightly to relieve the resulting internal tension.

Delftware: Dutch tin-glazed earthenware, named after the town of Delft. (The term is also applied to similar English ware.)

Double-gourd vase: Chinese vase shape, formed of two rounded 'gourd' parts, with a slim waist between.

Enamel colors: Metallic oxides in a glassy medium, applied over the glaze and fired at a low temperature.

Fabeltiere: German term for porcelain decorated with animal fables or exotic beasts.

Faceted ware: Any ware whose form is based on a number of flat surfaces or facets, for example a six-sided vessel.

Faience: Tin-glazed earthenware (like maiolica and delftware) from France, Germany or Scandinavia.

Famille: (French 'family'.) Nineteenth-century classification of Chinese porcelain decorated with enamels, based on the dominant enamel color present. Includes *famille rose*, an opaque pink to purplish-rose enamel; *famille verte*, a brilliant transparent green; *famille noire*, a black ground washed over with transparent green enamel.

Finial: Same as knop.

Filter press: Appliance for turning watery slip to plastic clay, by pressing through a series of filters.

Flambé: French term, used to describe reduced copper glazes.

Flange: Flat projecting rim.

Floral meander: Decorative border in the form of a winding, continuous line of flowers.

Floral swag: Decorative pattern in the form of a festoon or 'chain' of flowers.

Fluting: Ornament composed of shallow, rounded, parallel or radiating channels (flutes).

Flux: Substance added to glazes or vitrifiable clays to lower their melting point during firing, and thus aid flowing. Fluxes include soda, borax, bone-ash and various plant-ashes; many glazes are named after the main flux used.

Foot-rim: Slightly projecting rim on the base of a plate or vessel; may be an aid to identification.

Frit: Silica which has been fused into glass and the ground, for incorporation into a clay body or a glaze to aid vitrification.

Fukien ware: Porcelain made at Tê Hua (Fukien province): see *blanc de chine*.

Gadrooning: Relief border, consisting of a repeating pattern of parallel or twisted reeds; style and term taken from silversmithing.

Galena glaze: Glaze formed by dusting sulfide of lead onto slip-painted pottery, and then firing at a low temperature.

Gallipot: Small jar or vessel for ointments, sweetmeats, etc.

Garniture de cheminée: (French, 'chimney-piece decoration'.) Set of porcelain vases, designed to stand together on a mantelshelf; usually comprises three or five pieces.

Gilding: Application of gold to highlight or enrich decoration on porcelain. Various methods used, including honey-gilding, where gold is applied pounded with honey; mercuric gilding, where gold is amalgamated with mercury and applied by brush.

Glost fire: Firing of glaze onto ware which has previously been fired to a lower temperature.

Grisaille: Decorative painting in shades of grey, intended to simulate bas-relief.

Grog: Pulverized fired clay, added to clay body to give texture, and reduce shrinkage during firing.

Grotteschi: Italian term (English, grotesques), for fanciful part-human or -animal and part-foliage figures; a common motif in Baroque decoration.

Hexafoil: Six-lobed shape or ornament.

Impasto: Manner of applying colors so that they stand out from the surface in slight relief.

Indianische blumen: (German, 'Indian flowers'.) Style of decoration based on Japanese Kakiemon porcelain, depicting floral sprays on a white ground.

Istoriato: (Italian) Pictorial style of maiolica painting, illustrating historical, mythological, and biblical stories.

Jardinière: (French) Large ornamental vessel for cut flowers or for growing plants.

Kaolinite: White crystaline mineral, main ingredient of china clay, and thus essential to manufacture of hard-paste porcelain.

Kinrande: Japanese word for sixteenth-century Chinese porcelain, with underglaze blue and overglaze red decoration, enriched with gilding.

Knop: Ornament at the top of any object but, in particular, on the cover of a vessel, where it also serves as a handle. It comes in many forms such as an animal, figure, fruit or flower.

Ko-kutani ware: Japanese porcelain, attributed to kilns at Kutani, made in late seventeenth century.

Kufic: An angular Arabic script, associated with early copies of the Koran, and used on Islamic ceramics.

Lacquer: Resinous coloring, applied cold to some ceramics.

Lady in a pavilion: Chelsea Kakiemon pattern, depicting a lady in a draped pavilion with a birdcage and two escaped birds.

Lambrequin: Scalloped border pattern, incorporating drapery, scrollwork, stylized foliage and lace motifs.

Lobed: Formed with rounded projections.

Lund's Bristol (or Lowdin's): Porcelain made at Bristol from mid-eighteenth century, a forerunner of Worcester porcelain. William Lowdin owned the glasshouse where it was made; Benjamin Lund was concerned with the actual manufacture.

Luster: Decorative surface treatment, giving metallic or iridescent appearance; used as an overall ground or for part of a pattern.

Luting: Cementing parts of an object together, before firing, with a liquid slip.

Maiolica: Tin-glazed earthenware made in Italy from fourteenth century, in imitation of Islamic work.

Medici porcelain: First European artificial porcelain, in imitation of Chinese blue and white ware; made during late sixteenth century.

Mei-ping: Chinese vase shape, with short, narrow neck, made to hold a single spray of blossom.

Minai ware: Persian ware, decorated with narrative scenes derived from manuscript illumination, using both over- and under-glaze painting.

Mohammedan blue: Fourteenth- and fifteenth-century name for Chinese blue and white ware.

Monochrome: decorated in a single color.

Monteith: Large bowl for serving iced water with scallops on rim, used for suspending wine-glasses for cooling.

Montmorillionite: Mineral, found in residual clays decomposed from volcanic basalt.

Muffle: Inner container in which wares are enclosed to keep them away from flames or smoke during firing.

Nien-hao: Chinese inscription of four or six characters meaning 'in the reign of'.

Nishiki-de: Japanese term for elaborate brocade-pattern enamelled ware, made at Arita (Hizen province).

Ormolu: Alloy similar to brass, used from eighteenth century as mount or embellishment on certain ceramics.

Peach-bloom glaze: Reduced copper glaze developed in China during late seventeenth century; normally pink mottled with deeper red, but firing conditions may produce a green result.

Porcelain : White, translucent, vitrified ceramic body. Hard-paste — 'true porcelain' — is china clay, felspar and silica, given a low biscuit firing and a high glaze firing. Soft-paste — 'artificial porcelain' — is a mixture of white clay and ground frit or other flux; given a high biscuit firing and low glaze firing.

Porcellana, alla: Early Italian term for blue foliage decoration on maiolica, frequently used on reverse of dishes and inspired by Chinese decoration.

Powder-blue: Cobalt blue applied in powder form, as an underglaze color. Originally a Chinese techique.

Prunus: Plum-blossom, featuring in Chinese and Japanese decoration.

Raku: Low-fired, lead-glazed, Japanese earthenware, with soft porous body. Raku ware is handbuilt and is subject to rapid cooling during manufacture which produces random effects.

Repoussé: Silversmithing term, for ornament raised in relief by hammering with punches from the back; used for similar relief ornament on ceramics.

Reticulated: Patterned with a network of interlaced lines or pierced holes.

Sang-de-boeuf: (French, 'bull's blood'.) Deep red glaze, derived from reduction firing of cobalt oxide.

Scratch blue: White saltglazed stoneware, with incised decoration which is filled in with cobalt oxide before firing.

Sèvres ground colors: Distinctive ground colors introduced by the Sèvres factory, including: dark blue (*bleu lapis*, c. 1753-63, *bleu nouveau*, 1763); turquoise (*bleu céleste*, 1753); yellow (1753); green (1756); and pink (1757).

Silica: Hard, glassy, mineral, found as sand, quartz, and in other forms; the basic ingredient of all glasses, and hence of all glazes.

Spur: Support for holding pots in kiln with three legs and an upward point.

Stampino, a: Italian term for decoration where design is guided by a stencil.

String-rim: Projecting double lip on a vessel, to enable a lid or cover to be securely tied to it.

Swan Service: Meissen dinner service made 1737-41; commissioned by Augustus III for presentation to the factory's director, Count von Brühl. Highly modelled with swans and other water creatures, it is the most important dinner service made at Meissen.

Temmoku: Japanese oxidized iron glaze; black, breaking to rust where glaze is thin.

Thumb-piece: Flat area on a handle or plate-rim, to rest the holder's thumb for better support.

Transfer printing: Application of pattern from printed sheet of tissue paper. The pattern is printed in an oil-based oxide color; the tissue is rubbed down on the ware before firing, and burns off in the kiln, leaving the pattern behind.

Tulip vase: Vase with several tube-like mouths, each intended to hold a single tulip.

Underglaze colors: High-firing colors, painted direct onto the biscuited ware, then fired with the glaze on top of them.

Vaisseau à mât: (French, 'masted vessel'.) Type of pot-pourri vase, in form resembling a single-masted ship.

Vermiculé: Linear ground pattern, resembling a surface eaten by worms.

Well: The sunken central part of a plate or dish.

OUTLINE OF CHINESE DYNASTIES

The table below shows the modern Pinyin spellings — used throughout the book; years correspond to the Western Calendar.

Xia (Hsia)	2205-1766 B.C.
Shang	1766-1122 B.C.
Zhou (Chou)	1122-256 B.C.
Jin (Chin)	221-206 B.C.
Han	206 B.C. - 220 A.D.
Six Dynasties	221-589
Sui	589-618
Tang (T'ang)	618-906
Five Dynasties	907-959
Northern Song (Sung)	960-1130
Southern Song (Sung)	1131-1276
Yuan	1277-1367

Ming Dynasty

Hongwu (Hung Wu)	1368-1398
Jianwen (Chien Wen)	1399-1402
Yongle (Yung Lo)	1403-1424
Hongxi (Hung Hsi)	1425
Xuande (Hsuan Teh)	1426-1435
Zhengtong (Cheng T'ung)	1436-1449
Qingtai (Ch'ing T'ai)	1450-1456
Tianshun (T'ien Shun)	1457-1464
Chenghua (Ch'eng Hua)	1465-1487
Hongzhi (Hung Chih)	1488-1505
Zhengde (Chung Teh)	1506-1521
Jiajing (Chia Ching)	1522-1566
Longqing (Lung Ch'ing)	1567-1572
Wanli (Wen Li)	1573-1619
Tai Chang (T'ai Ch'ang)	1620
Tianqi (T'ien Ch'i)	1621-1627
Chongzheng (Ch'ung Cheng)	1628-1643

Qing Dynasty

Shungzhi (Shun Chih)	1644-1661
Kangxi (K'ang Hsi)	1662-1722
Yongzheng (Yung Cheng)	1723-1735
Qianlong (Ch'ien Lung)	1736-1796
Jiaqing (Chia Ch'ing)	1796-1820
Daoguang (Tao Kuang)	1821-1850
Xianfeng (Hsien Feng)	1851-1861
Tongzhi (T'ung Chih)	1862-1874
Guangxu (Kuang Hsu)	1875-1908
Xuantong (Hsuan T'ung)	1909-1911

Bibliography

Luster

La Maiolica Italiana Sino Alla Comparsa Della Porcellana Europa, *G. Liverani, Electa Editrice, Milano 1958*

Li Tre Libri dell'Arte del Vasareo, *Cav Cipriano Piccolpasso, translation and introduction by Bernard Rackham and Albert van de Put, London V & A 1934*

Lustreware of Spain, *Alice Wilson Frothingham, The Hispanic Society of America, New York 1951*

The Arabs in History, *B. Lewis, Hutchinson University Library, London, 1950*

The Arts of Japan, Catalogue of Exhibition, *Hayward Gallery, The Arts Council of Great Britain 1976*

William de Morgan, *William Gaunt & Clayton Stamm MDE, London 1971*

Gruppo di Bacini Islamici de Ciese Romaniche Pisaree, *Berti Graziella & Liana Tongiorgi, Atti IV Convegno Internazionale della Ceramica Albissola 1971*

Catalogo della Mostra — 1 Bacini delle Chiese Pisane, *Roma, Palazzo Brancaccio 1983*

Sèvres

Sèvres Porcelain from the Royal Collection, *Geoffrey de Bellaigue, The Queen's Gallery, London 1979*

Sèvres, Des origines à nos jours, *Marcelle Brunet & Tamara Préaud, Fribourg 1978*

Decorative Art from the Samuel H. Kress Collection at the Metropolitan Museum of Art, *Carl Christian Dauterman, James Parker & Edith Appleton Standen, London 1964*

The Wrightsman Collection: Porcelain, *Carl Christian Dauterman, Volume IV, New York 1970*

The James A. de Rothschild Collection at Waddesdon Manor: Sèvres Porcelain, *Svend Eriksen, Fribourg 1968*

Porcelaines de Vincennes, Les Origines de Sèvres, *Tamara Préaud & Antoinette Fay-Hallé, Grand Palais, Paris 1977*

European

Alte Deutsche Fayence-Krüge, *Wolfgang Schwarze, Dr Wolfgang Schwarze Verlag, Wuppertal, 1980*

European Ceramic Art, *William Bowyer Honey, Faber & Faber, 1949*

Dresden China, *William Bowyer Honey, A & C Black, 1934*

Meissen, *Hugo Morley-Fletcher, Ferndale Editions, 1971*

Delft Ceramics, *C. H. de Jonge, Pall Mall Press Ltd., 1970*

Aritaporzellan als Vorbild für Meissen, *Masako Shono, Editions Schneider, Munich, 1973*

Meissener Porzellan, *Rainer Rückert, Hirmer Verlag, Munich, 1966*

Johann Friedrich Böttger, *Staatliche Kunst-sammlung, Dresden, Edition Leipzig, 1982*

Franz Anton Bustelli, *Rainer Rückert, Hirmer Verlag, Munich, 1963*

English

Eighteenth Century English Porcelain, *George Savage, Rockcliffe Publishing & Co. Ltd. 1952*

Old English Porcelain, *William Bowyer Honey, A & C Black 1948*

English Blue and White Porcelain of the Eighteenth Century, *Dr Bernard Watney, Faber & Faber 1973*

Bow Porcelain, *Anton Gabszewicz & Geoffrey Freeman, Lund Humphries 1982*

Worcester Porcelain & Lund's Bristol, *Franklin A. Barret, Faber & Faber 1966*

Chelsea Porcelain, Triangle and Raised Anchor Wares, *F. Severne Mackenna, F. Lewis 1948*

Derby Porcelain, *John Twitchet, Barrie & Jenkins 1980*

Chelsea Porcelain at Williamsburg, *John C. Austin, Colonial Williamsburg Foundation 1977*

Chinese

China for the West, *David Howard & John Ayers, Sotheby Parke Bernet Publications 1978*

Chinese Armorial Porcelain, *David Sanctuary Howard, Faber & Faber 1974*

China-Trade Porcelain, *John Goldsmith Phillips, Harvard University Press*

Porcelain and the Dutch China Trade, *C.J.A. Jörg, Uitgeverij Martinus Nijhoff 1982*

Chinese Export Porcelain, Chine de Commande, *D.F. Lunsingh Scheurleer, Faber & Faber 1974*

China Trade Porcelain: Patterns of Exchange, *Clare le Corbeiller, Metropolitan Museum of Art 1974*

Japanese

Japanese Pottery, *Soame Jenyns, Faber & Faber 1971*

Tea Ceremony Utensils, Arts of Japan 3, *Ryōichi Fujioka, Weatherhill/Shibundo 1973*

The Way of Tea, *Rand Castile, Weatherhill 1971*

Japanese Porcelain, *Soame Jenyns, Faber & Faber 1965*

Early Japanese Porcelain, *Friedrich Reichel, Orbis Publishing London 1981*

Ceramic Art of Japan, *Tadanari Mitsuoka, Tokyo Tourist Library, Vol 8, Tokyo 1949*

The Ceramic Art of Japan, *Hugo Munsterberg, Charles E. Tuttle 1964*

The World of Japanese Ceramics, *Herbert H. Sanders, Kodansha International Ltd. 1967*

Japanese Ceramics from Ancient to Modern Times, *Editor: Fujio Koyama, Oakland Art Museum, California 1961*

A Survey of Japanese Ceramics, *Maria Penkala, Interbook International B.V. 1980*

The Art of Japanese Ceramics, *Tsugio Mikami, Weatherhill/Heibonsha 1972*

The Baur Collection Geneva: Japanese Ceramics, *John Ayers, Collections Baur 1982*

Craft Pottery

A Potter in Japan, *Bernard Leach, Faber & Faber 1960*

Hamada Potter, *Bernard Leach, Kodansha International 1975*

A Potter's Book, *Bernard Leach, Faber & Faber 1977*

The Art of the Modern Potter, *Tony Birks, Country Life Books 1976*

Hans Coper, *Tony Birks, Collins 1983*

Index

Numbers in italics refer to illustrations

Credits and Acknowledgements

Key:
(t) - top
(tl) - top left
(tr) - top right
(m) - middle
(b) - bottom
(bl) - bottom left
(r) - right
(l) - left

Picture Credits and Acknowledgements
Ashmolean Museum, Oxford 35
Bodleian Library, Oxford 38(r)
Burghley House Collection 103 (t and ml)
Cardew, Seth 169
Collection Haags Gemeentemuseum, The Hague 86(r)
Coper, Jane 157, 170, 171, 172, 173
Craft Council 156(r), 166(m and b)
Craft Study Centre, Holburne Museum (University of Bath) 168(t and r)
Evans, Mary Picture Library 58(t), 59(r), 60(l)
Fitzwilliam Museum, Cambridge 146(m)
Getty, J. Paul Museum, Malibu 31, 56, 57(t), 62, 63, 64(m), 65
Godman Collection, British Museum 34
Grog Collection 64(l)
Hammond, Henry 168(bl)
Hulton Picture Library 163(b)
Meissen 24, 28(bl), 29(bl and br), 146(t)
Museum of Fine Arts, Boston 67
National Trust, Waddesdon Manor 55, 56

Philadelphia Museum of Art 53
Réunion des Musées Nationaux, Paris 54
Royal Crown Derby Museum 129
Royal Worcester 20, 21, 23(r), 25(tr and b), 27(b), 28(l and r and br), 29(t)
Victoria and Albert Museum 14(r), 18(tr), 23(l), 36, 37(l and r), 38(t), 48(t and br), 49, 50, 51, 57(b), 60(t), 70, 84, 85, 90, 93(l and r), 112, 115, 119, 128, 130(t), 150, 151(l), 152(m)

Reproduced by permission of the Trustees, the Wallace Collection, London 42(t and bl), 45(t)

By kind permission of the Marquess of Tavistock and the Trustees of the Bedford Estate 58(m)

Reproduced by gracious permission of Her Majesty the Queen 59(l), 61

All other pictures have been supplied by Christie's, London and Quarto Publishing Ltd.

While every effort has been made to acknowledge all copyright holders, we apologize if any omissions have been made.